Music and guitar theory can seem intimidating, but my goal is to make it fun, clear, and approachable. As I was writing this book, many people asked me what my "angle" was. Honestly, I didn't have a straightforward answer other than this: I believe the way I explain these concepts is clearer and more engaging than what you might find elsewhere.

This book assumes you already have some familiarity with the guitar and want to deepen your understanding, filling in any gaps that may have occurred along the way.

Learning is a lifelong journey, not a destination. Think of each chapter as a stop along the way—you might linger in some places, explore deeply, or simply pass through. You may also find yourself returning to chapters to see them from a new angle. This is your journey, and I hope this book can guide you, provide fresh insights, and make sense of things you might already know, while also introducing you to new ideas.

Copyright © 2025 by Mark Wade
All rights reserved.

No portion of this book may be reproduced in any form without written permission from the publisher or author, except as permitted by U.S. copyright law.

GUITAR THEORY SIMPLIFIED

STRING NAMES..........1
NOTE NAMES............2
TABLATURE.............9
RHYTHM............18
TIME SIGNATURES.............25
STRUMMING............30
INTERVALS...........40
TRIADS..........46
OPEN CHORDS..........47
BARRE CHORDS...........49
OCTAVE PATTERNS............54
PENTATONIC SCALES............58
MINOR PENTATONIC PATTERNS.............59
MINOR PENTATONIC LEAD PATTERNS....83
CAGED....88
MAJOR PENTATONIC PATTERNS....96
MAJOR PENTATONIC LEAD PATTERNS....110
MINOR CAGED.....123
INVERSIONS....124
GENERAL MUSIC THEORY....141
CIRCLE OF 5THS AND 4THS.........146
CHORDS IN A KEY.....153
NASHVILLE NUMBER SYSTEM....158
FINDING THE KEY OF A SONG USING CHORDS...160
RELATIVE MINORS......162
DIATONIC VS. NON-DIATONIC...165
PLAYING BARRE CHORDS IN A KEY....170
OPEN CHORD DICTIONARY..178

STRING NAMES

First, it is important to learn the string names. Don't skip this step; you will need to know them for every section in this book. And hey, while you're at it, tune your guitar! Tune every time you sit down to play. Your guitar can go out of tune because of temperature and humidity, not just when a peg gets accidentally bumped.

Here are the open string names:

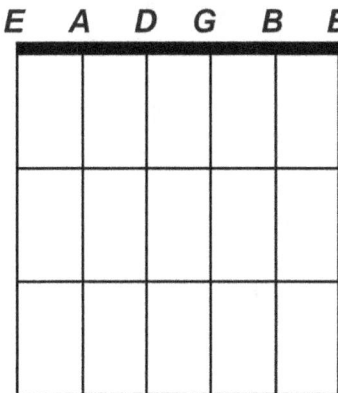

You can use a saying to remember your string names; a couple of examples are:

Elephants And Donkeys Grow Big Ears

or

Eddie Ate Dynamite Good Bye Eddie

We will also refer to strings as numbers. The string closest to the floor is string 1; the one closest to the ceiling is string 6.

1

NOTE NAMES

Note names are extremely important. If you don't learn them, then most things in this book are pointless. You don't need to learn all of your note names on the entire fretboard all at once, but it should be something that you're constantly working toward.

Here is the musical alphabet:

A B C D E F G

Each note has a fret between it and the adjacent note *EXCEPT* **B & C and E & F**. Those two groupings are right next to each other on the fretboard and don't have a fret between them.

To help remember this you can use the saying:

BeCause Elephants Fly

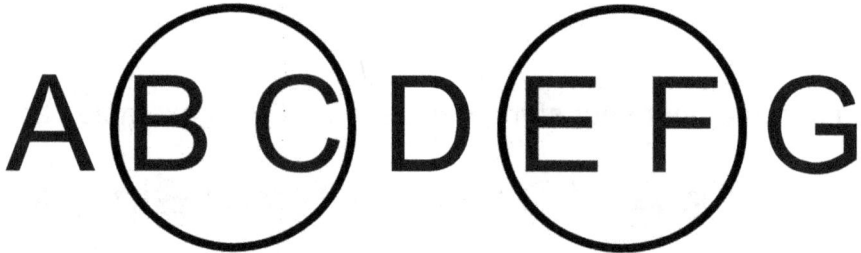

Whole step = 2 frets
Half step = 1 fret

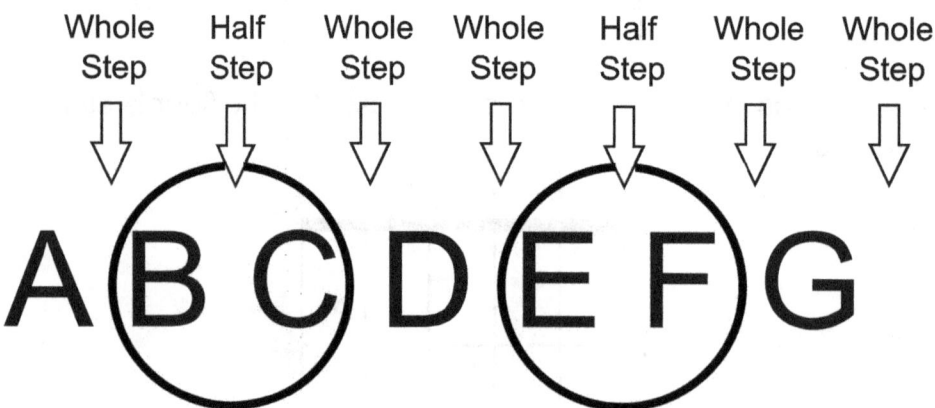

2

OCTAVES

The word *octave* comes from the Latin word *octo*, meaning "eight." Fun fact: my birthday is in October, which made me wonder—why isn't October the 8th month? Well, in the original Roman calendar, it was. But when Julius Caesar reformed the calendar, he added January and February to the beginning of the year, pushing October to month number 10.

Back to music…

In music, an *octave* means moving from one note to the next note with the **same letter name**, higher or lower in pitch. The musical alphabet has seven letters: **A, B, C, D, E, F, G**.

So, if we start on **A** and go upward:
A → B → C → D → E → F → G → **A**

That last A is the *octave* of the first A—same note name, but higher in pitch. This works for any starting note.

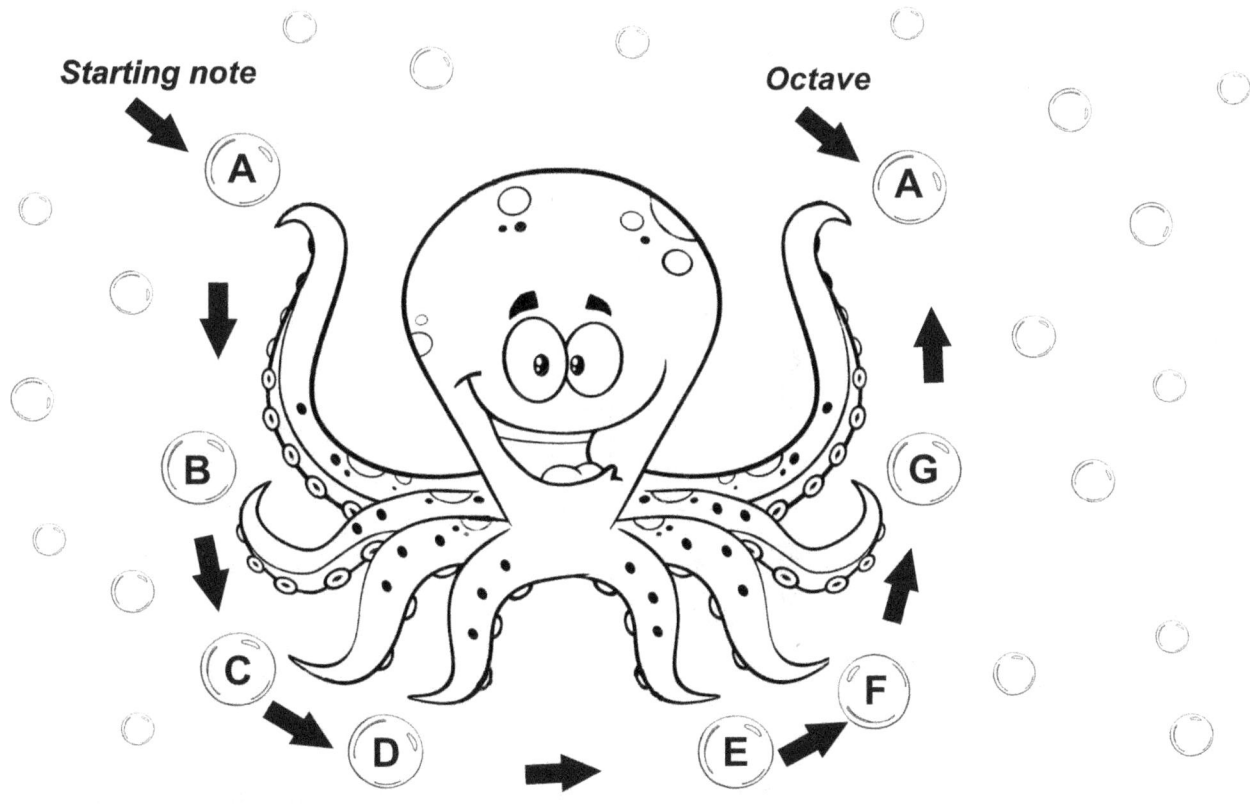

A few songs that use octaves in the opening guitar riff:
• *Bulls On Parade* - Rage Against the Machine
• *My Sharona* - The Knack
• *Immigrant Song* - Led Zeppelin

Here are the natural (not sharped or flatted) notes on the E string:

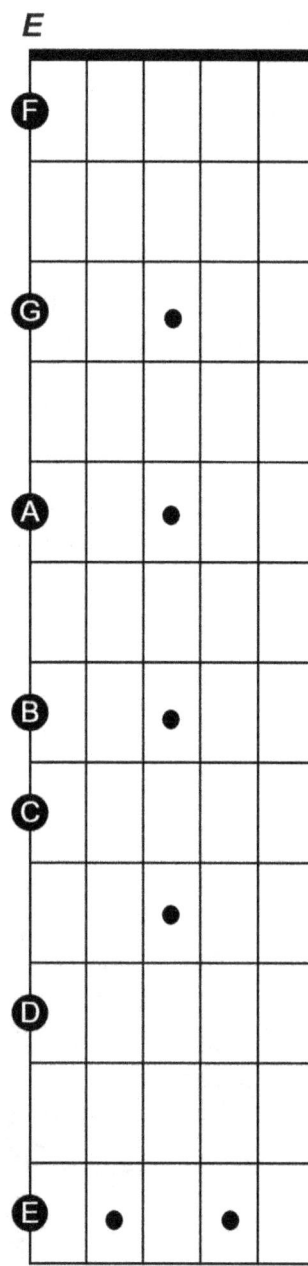

Helpful tip: On the guitar, *"up the neck"* means moving toward the **body of the guitar**, while *"down the neck"* means moving **toward the headstock**. This terminology comes from **pitch**, not physical direction—when you move *up* the neck, the notes get **higher in pitch**; when you move *down*, the notes get **lower**.

Exercise

Start with the **open E string** and work your way up:

- **E** (open)

- +1 fret → **F**

- +2 frets → **G**

- +2 frets → **A**

- +2 frets → **B**

- +1 fret → **C**

- +2 frets → **D**

- +2 frets → **E** (one octave higher)

Then work your way **backward** down the string.

Tip: Use the fretboard dots as landmarks to help you remember note locations.

Once you're comfortable going up and down, **pick a note at random** and try to find it *without* playing the notes leading up to it. This helps train your brain to recognize notes instantly, rather than by counting frets.

<u>**Helpful tip:**</u>
The **double dot** on your fretboard marks the **octave** on every string—which means it's the same note name as the open string. Use it as a quick reference point when finding notes.

For example:
If you need to find a **D** on the **E string**, don't start counting from the 1st fret. Instead, jump to the **double dot E** (12th fret) and go *down* two frets—that's your D.

The double dot also marks the point where **note names repeat** on each string:

- The 13th fret has the same note name as the 1st fret.

- The 14th fret matches the 2nd fret, and so on.

Once you see the pattern, navigating the neck becomes much faster.

After you feel comfortable with the natural notes on the E string, move to the A string. The same concept applies with the spacing between notes.

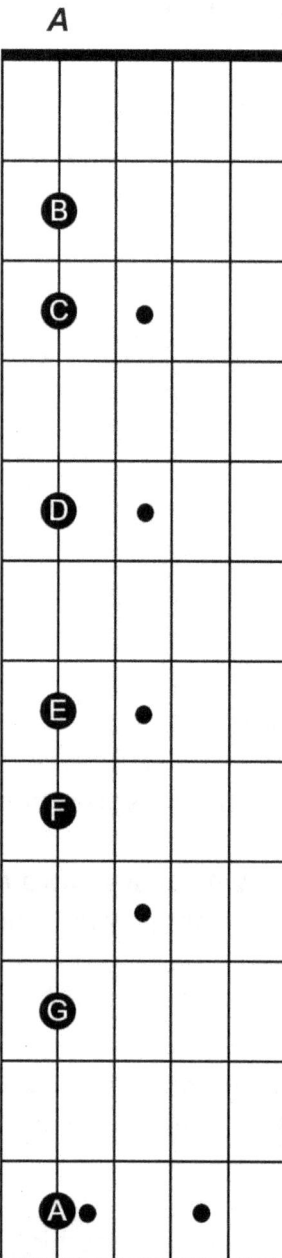

All of your strings will use this same concept. It is most important to start with the E and A strings, because we will be using these string notes first for the octave patterns and barre chords.

Exercise

• Find a C on the E string, then find a C on the A string. These two notes will sound exactly the same.

• Find an F on the E string, then find an F on the A string. The F on the A string will sound an octave higher than the F on the E string.

• Be comfortable finding any note pairing between the E and A strings.

Hey, what about all of the notes in between that we haven't named yet?

Sharp

Flat

The notes we haven't named yet are the **sharps** (#) and **flats** (♭).

• A **sharp** raises a note by a half step (1 fret).

• A **flat** lowers a note by a half step (1 fret).

For example:

• Take an F and move it up one fret (toward the guitar body) → it becomes F#.

• Take a G and move it down one fret (toward the headstock) ← it becomes G♭.

You might notice that F# and G♭ are on the same fret and sound the same. This is called an **enharmonic equivalent**. Which name you use depends on the key you're in and how that note functions alongside the others in the music.

An easy way to remember the difference between a sharp and flat:

Sharp: When you *sharpen* a pencil you *raise* the point.

Flat: When you get a *flat* tire, it goes *lower*.

To practice locating sharps, start on the F on the 1st fret of the E string. Play every fret going up the neck and name each note out loud up to the 12th fret E. Use only natural notes and sharps.

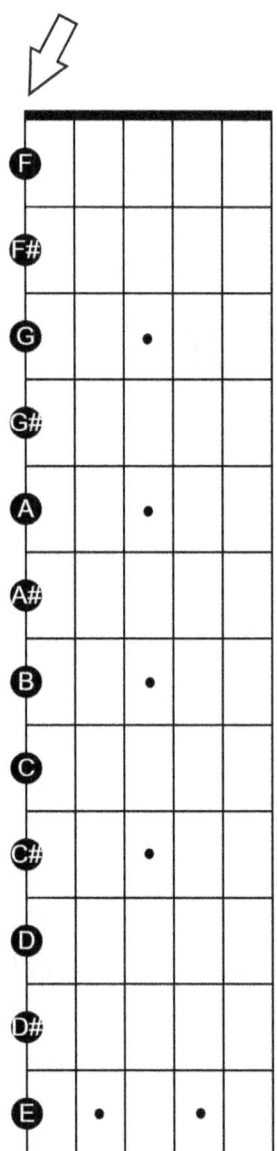

To practice playing flats, start on the E on the 12th fret of the E string. Play every fret going down the neck and name each note out loud. Use only natural notes and flats.

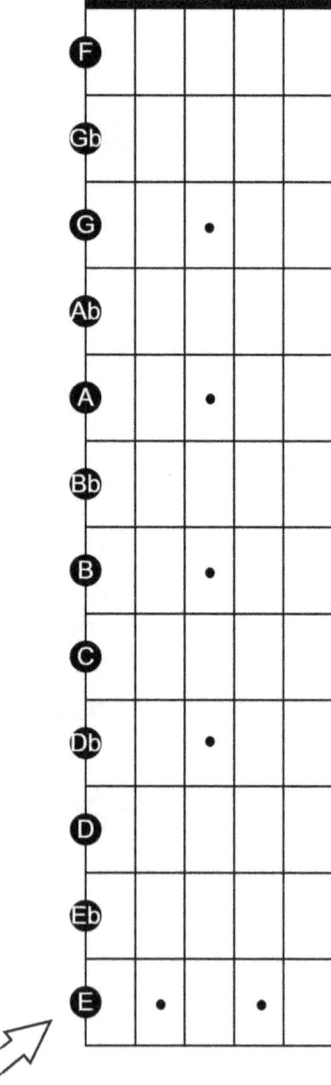

Helpful tip: Practice saying the alphabet backward from G to A. This will help you when working backward on the fretboard.

TABLATURE

Tablature (or "tab") is a number-based notation system that originated in the 1300s for organ music. Guitar tab tells you what fret to play on which string. Standard notation—which uses notes on a staff—tells you what pitch to play and the rhythm. I recommend (at the very least) that you learn how to read rhythms in standard notation because a lot of tab will include rhythmic elements from standard notation. Below are both pros and cons of each system.

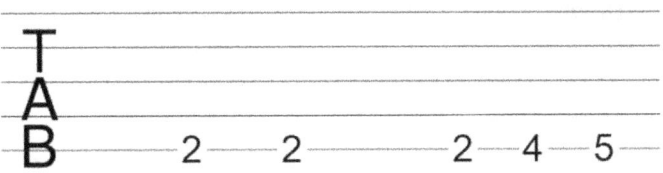 

Guitar tab  vs.  Standard notation

PROs:
- Tells you exactly where to play a note
- Easy to read
- Might help you see patterns on the guitar
- Beginner-friendly
- Easier to read a chord
- Instant gratification

CONs:
- Rhythmic value not always attached to it
- You might not know what note you are playing, just the number
- Doesn't translate to non-fretted instruments
- Doesn't teach you music theory
- Dynamics and articulation commonly left off
- Can be confusing thinking about tab number, fret number, string number, and finger number

PROs:
- Rhythmic values attached to notes
- Can be read by all instruments in the same clef
- Teaches you music theory and note names on your instrument
- Helps with ear training
- Facilitates a stronger connection with the music you are playing
- Easier to see intervals

CONs:
- Does not tell you where on your instrument to play the note (you may have multiple places to play the same note on the guitar)
- Longer process to become proficient
- Might not ever need to use it depending on your goals

When you read tab, each line represents a string.

String closest to floor →
```
---E---
T  B
A  G
   D
B  A
---E---
```
String closest to ceiling →

Helpful tip: At first you may struggle with how tab is written. If you lay your guitar on your lap with the strings facing towards the ceiling, and then lay the tab sheet on your guitar, that will tell you what strings to play the notes on and might help you get oriented.

The number represents which fret to play, with the exception of a zero. A zero means you play the string open without holding down a fret.

Play the 3rd fret of this string (D); then play this string open → ——3——0——

When you see notes stacked on top of each other you play those notes at the same time. This is what a G chord looks like when tabbed:

Form the chord and strum all 6 strings →
```
———3———
———0———
———0———
———0———
———2———
———3———
```

On the following pages you will learn about different symbols and techniques used in tablature. You will see two different versions of the same symbols. The one on the left is more official, the one on the right is more DIY and done with text only, but they both mean the same thing.

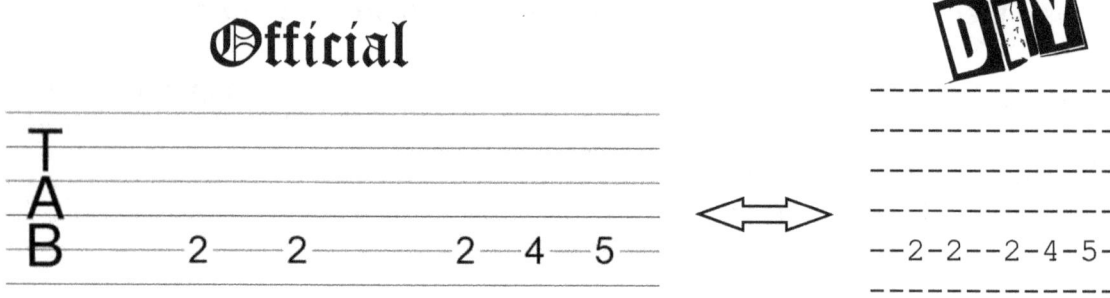

Official — TAB: —2—2——2—4—5—   ⟷   **DIY** — --2-2--2-4-5-

Hammer-on (h)

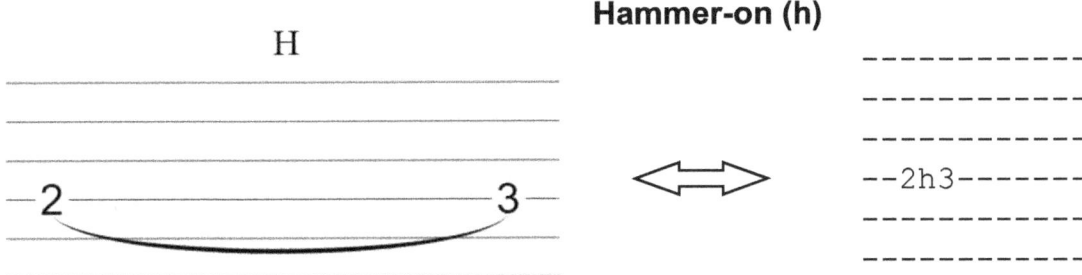

A **hammer-on** is when you use your fretting hand to strike a note without picking it. To play the above notes, pick the 2 and then use your fretting hand to hammer down on the 3 without picking it.

Pull-off (p)

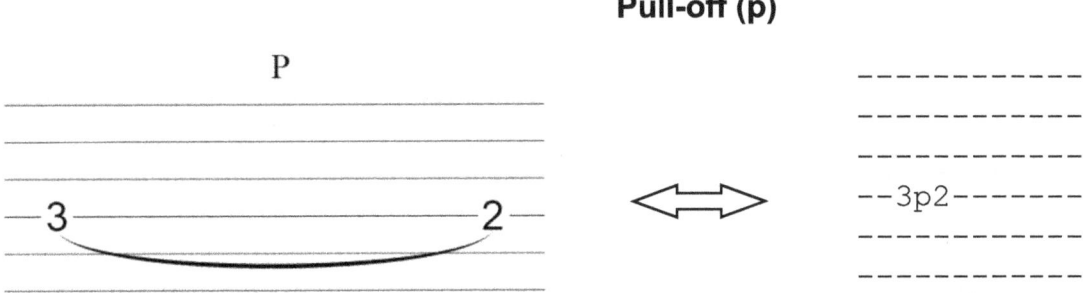

A **pull-off** is when you use your fretting hand to pull off of a note using a plucking motion to a note below it without picking it. To play the above notes, pick the 3 and then use your fretting hand to pull off the 3, in turn playing the 2 without picking it.

Hammer-on pull-off hammer-on

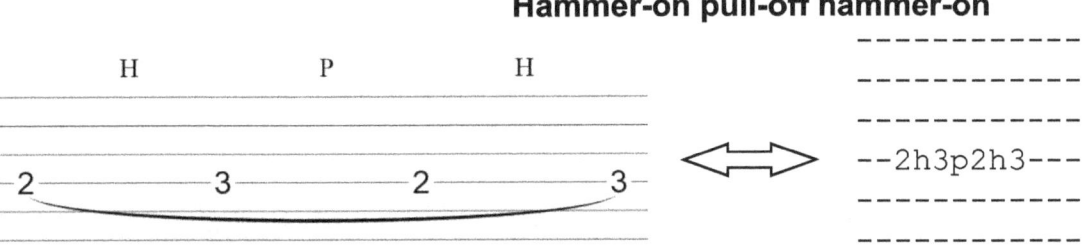

To play this sequence of notes you only pick the first 2, then hammer your finger down to the 3, pull the 3 off to the 2, then hammer the 3 back down.

Exercise

Play this sequence of notes using fingers 1, 2, 3, and 4 in order. Pick the first note and hammer the rest. Make sure they are all equal rhythmically and are the same volume.

```
------------------------------------------5h6h7h8-
------------------------------------5h6h7h8---------
------------------------------5h6h7h8---------------
------------------------5h6h7h8---------------------
------------------5h6h7h8---------------------------
--5h6h7h8-------------------------------------------
```

Slide up (/)

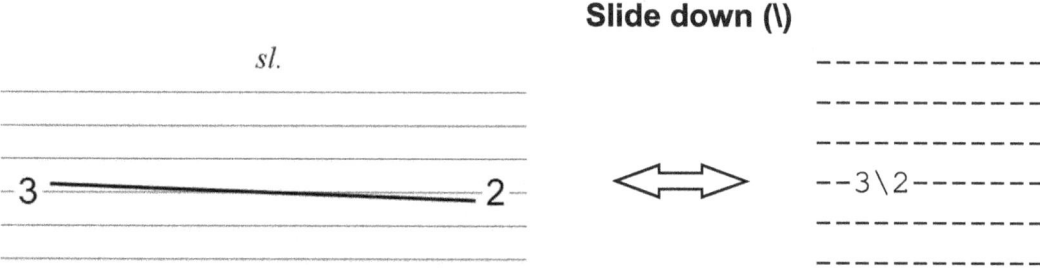

```
------------
------------
------------
--2/3-------
------------
------------
```

A **slide up** is when you use your fretting hand to slide from one note to the next without picking it. To play the above notes, pick the 2 and then slide to the 3 without picking it.

Slide down (\)

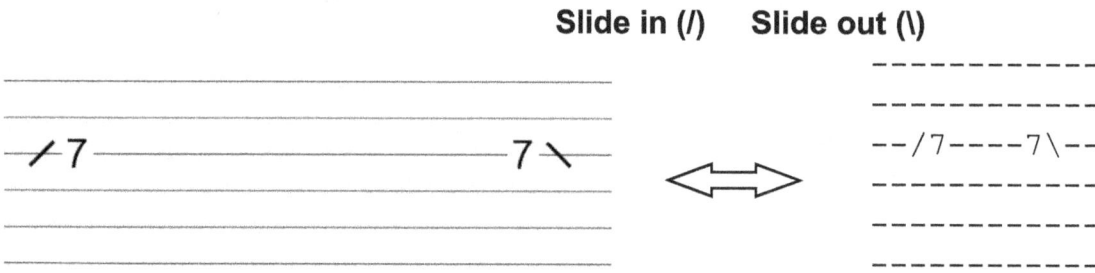

```
------------
------------
------------
--3\2-------
------------
------------
```

A **slide down** is when you use your fretting hand to slide from one note to the next without picking it. To play the above notes, pick the 3 and slide to the 2 without picking it.

Slide in (/) Slide out (\)

```
------------
------------
--/7----7\--
------------
------------
------------
```

A **slide in** is when you use your fretting hand to slide into a note from an undetermined starting point. As a general rule, two frets below the note you are sliding into is a good starting point. A **slide out** is when you slide out of a note to an undetermined stopping point but release the pressure to stop the note before you stop your slide.

Hold ( )

```
------------
------------
------------
------------
----3---(3)-
------------
```

Play the first note and hold it; do not pick the (3).

Half bend (b)

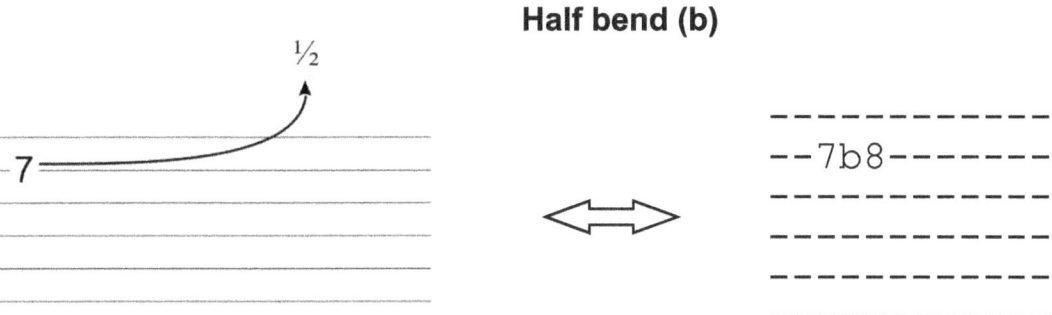

A **half bend** is when you take a note you've played and push or pull the string to make the pitch 1 fret higher. To play the above notes, pick the 7 and then push or pull the string so it sounds like an 8 without picking it.

Full bend (b)

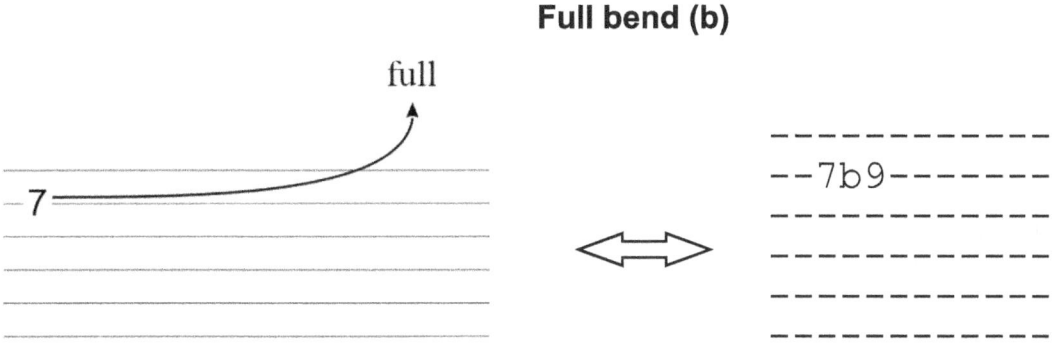

A **full bend** is when you take a note you've played and push or pull the string to make the pitch 2 frets higher. To play the above notes, pick the 7 and then push or pull the string so it sounds like a 9 without picking it.

Bend and release (br)

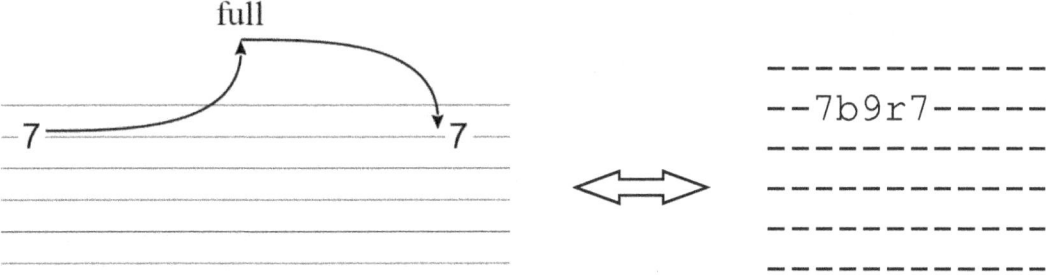

A **bend and release** is when you take a note you've played and push or pull the string to the higher pitch and then release the bend to the original note. To play the above notes, pick the 7, push the string so it sounds like a 9, and then release the bend to return it to the 7. Make sure to hold the string down the whole time.

> ***Helpful tip:*** When performing a bend, grip your guitar neck as if it were a bat, with your thumb wrapped so it is next to your 6th string. Use your 2nd and 3rd fingers to bend the string using leverage from your thumb.

Pre-bend release (pbr)

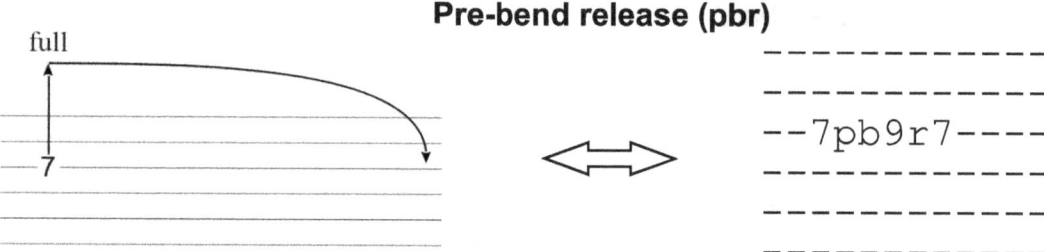

```
------------
------------
--7pb9r7----
------------
------------
------------
```

A **pre-bend release** is when you bend the string to a note prior to playing it, then pick the note and release it back to its original fret. To play the above notes, put your finger on the 7, bend it to the 9, play the note, and then release the bend back to the 7.

Unison bend

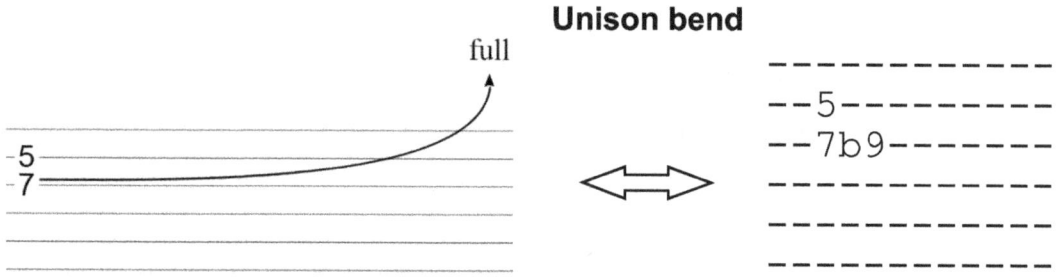

```
------------
--5---------
--7b9-------
------------
------------
------------
```

A **unison bend** is when you play 2 notes and then bend the lower of the 2 notes to be in unison with the higher. To play the above notes, put your first finger on the 5 and third finger on the 7, then pick both notes and bend the 7 to the 9.

Bend slow release

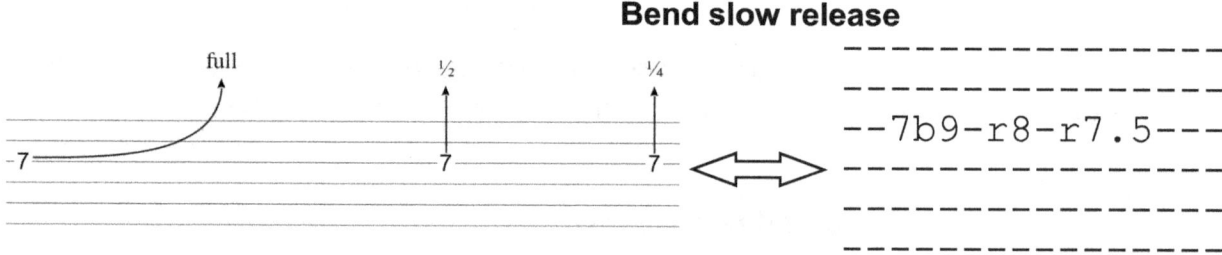

```
------------------
------------------
--7b9-r8-r7.5---
------------------
------------------
------------------
```

A **bend slow release** is when you play a bend and then incrementally release it while playing it. To play the above notes you will pick the 7, bend to the 9, release it to the 8 and play it again. Then, barely release it to not quite the 7 and play it again.

Helpful tips:
• Default to pushing the string to the ceiling for a bend unless the note after the bend is on a lower string. In this case you should pull the string to the floor so you aren't bending into that string.

• If you are having trouble bending, try lighter gauge strings such as 9s.

• Bends are generally easier on an electric guitar.

Exercise

Practicing Bends on the Guitar

Half Bend (One Semitone)
1. *Play the starting note*: Play the 12th fret of the high E string.

2. *Hear the goal*: Play the 13th fret so you know the pitch you're aiming for (F).

3. *Bend to match*: Go back to the 12th fret and bend the string until it matches the pitch of the 13th fret.

4. *Check accuracy*: Use a digital tuner if you're unsure whether you've hit the note.

5. *Challenge yourself*: Once you're comfortable here, practice the same bend on lower frets—bending gets harder as you move toward the nut.

Full Bend (Two Semitones)
1. *Play the starting note*: Play the 12th fret of the high E string.

2. *Hear the goal*: Play the 14th fret so you know the pitch you're aiming for (F#).

3. *Bend to match*: Go back to the 12th fret and bend the string until it matches the pitch of the 14th fret.

4. *Check accuracy*: Use a digital tuner for confirmation.

5. *Challenge yourself*: Once you're comfortable, move to lower frets—full bends are even harder lower on the neck.

Tip: Keep your thumb anchored next to the 6th string and use multiple fingers to help push the string for control and accuracy.

> *Helpful tip:* Practice bends alone where no one can hear you.

Palm mute (PM)

```
P.M. -----------------------------|             P.M.
                                                ----------------
                                                ----------------
--5--------5--------5--------5---      <──>     ----------------
                                                --5--5--5--5----
                                                ----------------
                                                ----------------
```

Palm muting is a picking hand technique where you lightly rest the side of your palm on the strings near the bridge to produce a muted sound when the strings are picked. This is usually done with all down picks.

Harmonic (< >)

```
                                                ----------------
                                                ----------------
                                                ----------------
--<7>----------------------------      <──>     --<7>-----------
                                                ----------------
                                                ----------------
```

To play a ***harmonic***, you lightly touch the string directly on top of the fret wire and pick the string. Do not hold the string down.

Vibrato (~)

```
  ~~~~~~~~~~~~~~~~~~~~~                         ----------------
                                                ----------------
                                                ----------------
                                        <──>    ---7~~~~~-------
--7------------------------------               ----------------
                                                ----------------
```

Vibrato is a fretting hand technique where you rapidly change the pitch of a note to create a pulsing sound effect. There are 3 ways to do vibrato on the guitar: bending and releasing the string repeatedly and rapidly, rolling the fingertip, or shaking the neck of the guitar.

Trill (tr)

```
       tr~~~~~                                  ----------------
                                                ----------------
                                                ----------------
                                        <──>    ---7tr8---------
-------7 (8)---------------------               ----------------
                                                ----------------
```

A ***trill*** is when you repeatedly do a hammer-on and pull-off as fast as possible for the duration of the note. To play this, pick the 7, hammer-on to the 8, pull-off to the 7, hammer-on to the 8, pull-off to the 7, etc.

Dead note (x)

A **dead note**—also know as a **ghost note** or **scratching**—is a muted, percussive, non-pitched technique where you lightly rest your fretting hand on the string(s) and then pick those strings. This technique can also be done with your picking hand by resting the palm on the strings before strumming. This is commonly done when playing open chords.

Exercise

Dead Strum Practice

1. Strumming-Hand Dead Strum
- Start with an **open G chord** and strum **four downstrokes**: ↓ ↓ ↓ ↓

- Now replace the **2nd** and **4th** downstrokes with dead strums by **resting your strumming hand** lightly on the strings just before you hit them: ↓ x ↓ x
("x" = dead strum)

2. Fretting-Hand Dead Strum
- Play an **open F chord** and strum normally.

- Without lifting your fingers off the strings, **release the pressure** so the notes are muted.

- Strum again to get a **dead, percussive sound** instead of ringing notes.

Helpful tip: Dead strums are about *timing* and *feel*. Keep your strumming motion smooth—don't stop your arm when muting.

RHYTHM

Rhythm is a fundamental element of music. A melody cannot exist without rhythm. You should have an understanding of all of the note types on this page even if you never plan to read sheet music.

⇒ Whole note, worth 4 beats

⇒ Half note, worth 2 beats

⇒ Quarter note, worth 1 beat

⇒ Eighth note, worth 1/2 a beat

⇒ Sixteenth note, worth 1/4 a beat

Note equivalents:

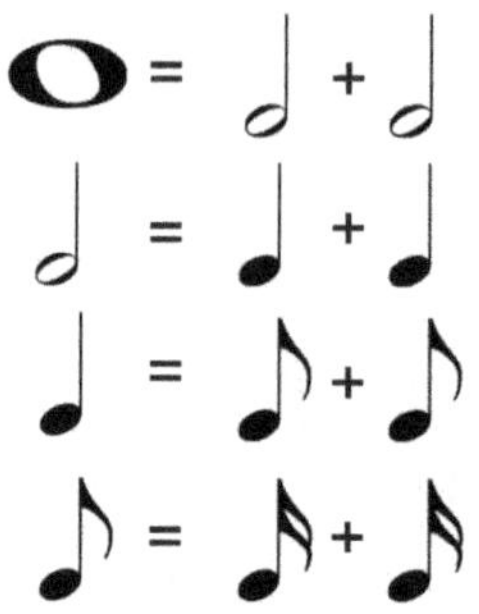

𝍫 = ♩ + ♩

♩ = ♪ + ♪

♪ = 𝅘𝅥𝅯 + 𝅘𝅥𝅯

Each note is cut in half to equal the value below it.

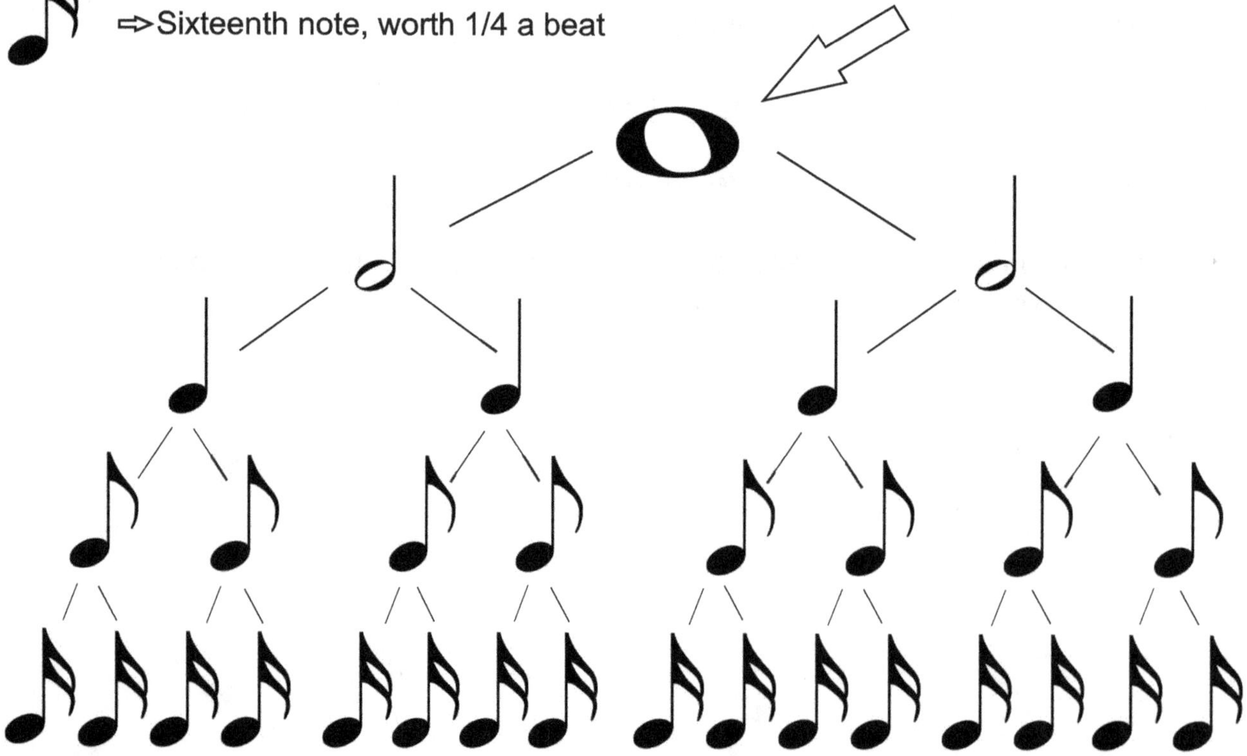

Helpful tip: When looking at sheet music, eighth notes and sixteenth notes will usually have a beam above them, grouping them in beats. A single bar will indicate eighth notes ♫ while a double bar will indicate sixteenth notes 𝅘𝅥𝅯𝅘𝅥𝅯𝅘𝅥𝅯𝅘𝅥𝅯.

COUNTING RHYTHMS

The type of rhythms in a measure will determine *how you count*.

• If a bar has **both eighth notes** and **quarter notes**, it can help to **count in eighth notes** the whole time—even during the quarter notes.

• If a bar has **both eighth notes** and **sixteenth notes**, you might want to **count in sixteenth notes** throughout.

This technique is called **subdivision**—breaking each beat into **smaller, equal parts** so your timing stays steady.

Example:

• Quarter notes → count "1 2 3 4"

• Eighth notes → count "1 & 2 & 3 & 4 &"

• Sixteenth notes → count "1 e & a 2 e & a 3 e & a 4 e & a"

Tip: Counting the smallest note value in the bar will make it easier to place all the other rhythms correctly.

Note Value	Beats per Note	How It Fits in 1 Beat	Counting a Full Bar
Quarter note	1	♩	1 2 3 4
Eighth note	½	♪♪	1 & 2 & 3 & 4 &
Sixteenth note	¼	♪♪♪♪	1 e & a 2 e & a 3 e & a 4 e & a

How to apply this chart:

1. Look at the **smallest note value** in your measure.

2. Use that note's counting method for the whole bar.

3. This keeps your timing locked in—especially when switching between different rhythms.

Eighth notes:

When counting a bar of eighth notes, count 1 & 2 & 3 & 4 &. This means that every beat gets a *number* and an *&*.

 A single eighth note is worth 1/2 a beat, and will either get a *number* (1, 2, 3, or 4), or an *&* depending on where it falls within a bar.

 Two beamed eighth notes are worth 1 beat, and are counted as *1&*, *2&*, *3&*, or *4&*, depending on where they fall within a bar.

 Four beamed eighth notes are worth 2 beats and are counted as *1&2&*, *2&3&*, or *3&4&*, depending on where they fall within a bar.

A full bar of eighth notes will look like either one of these:

Exercise

Count out loud (1&2&3&4&) as you clap these rhythms:

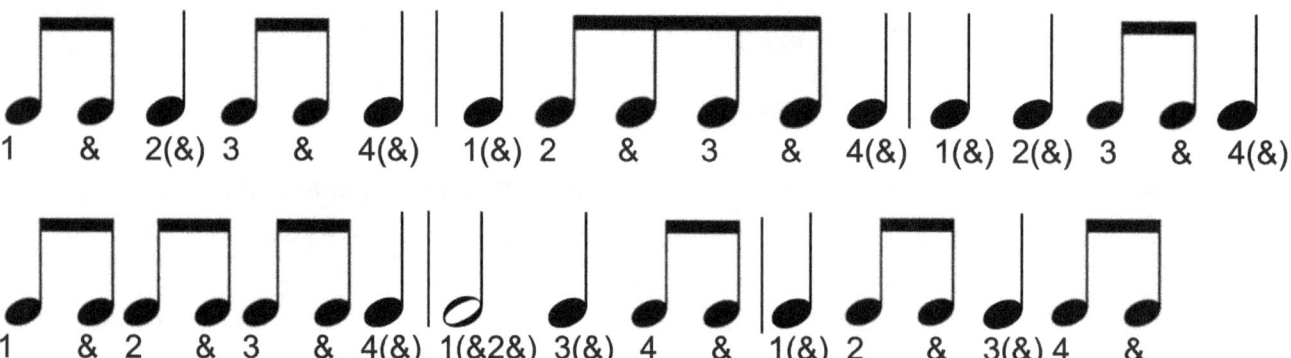

20

Sixteenth notes:

When counting a bar of sixteenth notes, count 1e&a 2e&a 3e&a 4e&a. This means that every beat gets a *number*, an *e*, an *&*, and an *a*.

 A single sixteenth note is worth 1/4 a beat, and will either get a *number* (1, 2, 3, or 4), an *e*, an *&*, or an *a* depending on where it falls within a bar.

 Two beamed sixteenth notes together are worth 1/2 a beat, and will either get a *number* and an *e* (1e, 2e, 3e, or 4e), an *e* and an *&*, or an *&* and an *a* depending on where they fall within a bar.

 Four beamed sixteenth notes together are worth 1 beat, and will get a *number* and an *e*, an *&*, and an *a* (1e&a, 2e&a, 3e&a, or 4e&a).

This represents a full bar of sixteenth notes:

Exercise

Count out loud (1e&a2e&a3e&a4e&a) as you clap these rhythms:

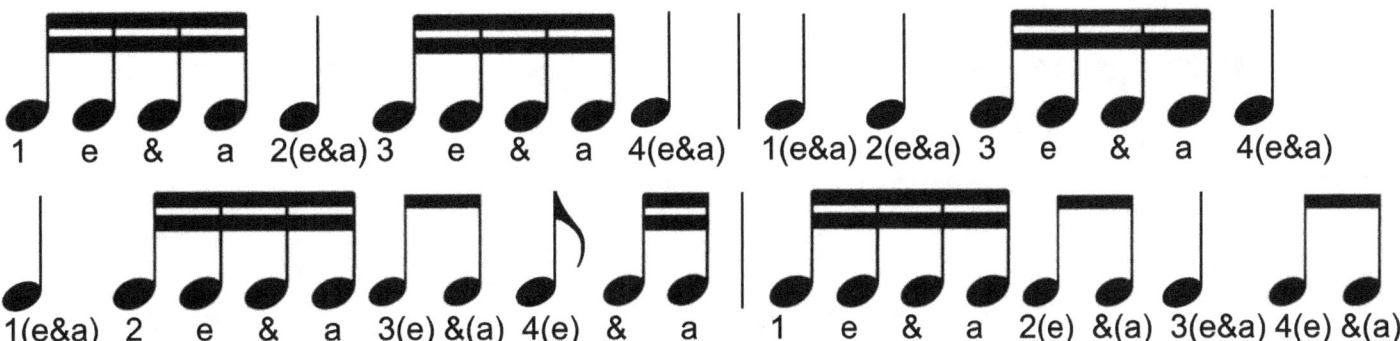

21

Rests:

A rest is when you are not playing and your instrument is silent. It is important to count during rests so you know when to play again.

 Whole note rest = 4 beats

Half note rest = 2 beats

Quarter note rest = 1 beat

Eighth note rest = 1/2 beat

Sixteenth note rest = 1/4 beat

Exercise

Count out loud as you clap these rhythms:

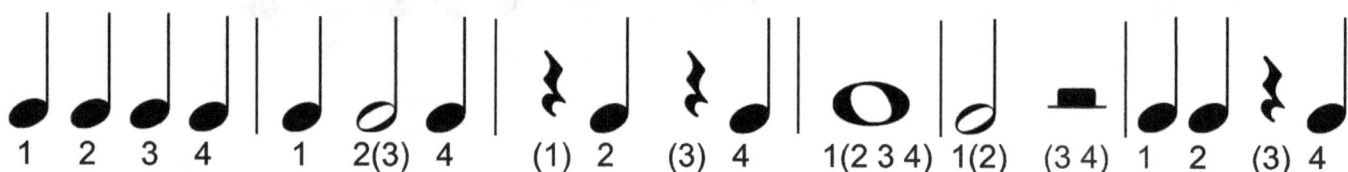

1 2 3 4 | 1 2(3) 4 | (1) 2 (3) 4 | 1(2 3 4) | 1(2) (3 4) | 1 2 (3) 4

Count out loud (1&2&3&4&) as you clap these rhythms:

1 & (2&) 3 & 4(&) | 1 & 2 & (3&) 4 & | 1(&) 2 & (3&) 4 &

Count out loud (1e&a2e&a3e&a4e&a) as you clap these rhythms:

1 e & a 2(e) &(a) 3(e&a) 4 e & a | 1 e (&a) 2 e &(a) 3(e) &(a) (4e&a)

Dotted notes:

A dotted note is a note with a small dot written after it. When you see this you increase the value of the note by half of its original value.

We'll use a dotted half note as an example: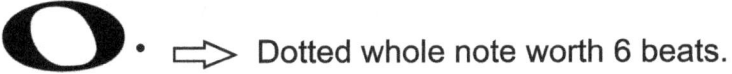

A half note gets 2 beats. Half of 2 is 1, so we add 1 beat making the dotted half note worth 3 beats.

○. ⇒ Dotted whole note worth 6 beats.

𝅗𝅥. ⇒ Dotted half note worth 3 beats.

♩. ⇒ Dotted quarter note worth 1 1/2 beats. Counted as 1&2.

♪. ⇒ Dotted eighth note worth 3/4 beats. Counted as 1e&.

Exercise

Count out loud (1 2 3 4) as you clap these rhythms:

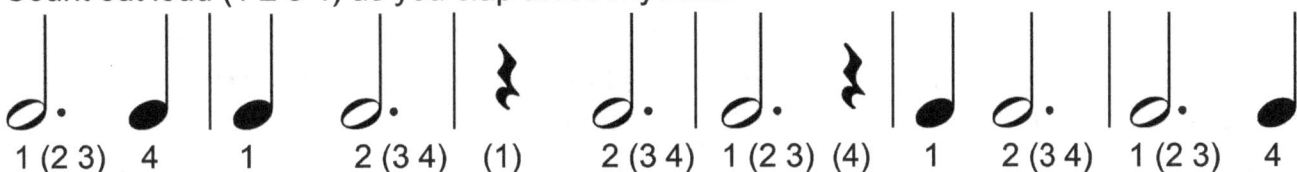

Count out loud (1&2&3&4&) as you clap these rhythms:

Count out loud (1e&a2e&a3e&a4e&a) as you clap these rhythms:

SYNCOPATION

Syncopation is when the weaker beats of a bar are accented or emphasized. When counting eighth notes the **&'s** are the weaker beats. When counting sixteenth notes the **e's** and **a's** are the weaker beats.

Exercise

• Count eighth notes (1& 2& 3& 4&) while tapping your foot. Your foot will go down on a number and up on an &. Next, clap the rhythms listed:

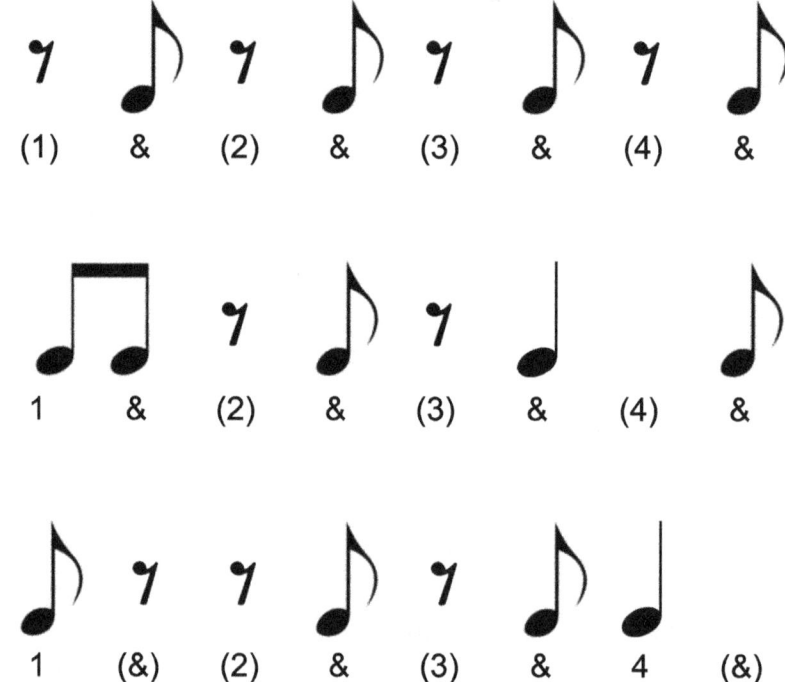

• Count sixteenth notes (1e&a 2e&a 3e&a 4e&a) while tapping your foot. Your foot will go down on a number and up on an &. Next, clap the rhythms listed:

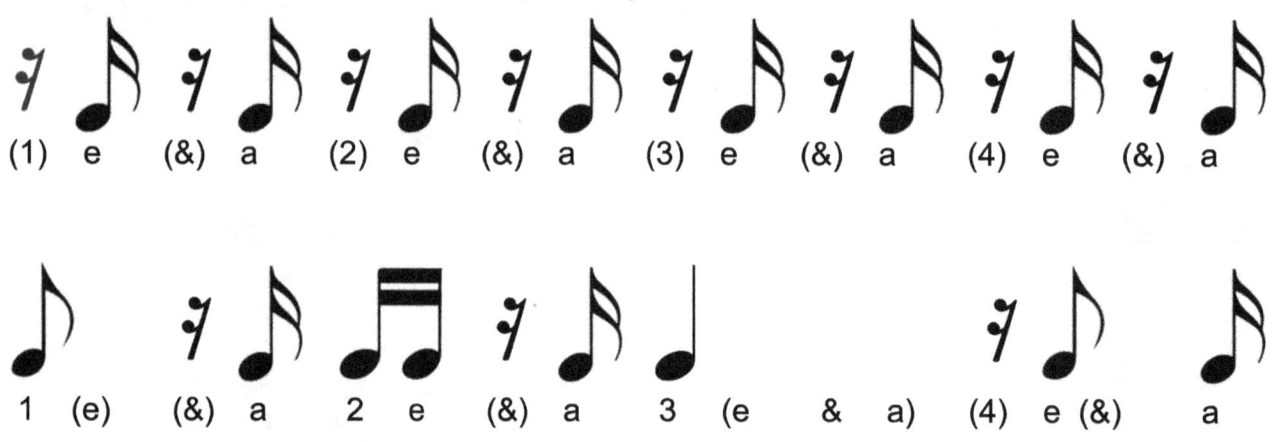

Helpful tip: When counting sixteenth notes you can also tap on the number and the &. This will put your foot going up on the e's and a's making it easier to clap the syncopation.

24

TIME SIGNATURES

The top number of a time signature will tell you how many beats are in a bar (also known as a measure). The bottom number will tell you what type of note receives one beat in a measure. The most common time signatures are:

2/4   **2** = 2 beats in a measure
            4 = quarter note gets one beat

Waltz time signature ⇒ **3/4**   **3** = 3 beats in a measure
                                 4 = quarter note gets one beat

Also commonly listed as **C** for "common time" ⇒ **4/4**   **4** = 4 beats in a measure
                                                     4 = quarter note gets one beat

6/8   **6** = 6 beats in a measure
            8 = eighth note gets one beat

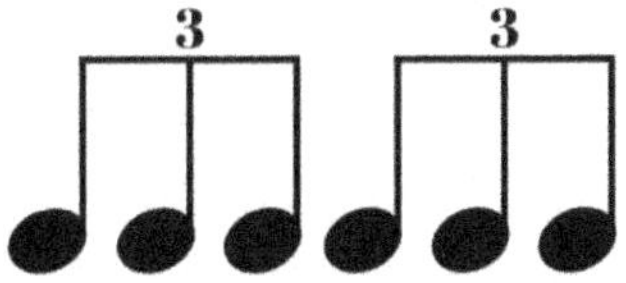

12/8   **12** = 12 beats in a measure
              8 = eighth note gets one beat

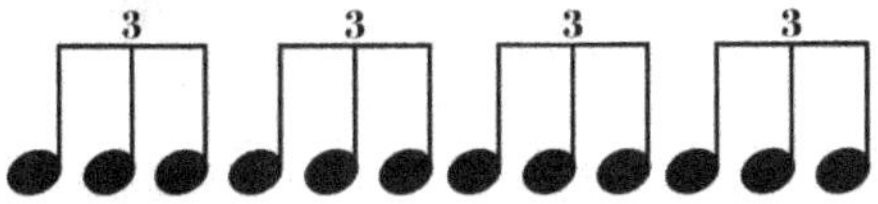

In *6/8 time*, think of the rhythm as *two big beats per measure*, each divided into three smaller notes (a triplet feel). If you count all six notes, the accents naturally land on *1* and *4*.

In *12/8 time*, the feel is the same—triplets—but now there are *four big beats per measure*. Counting all twelve notes, the accents fall on *1*, *4*, *7*, and *10*.

A fun way to tell them apart: if you can imagine *swaying your drink* side to side in time with the music, you're probably in one of these time signatures. The difference is whether you sway twice (6/8) or four times (12/8) before starting the next measure.

DETERMINING A TIME SIGNATURE

Figuring out a song's time signature can be tricky. Listen for a few key things and use a counting method.

What to listen for:
- *Drum accents* (kick/snare), they often mark the strong beats.

- *Where the chords change* and *when the riff repeats*.

- *Melody and bass phrasing*—when a melody or bass phrase starts over.

- *How the accents group* (do they come in twos, threes, fours, or something odd?).

A step-by-step check:
1. *Pick a clear section* (intro riff or groove without big fills).

2. *Loop it and tap or clap* steadily on the perceived pulse. Count the pulses aloud: 1, 2, 3…until the riff comes back to the same point. That number is your measure length (the top number of the time signature).

3. *Listen for accent groupings*. If the accents fall on 1 and 4 when you count to 6, you're feeling the two-beat triplet feel of 6/8. If accents fall on 1–4–7–10 when you count to 12, you're feeling 12/8 (four beats of three).

4. *Decide simple vs. compound*: If you naturally count in threes inside each big beat, it's compound (6/8, 12/8, etc.). If you count 1 & 2 & 3 & 4 &, it's simple (4/4, 3/4, etc.).

5. *Double-check by tapping and singing* the root or the first chord—where it feels like "home" is often beat 1.

Example:
A classic example is Pink Floyd's "*Money*." Listen to the riff and count until it repeats—you'll hear a grouping of seven pulses, which is why the groove feels unusual compared to common 4/4 tunes. It is in 7/4, seven beats per measure and each pulse is a quarter note.

COUNTING TO DRUMS

When hearing a drum beat, it is helpful to be able to distinguish the different drums and cymbals that are being played. This can help you count along to the music and communicate with a drummer.

Kick or Bass Drum
- Typically played on beats 1 and 3 in 4/4 time
- Typically played on beat 1 in 3/4 and 6/8 time, and 1 and 7 in 12/8 time
- Played with foot
- Lowest sounding drum

Snare Drum
- Typically played on beats 2 and 4 in 4/4 time
- Typically played on beat 4 in 6/8 time, and beats 4 and 10 in 12/8 time
- Typically played on beats 2 and 3 in 3/4 time
- Has stiff wires on the underside of it to give it a rattly sound

Hi-Hat
- Typically played as eighth notes on every beat in 4/4 time
- Typically played on every beat in 6/8 and 12/8 time
- Played with a drumstick, but also has a foot pedal that is used for opening and closing

Toms
- Typically used for fills, but can also take the place of the hi-hat in a drum beat

Cymbals
- Ride cymbal: Typically used in place of a hi-hat in a drum beat
- Crash cymbal: Typically used at the end of a drum fill, or to signal a new section in a song

TAP AND CLAP

For this exercise, you'll mimic a drum beat by tapping your foot for the kick drum and clapping your hands for the snare drum. Count out loud as you mimic these drum beats in different time signatures.

3/4 = kick (1) snare (2) snare (3)

4/4 = kick (1) snare (2) kick (3) snare (4)

5/4 = kick (1) snare (2) kick (3) snare (4) snare (5)

6/8 = kick (1) 2 3 snare (4) 5 6

12/8 = kick (1) 2 3 snare (4) 5 6 kick (7) 8 9 snare (10) 11 12

Exercise

Listen to the following songs and count along by listening to the drum beat. These songs will either be in 3/4, 4/4, 6/8, or 12/8. The answers are listed at the bottom of the page.

$$\frac{3}{4} \qquad \frac{12}{8} \qquad \frac{4}{4} \qquad \frac{6}{8}$$

1. *Waltz #2 (XO)* - Elliot Smith

2. *Back In Black* - AC/DC

3. *We Are The Champions* - Queen

4. *Fool in the Rain* - Led Zeppelin

5. *I Hate Myself for Loving You* - Joan Jett & the Blackhearts

6. *Everybody Wants To Rule The World* - Tears For Fears

7. *Dreams* - Fleetwood Mac

8. *Fallin'* - Alicia Keys

9. *Gold Lion* - Yeah Yeah Yeahs

10. *Crazy* - Aerosmith

Answers:
1. 3/4
2. 4/4
3. 6/8
4. 12/8
5. 4/4
6. 12/8
7. 4/4
8. 12/8
9. 4/4
10. 6/8

STRUMMING

"What is the strum pattern?" is one of the top questions I get asked from students learning a new song. The answer is sometimes easy, but often times it's either difficult to hear what strum the artist is doing, or they are varying the strum so much that it's impossible to copy it. I like to give students a few templates to start with. These general strum patterns can easily be modified and adjusted to fit most songs. Let's assume that the song is in 4/4 time, which means there are 4 beats per bar (or measure) and each beat is a quarter note.

Strum Pattern 1 : Eighth note strum

First, start out by counting: 1 - 2 - 3 - 4

Now do a down strum on each number. By doing down strums on the numbers, you are automatically doing up strums on the &'s. Now strum the downs and ups and count:

You are now strumming eighth notes.

The most common eighth note strum to know is:

This is commonly referred to as the "folk strum."

For bars that have 2 chords per measure, each being worth 2 beats, with the first chord on the 1 and the second chord on the 3, you can default to this strum:

Practice tapping your foot with these strums. You will tap down on the downbeats (numbers) and up on the upbeats (&'s). If your foot is going down, your pick is going down. If your foot is going up, your pick is going up.

Exercise

For the next set of strum patterns, practice keeping your arm swinging during the counts when you aren't strumming the strings—essentially air strumming. This will help make you a more solid rhythm player, and will help you play different strum patterns.

Strum the strings on (⬇) and (⬆); air strum during ⇩ and ⇧.

(⬇) ⇧ ⇩ (⬆) (⬇) (⬆) ⇩ ⇧
1 & 2 & 3 & 4 &

(⬇) (⬆) ⇩ ⇧ (⬇) (⬆) ⇩ (⬆)
1 & 2 & 3 & 4 &

⇩ (⬆) ⇩ (⬆) ⇩ (⬆) (⬇) (⬆)
1 & 2 & 3 & 4 &

(⬇) ⇧ ⇩ ⇧ ⇩ ⇧ ⇩ (⬆)
1 & 2 & 3 & 4 &

Strum Pattern 2 : Sixteenth note strum

First start out by counting: 1 & 2 & 3 & 4 &

Now, down strum on each number and each &, and count:

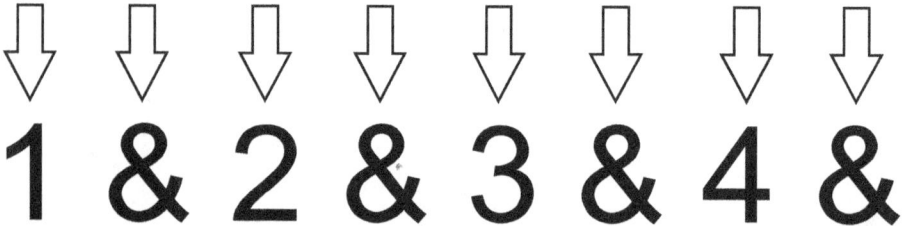

By doing this strum, you are automatically strumming ups in between your downs. When counting sixteenth notes, you are counting: 1e&a2e&a3e&a4e&a. You will be strumming up on each "e" and "a." Now strum all of the downs and ups and count:

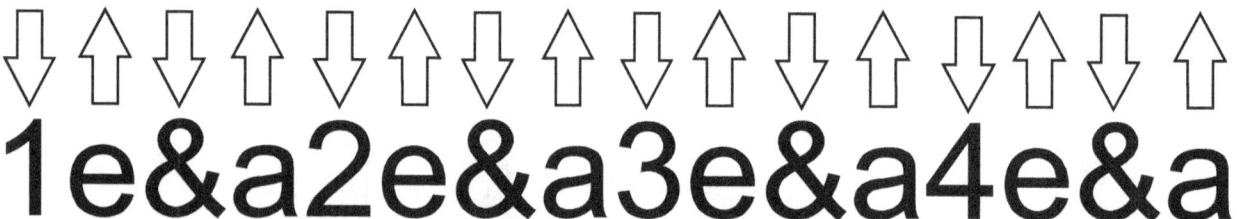

You are now strumming sixteenth notes. Here is a common sixteenth note strum pattern:

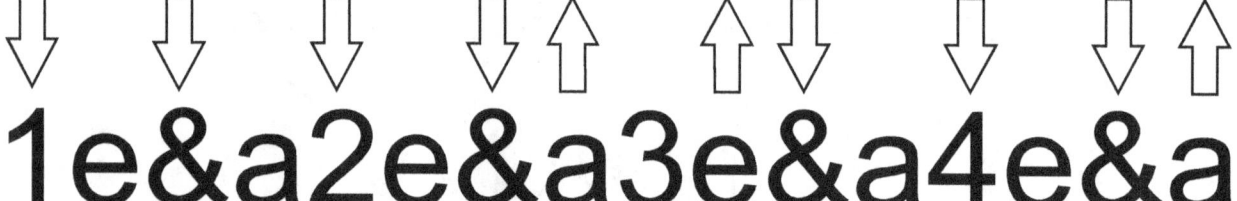

Here is another common sixteenth note strum pattern, especially when you have 2 chords per bar:

Helpful tip: The most important thing to remember while doing any strum is to **keep your arm swinging**. Where the arrows are missing, you are still strumming, just not hitting the strings. Variations on these strums will go virtually unnoticed when played with other instruments. So, if you accidentally add in an extra strum, or leave one out, it won't matter, just as long as you are swinging your arm to the beat. Most guitarists aren't rigid with their strumming; they will add or subtract downs and ups for variety.

Exercise

For the next set of strum patterns, again practice keeping your arm swinging during the counts when you aren't strumming the strings—essentially air strumming. This will help make you a more solid rhythm player, and will help you play different strum patterns.

Strum the strings on ⬇ and ⬆; air strum during ⇩ and ⇧.

⬇⬆⇩⇧⬇⬆⇩⇧⬇⬆⇩⇧⬇⬆⬇⬆
1 e & a 2 e & a 3 e & a 4 e & a

⬇⇧⇩⬆⬇⇧⇩⬆⬇⇧⇩⬆⬇⇩⇩⬆
1 e & a 2 e & a 3 e & a 4 e & a

⬇⇧⇩⬆⇩⬆⬇⇧⇩⬆⬇⇧⇩⬆⇩⬆⬇⇧⇩⬆
1 e & a 2 e & a 3 e & a 4 e & a

⬇⬆⬇⇧⇩⇧⇩⬆⬇⬆⬇⇧⇩⇧⬇⬆
1 e & a 2 e & a 3 e & a 4 e & a

You can also try the above strums with scratch mutes in place of the air strums. Rest your fretting hand fingers gently on the strings and strum to produce a rhythmic sound where you were previously missing the strings.

Strum Pattern 3 : 6/8 or 12/8

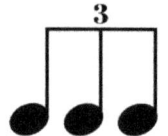 

When in 6/8, the beat is felt in 2 big beats, and each beat is a triplet. When in 12/8, the beat is felt in 4 big beats, and each beat is also a triplet. A common rhythm for a song in these time signatures is swung eighth notes. Swung eighth notes is when you play the first note of a triplet and hold (or rest) during the 2nd note, then play the 3rd note.

6/8 with swung eighths:

When playing swung eighth notes think "long-short."

First start out by counting: 1 - 2 - 3 - 4 - 5 - 6

Now do a down strum on numbers 1 and 4. Then do an up strum on numbers 3 and 6 and count:

⬇ ⬆ ⬇ ⬆
1 2 3 4 5 6

You can also feel this as 1 & 2 &, or "long-short-long-short."

6/8 with sixteenths:

Another way to strum in 6/8 is to strum sixteenth notes. Remember, each beat is already an eighth note, so to strum sixteenth notes, we'll only need two strums per beat: a down and an up.

First start out by counting: 1 - 2 - 3 - 4 - 5 - 6

Now do a down strum on each number. By doing down strums on the numbers, you are automatically doing up strums on the &'s. Now strum the downs and ups and count:

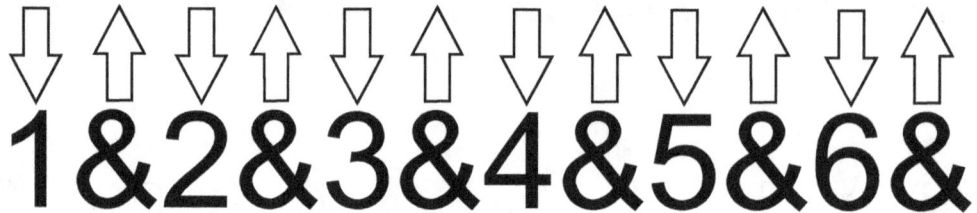

Below is a popular strum using this concept:

<u>Helpful tip</u>: Accent the 1 and 4 when strumming sixteenth notes in 6/8.

12/8 with swung eighths:

First start out by counting: 1 - 2 - 3 - 4 - 5 - 6 - 7 - 8 - 9 - 10 - 11 - 12

Now do a down strum on numbers 1, 4, 7, and 10. Then do an up strum on numbers 3, 6, 9, and 12, and count:

You can also feel this as 1 & 2 & 3 & 4 &, or "long-short-long-short-long-short-long-short."

12/8 with sixteenths:

Another way to strum in 12/8 is to strum sixteenth notes. Remember, each beat is already an eighth note, so to strum sixteenth notes we'll only need two strums per beat: a down and an up.

First start out by counting: 1 - 2 - 3 - 4 - 5 - 6 - 7 - 8 - 9 - 10 - 11 - 12

Now do a down strum on each number. By doing down strums on the numbers, you are automatically doing up strums on the &'s. Now strum the downs and ups and count:

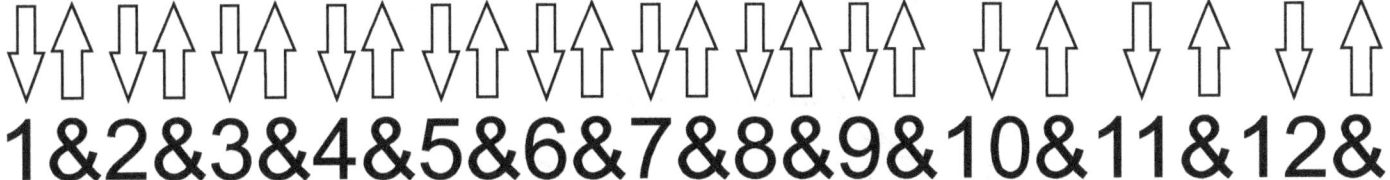

Below is a popular strum using this concept:

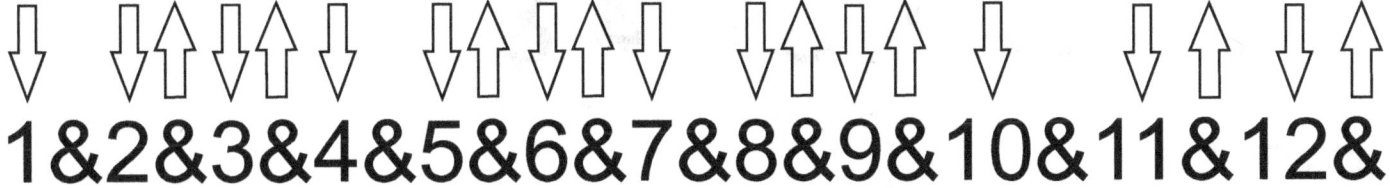

<u>Helpful tip:</u> Accent the 1, 4, 7, and 10 when strumming sixteenth notes in 12/8.

Transition strum:

In order for a chord progression to sound smooth, you will usually need to add in a *transition strum*. When changing from one chord to the next, you will **lift your fretting hand** during the *last up strum* of a measure. This will cause you to strum the strings open on the & of the last beat to get to the next chord. We will use our common eighth note strum in 4/4 as an example:

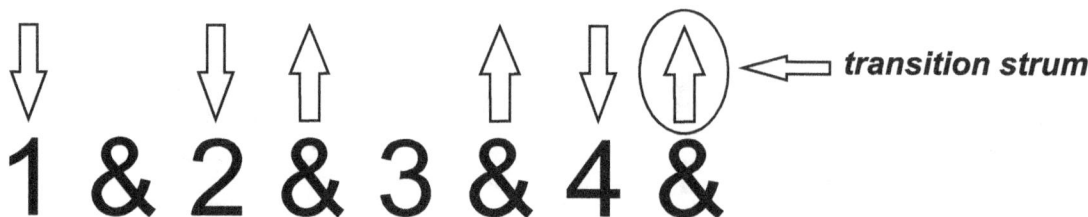

Exercise

• Form a G chord and do the above strum pattern, lifting all of your fingers off the strings on the last up strum.

• Try to transition smoothly from a G chord to a C chord using the above strum pattern. Use the transition strum to position your fingers for the next chord.

You can also use transition strums in between chord changes within a measure. Here is an example of a popular eighth note strum with transition strums:

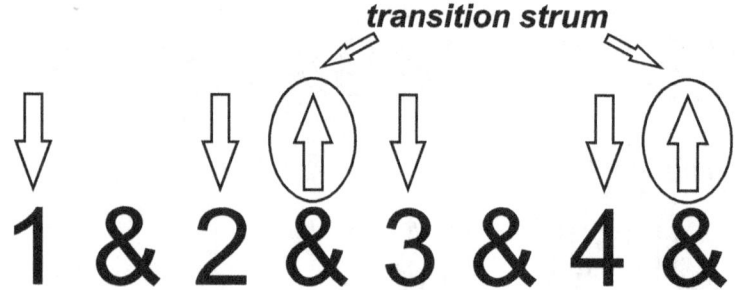

Exercise

• Form a G chord and strum down, down (↓ ↓).

• Lift all your fingers off the strings and strum an up (↑) on the open strings.

• Quickly form a C chord and strum down, down (↓ ↓).

• Lift all your fingers off the strings again and strum an up (↑) on the open strings.

• Repeat the pattern, keeping a steady rhythm with no pause as you switch chords.

Determining which strum pattern to use might take a bit of trial and error. It will matter how fast or slow you are counting the song. You might be hearing a bar as a fast 4, when it is actually only the first 2 beats of the bar at a slow tempo. If the song has drums, they will be able to help you determine the count of the song.

Let's take the song "Let it Be" by The Beatles as an example. You *could* count each chord getting 4 beats as its own bar, but you *should* count it as each chord getting 2 beats with 2 chords in each bar. If you tried to use an eighth note strum it wouldn't sound right with the song. Using a sixteenth note strum would be the right choice.

Let It Be - The Beatles

↓ ↓ ↓ ↓↑↓ ↓ ↓ ↓↑ | ↓ ↓ ↓ ↓↑↓ ↓ ↓ ↓↑
C   G   Am   F

↓ ↓ ↓ ↓↑↓ ↓ ↓ ↓↑ | ↓ ↓ ↓ ↓↑↓ ↓ ↓ ↓↑
C   G   F   C

Generally speaking, if a song is at a slow tempo, try a sixteenth note strum pattern.

Tempo = Speed of a song

BPM = Beats Per Minute

Drummer - "What is the tempo of the new song you wrote?"
Guitarist - "It's 120 bpm."
Drummer - "Cool."

Helpful tips:

• You don't have to strum all of your strings with a down or up strum. In fact, it will often sound more musical and dynamic if you are only strumming some of the strings. An example would be strumming strings 6, 5, and 4 with a down strum and 1, 2, and 3 with an up strum.

• A bass strum is when you are only picking the lowest note of a chord. A lot of artists will substitute a bass strum for the first down strum in a bar. You will commonly see it written like this: B ↓↑ ↑↓↑.

Exercise

Here are some examples of songs with strum patterns you can try:

Eighth note strum patterns

Last Kiss - Pearl Jam

↓ ↓↑ ↑↓↑ | ↓ ↑↓ ↑↓↑↓ | ↓ ↑↑ ↑↓↑↓ | ↓ ↑↑ ↑↓↑
G   Em   C   D

Good Riddance - Green Day

↓ ↓↑ ↑↓↑↓ | ↓ ↑↓ ↑↓↑↓ | ↓ ↑↑ ↑↓↑↓ | ↓ ↑↑ ↑↓↑
G   G   Cadd9   D

After Hours - The Velvet Underground (swung 8ths)

↓↑↓↑↓↑↓↑ | ↓↑↓↑↓↑↓↑ | ↓↑↓↑↓↑↓↑ | ↓↑↓↑↓↑↓↑
C   A7   Dm   G

Sixteenth note strum patterns

Fade Into You - Mazzy Star (in 6/8)

↓ ↑↓↑↓ ↑↓↑↓ | ↑↓↑↓ ↑↓↑↓ | ↑↓↑↓ ↑↓↑↓ | ↑↓↑
A   E   Bm   Bm

Wish You Were Here - Pink Floyd

↓ ↓↑↑↓ ↑↓↑↓ | ↓ ↑↓ ↓ ↑↓↑↓ | ↓ ↑↓ ↓ ↑↓↑↓ | ↓ ↑↓ ↓ ↑↓↑
C/G   D/F#   Am   G

22 - Taylor Swift

↓ ↓ ↓ ↓↑↓↑↓ | ↓ ↓↑↓ ↓ ↓ ↓↑↓↑↓ | ↓ ↓↑
G   D   C   D

Heart of Gold - Neil Young

↓ ↓ ↓ ↓↑↓ | ↓ ↓ ↓↑↓ | ↓ ↓ ↓↑↓ | ↓ ↓ ↓↑
Em   C   D   G

Yoshimi Battles the Pink Robots, Pt. 1 - The Flaming Lips

↓↑↓↑↓ ↓↑ ↑↓ ↓ | ↓↑↓↑↓ ↓↑ ↑↓ ↓ | ↓↑↓↑↓↑↓↑↓↑↓↑↓↑↓↑ | ↑↓ ↓↑↓↑↓ ↓↑
C   Em   Dm   F   G

PICKING INDIVIDUAL NOTES

Down pick
(aka down strum)

Up pick
(aka up strum)

You have a few options when picking individual notes on the guitar:

• **Alternate picking:** When you consistently alternate between down and up picks based on the rhythm. This technique follows what was just covered with strumming: **down** on **downbeats** and **up** on **upbeats**.

Examples:

 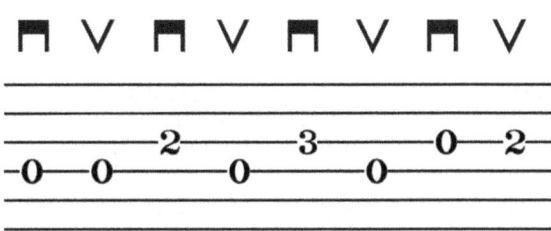

• **Economy picking:** When you pick in the direction of the next note you are playing. This is often used when arpeggiating chords, or playing each note individually in a chord.

Examples:

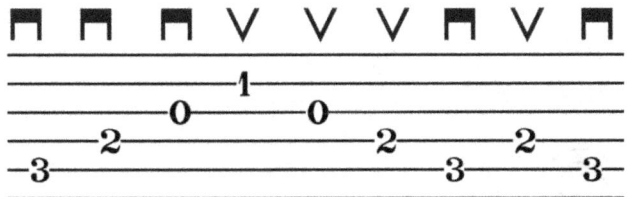 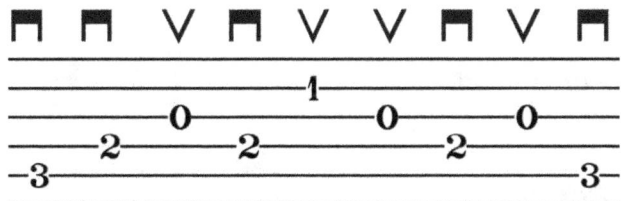

<u>**Helpful tip:**</u> Be intentional with your picking. Generally speaking, you will usually either be doing alternate picking or economy picking.

INTERVALS

An interval is the distance between 2 notes. Intervals are important because they are the building blocks of both melodies and chords. There are 2 different ways to play an interval on the guitar.

> **_Melodic Interval:_** This is when you are playing a melody, or one note at a time.
>
> **_Harmonic Interval:_** This is when you are playing 2 or more notes at the same time, or a chord.

First, we will look at three different types of intervals.

• *Major intervals*: As a general rule, major intervals sound happy. You can use a major scale to find major intervals. But not every interval is major in a major scale. ☺

• *Minor intervals*: As a general rule, minor intervals sound sad. To find minor intervals, we take major intervals and lower them by a half step (one fret). ☹

• *Perfect intervals*: These are not major or minor. Their sound quality is pure or simple. We will also be using the major scale to find perfect intervals.

Below are the notes in a C major scale with the intervals. These are all ascending intervals, measured from the lowest C.

C major scale →	C	D	E	F	G	A	B	C
Major 2nd →	Ⓒ	Ⓓ	E	F	G	A	B	C
Major 3rd →	Ⓒ	D	Ⓔ	F	G	A	B	C
Perfect 4th →	Ⓒ	D	E	Ⓕ	G	A	B	C
Perfect 5th →	Ⓒ	D	E	F	Ⓖ	A	B	C
Major 6th →	Ⓒ	D	E	F	G	Ⓐ	B	C
Major 7th →	Ⓒ	D	E	F	G	A	Ⓑ	C
Perfect octave →	Ⓒ	D	E	F	G	A	B	Ⓒ

MAJOR AND PERFECT INTERVALS

Now let's look at how to play these intervals. We will use a one-octave major scale to play the major and perfect intervals. Another name for a major scale is an *Ionian* scale.

The numbers are the fingering:

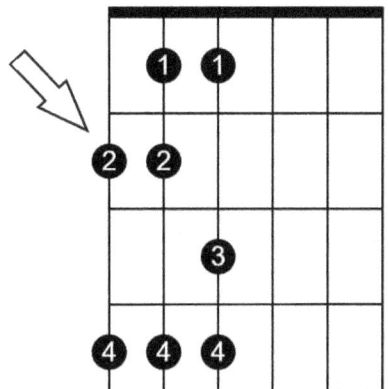

Here the numbers are the intervals:

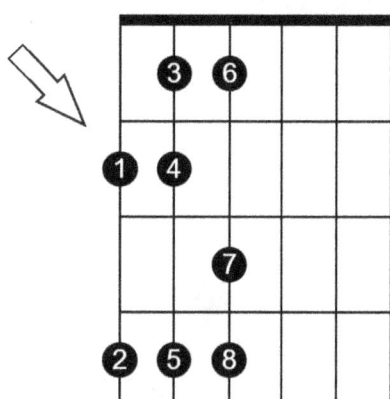

By playing from the first note of the major scale to any other degree of the scale, you'll be playing that interval. Below are the intervals listed out separately. Use the major scale fingering to play these intervals.

Major intervals:

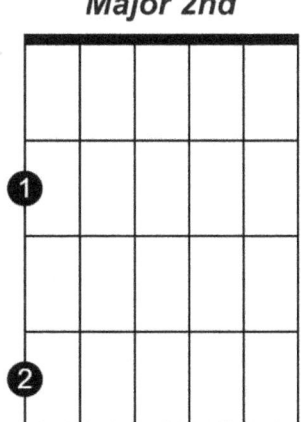
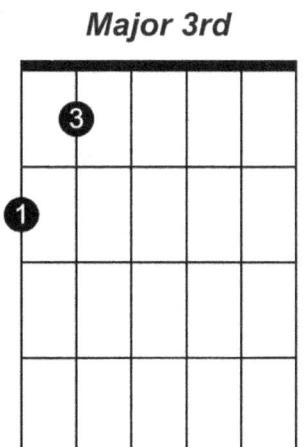
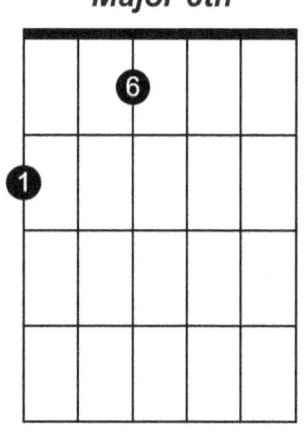
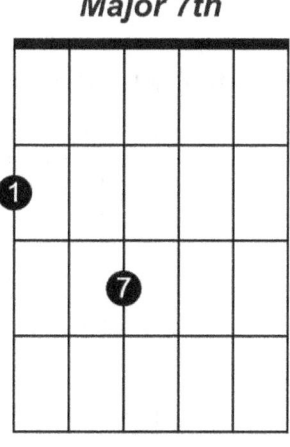

Perfect intervals:

Perfect intervals are the same in both a major and minor scale. More is covered on the next page when you alter a 4th or 5th.

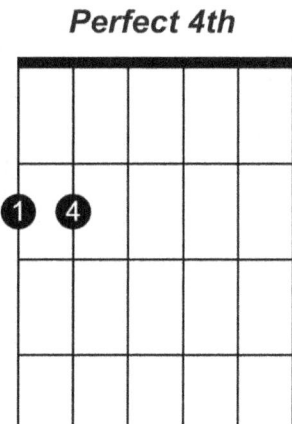
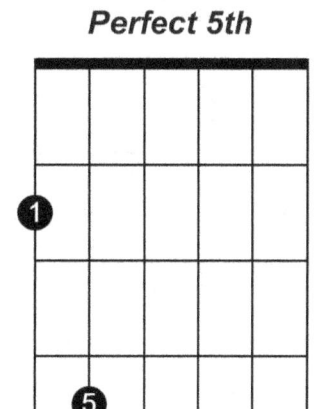

41

The great part about learning the intervals like this is that these are all moveable shapes. It doesn't matter what note you start on, they will always be the correct interval. It will be easiest to learn and remember these intervals by using your major scale fingering. This won't always be the way you ultimately play them, as it will depend on the context of what you are playing.

MINOR INTERVALS

Next, let's look at minor intervals. Instead of using a scale, we'll focus on lowering the major intervals. To make a major interval minor, you just need to lower it by 1 fret.

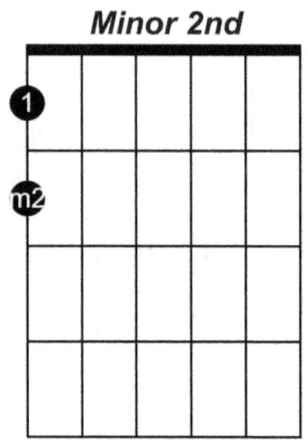
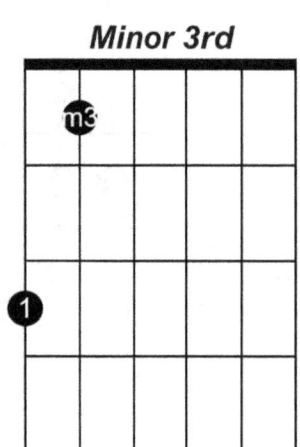
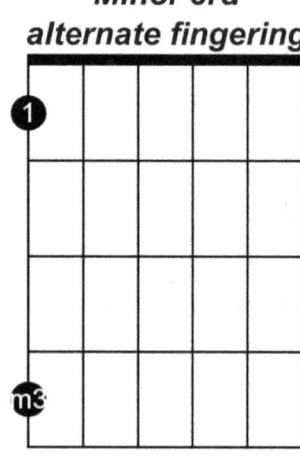
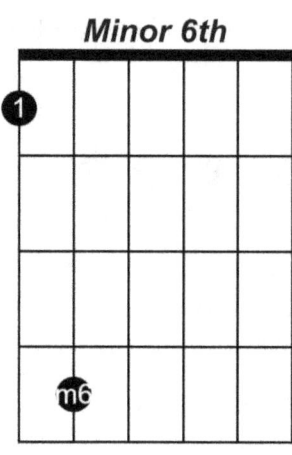

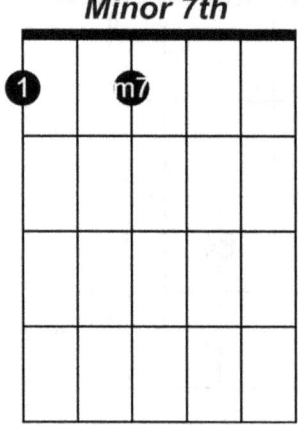

You can also use a **Phrygian** scale (minor scale with a lowered 2) to identify minor intervals:

The numbers are the fingering: Here the numbers are the intervals:

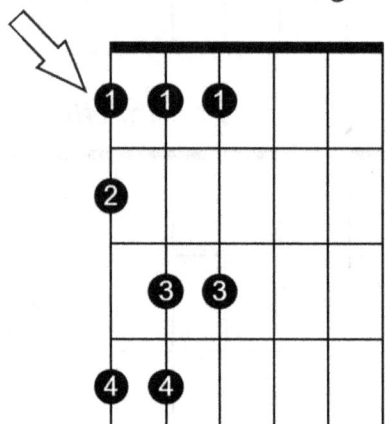
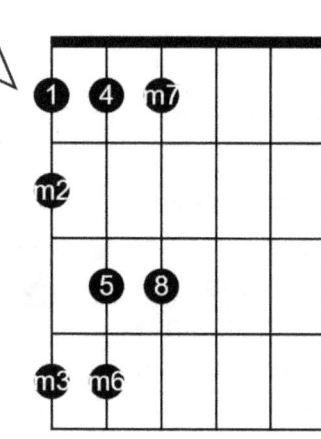

One important interval that has not been mentioned yet is a *tritone*. A tritone occurs when you **raise a perfect 4th** by 1 fret, making it **augmented**, or **lowering a perfect 5th** by 1 fret, making in **diminished**. This interval by itself sounds very dissonant and unstable, or unresolved. It is said to be the devil's interval, and rumored to be banned in churches long ago. This interval produces the "blue note" when played in a minor pentatonic scale. To hear a **harmonic tritone** in action, listen to the first 2 bars of "Purple Haze" by Jimi Hendrix. Noel Redding, the bass player, is playing an E note while Jimi is playing a B♭ note, so together they are playing a tritone. To hear a **melodic tritone** in action, listen to the opening of "YYZ" by Rush. Both Geddy Lee and Alex Lifeson are playing a tritone riff together.

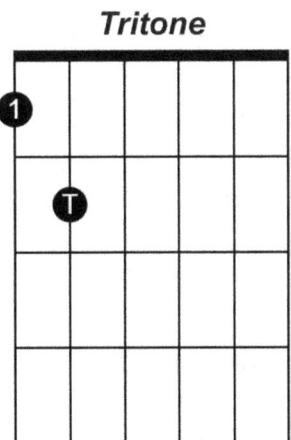

Exercise

Practice playing each of these intervals:

- Major 3rd
- Major 6th
- Major 2nd
- Major 7th
- Perfect 5th
- Minor 3rd
- Minor 7th
- Minor 2nd
- Minor 6th
- Perfect 4th
- Tritone

INTERVAL FORMULAS

Intervals are measured by whole and half steps. Remember that on the guitar, 1 fret is a half step while 2 frets is a whole step. Intervals are formulaic, so once you know the formula of whole and/or half steps for an interval, it will always be the same. These formulas tell you how to get to a specific interval from a root note. Here are the formulas for the intervals you've learned:

Unison = same note

Minor 2nd = ⇨ 1 half step

Major 2nd = ⇨ 1 whole step or 2 half steps

Minor 3rd = ⇨ 1 whole step and 1 half step or 3 half steps

Major 3rd = ⇨ 2 whole steps or 4 half steps

Perfect 4th = ⇨ 2 whole steps and 1 half step or 5 half steps

Tritone = ⇨ 3 whole steps or 6 half steps

Perfect 5th = ⇨ 3 whole steps and 1 half step or 7 half steps

Minor 6th = ⇨ 4 whole steps or 8 half steps

Major 6th = ⇨ 4 whole steps and 1 half step or 9 half steps

Minor 7th = ⇨ 5 whole steps or 10 half steps

Major 7th = ⇨ 5 whole steps and 1 half step or 11 half steps

Octave = ⇨ 6 whole steps or 12 half steps

You don't need to have all of these memorized, but you should understand the concept.

I cannot stress enough the importance of learning and being fluid with intervals. Understanding intervals will make everything you do on the guitar easier to understand, from playing by ear and learning modes to understanding chords and even figuring out vocal harmonies.

One other important distinction on intervals is the note names you give them.

Example 1
For this example we'll look at a minor 3rd from a C. If you were only going by the formula, which is going up 3 frets from the root, you might want to call that a D#. This would be incorrect because from a C to a D is only a 2nd. Therefore a D# would be considered an augmented 2nd, not a minor 3rd. You should call a minor 3rd of a C an E♭.

Major 3rd

Minor 3rd

Example 2
Let's take a major third from D for this example. If you were only going by the formula, which is going up 4 frets from the root, you might want to call that a G♭. This would be incorrect because from a D to a G is a 4th. Therefore a G♭ would be considered an diminished 4th, not a major 3rd. You should call a major 3rd of a D an F#.

Minor 3rd

Major 3rd

<u>*Helpful tip:*</u> If you use the musical alphabet, you will always land on the right letter name by counting up from your root. Then you will just need to determine whether the note is natural, flatted, or sharped.

TRIADS

A *triad* is a chord made of three notes stacked in intervals of a third. In other words, it's the three notes that make up a major, minor, augmented, or diminished chord. On the guitar, there are many ways and positions to play triads, but for now we'll focus on shapes rooted on the **E string**.

Learning these shapes is useful because it helps you identify the notes that form each chord. Under each diagram, you'll see how the triad is built by stacking thirds: the first interval is from the *root* to the *third*, and the second is from the *third* to the *fifth*.

Major Triad

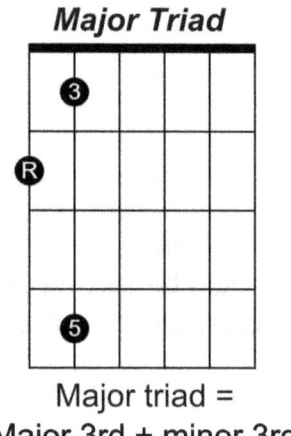

Major triad =
Major 3rd + minor 3rd

Minor Triad

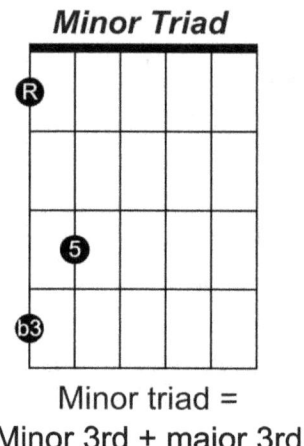

Minor triad =
Minor 3rd + major 3rd

Augmented Triad

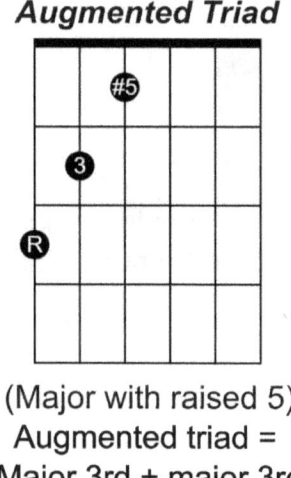

(Major with raised 5)
Augmented triad =
Major 3rd + major 3rd

Diminished Triad

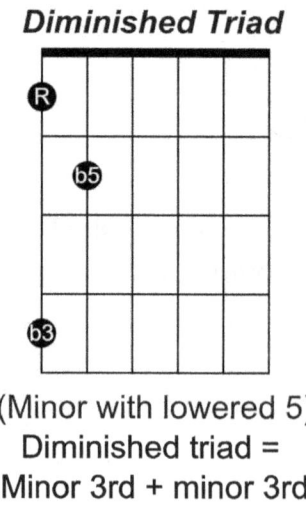

(Minor with lowered 5)
Diminished triad =
Minor 3rd + minor 3rd

You will have more context for these as you work further along in the book. These shapes are all transferable to roots on the A and D strings as well.

OPEN CHORDS

An **open chord** is a chord that uses one or more open strings. These are usually the first chords you learn on guitar and are often nicknamed "**cowboy chords**." Thousands of songs have been written using nothing more than open chords.

Open chords are named after their **lowest sounding note**—which isn't always the lowest note you fret. For example, in an open **E major chord**, the lowest fretted note is the 2nd fret of the A string (a B). But because the low E string is played open, **E** is the lowest sounding note, and that's why the chord is called E major.

All major and minor chords are built from just three notes, called a **triad**:

- **1 (Root)** – the note the chord is named after

- **3 (Third)** – either a major 3rd (two whole steps) or a minor 3rd (a step and a half)

- **5 (Fifth)** – a perfect 5th (three and a half steps above the root)

The **only difference** between a major and minor chord is the quality of the **3rd**. Major chords have a major 3rd, while minor chords have a minor 3rd.

You might wonder: "*If a chord only has three notes, why am I strumming five or six strings?*" The answer is that some of those strings are repeating the same notes in different **octaves**.

Let's look at the open **C major chord** as an example.

- Start on **C** (the root).

- Go up a major 3rd → **E**.

- Go up a minor 3rd (a step and a half) → **G**.

So, the notes in a C chord are **C–E–G**. When you strum the open C shape, you're just playing these three notes, repeated across different strings. Here are 2 different versions of an open C chord:

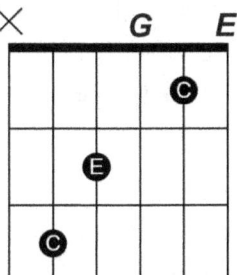 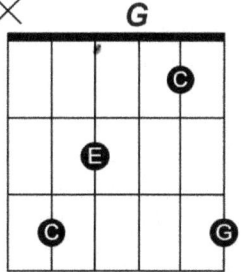

The only notes in this chord are C, E, and G. But we have octaves of both C and E.

In this version of the chord, we swapped out a G for the open E string. Since we still have all 3 notes represented, it is still considered an open C chord.

Next, let's look at the open G chord. You've probably already seen a few different versions of this shape, and understanding the notes inside the chord will explain why these variations work.

The notes that make up a **G major chord** are:

G (the root)

B (the major 3rd, a major 3rd above G)

D (the perfect 5th, a 5th above G)

Every version of the open G chord contains **only these 3 notes**, sometimes repeated in different octaves.

We'll start with the most common version:

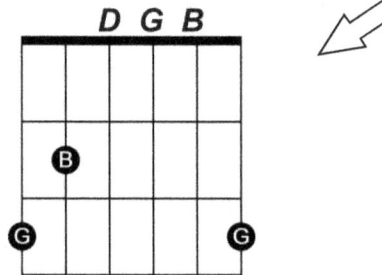

In this version of a G chord, we have 3 G's, 2 B's, and a D.

Another popular way to play an open G chord is:

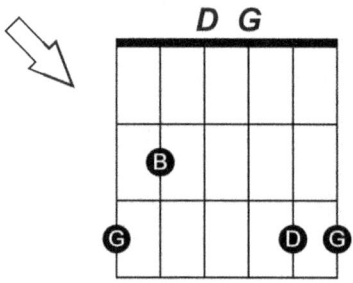

In this version of a G chord, we have 3 G's, 1 B, and 2 D's. You would call this a different voicing of a G chord compared to the first one.

A lot of people play their open G chord like this as well:

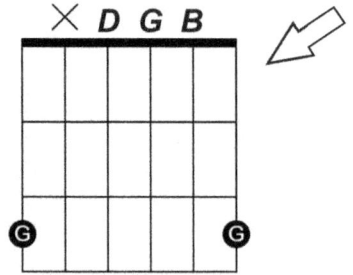

In this version of a G chord, we have 3 G's, 1 B, and 1 D.

All 3 of these are acceptable ways to play the open G chord. You will probably gravitate toward one, and then use one of the others when a song specifically calls for it.

At first, most guitarists struggle with the concept of having many ways to play the same chord, and knowing when to use which version. Eventually, you will know many more ways to play chords, and when you are fluid at it, it won't be as daunting. You can find an open chord dictionary at the end of this book.

BARRE CHORDS

A **barre chord** is a moveable chord shape where you press down on every string with your fretting hand, replacing the open strings you'd normally use in an open chord. This makes the chord **moveable** anywhere on the neck. In contrast, open chords use open strings and stay fixed in one position.

The two most common barre chord shapes are based on the open **E chord** and the open **A chord**. These are called the "**E shape**" and the "**A shape**."

Before trying to play these barre chord forms, make sure you're comfortable with their open chord versions first—this will help you understand how the shapes work when moved up the neck.

OPEN E CHORDS

E Major

E Major 7

E Dominant 7 (E7) V1

E Dominant 7 (E7) V2

E Minor

E Minor 7

E SHAPE BARRE CHORDS

With barre chords, your index finger essentially becomes the nut. These are called "shapes" or "forms" because it isn't technically an E chord unless you are placing the barre at the 12th fret.

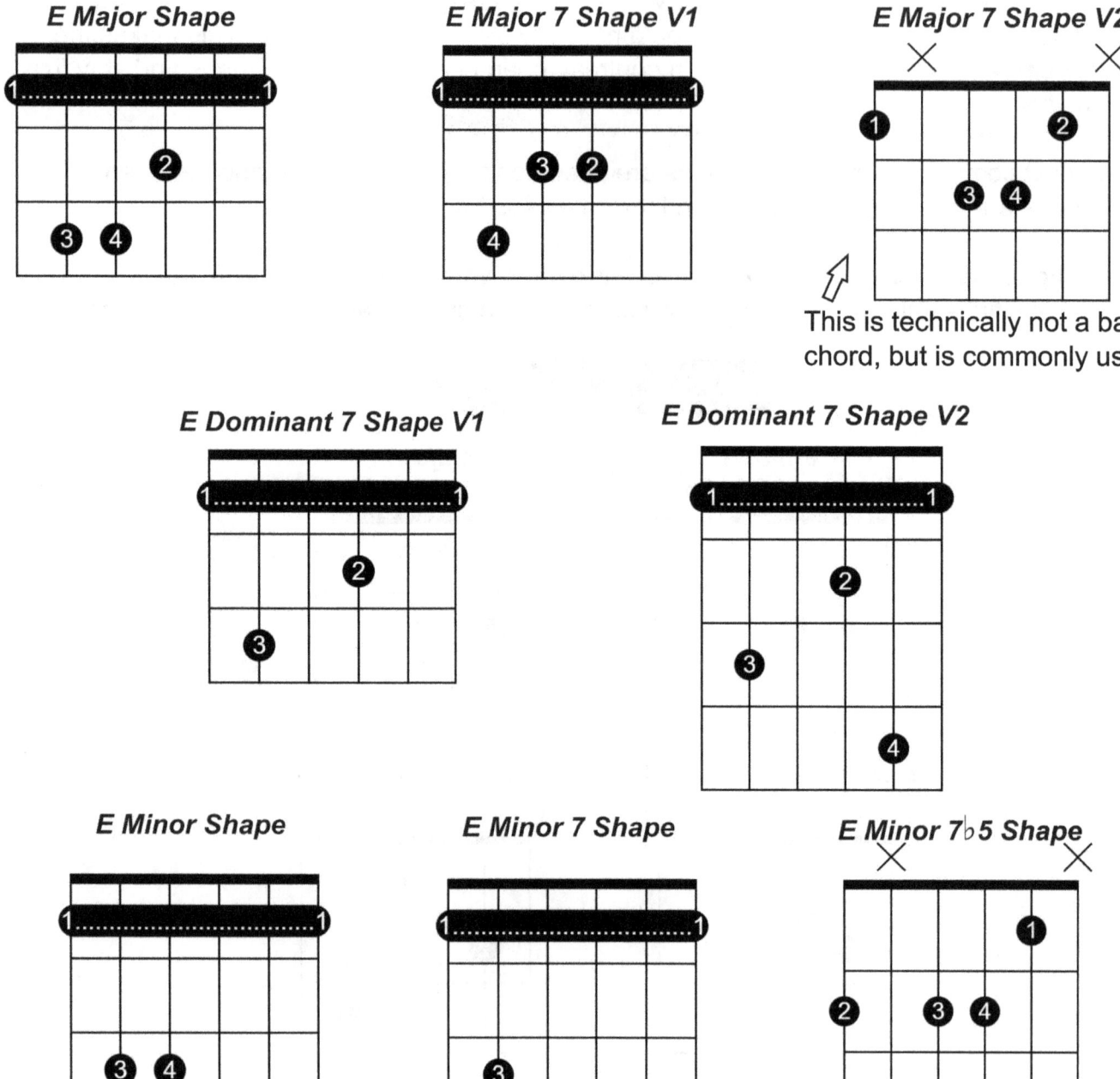

This is technically not a barre chord, but is commonly used.

To use these, first find the root note of the chord on the low E string, and then place the shape from that note. For instance, if you need a G minor chord, find the G on the E string (3rd fret)—this is where the index finger will barre across—and then place the rest of the shape from there. You are now playing a G minor chord using the E minor shape.

<u>**Simple rule**</u>*:* If the root is on the E string, use an E shape.

OPEN A CHORDS

A Major
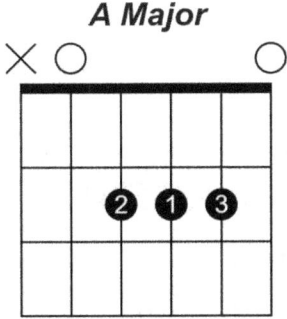

A Major 7
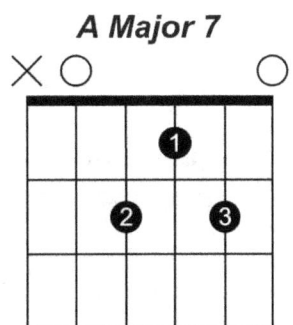

A Dominant 7 (A7) V1
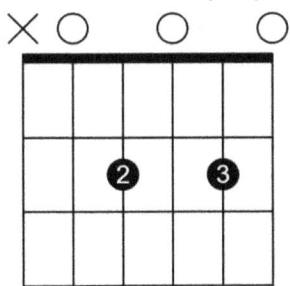

A Dominant 7 (A7) V2
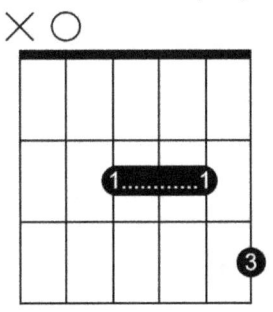

A Minor
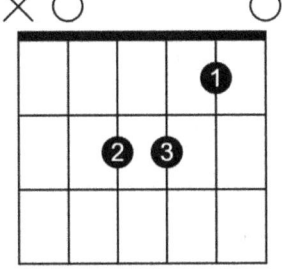

A Minor 7 V1
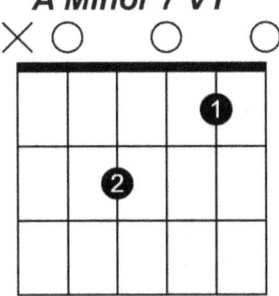

A Minor 7 V2
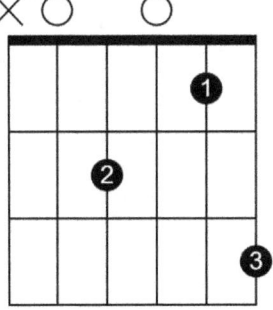

A Minor 7♭5
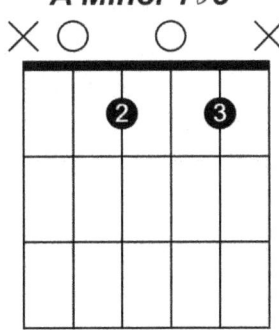

A SHAPE BARRE CHORDS

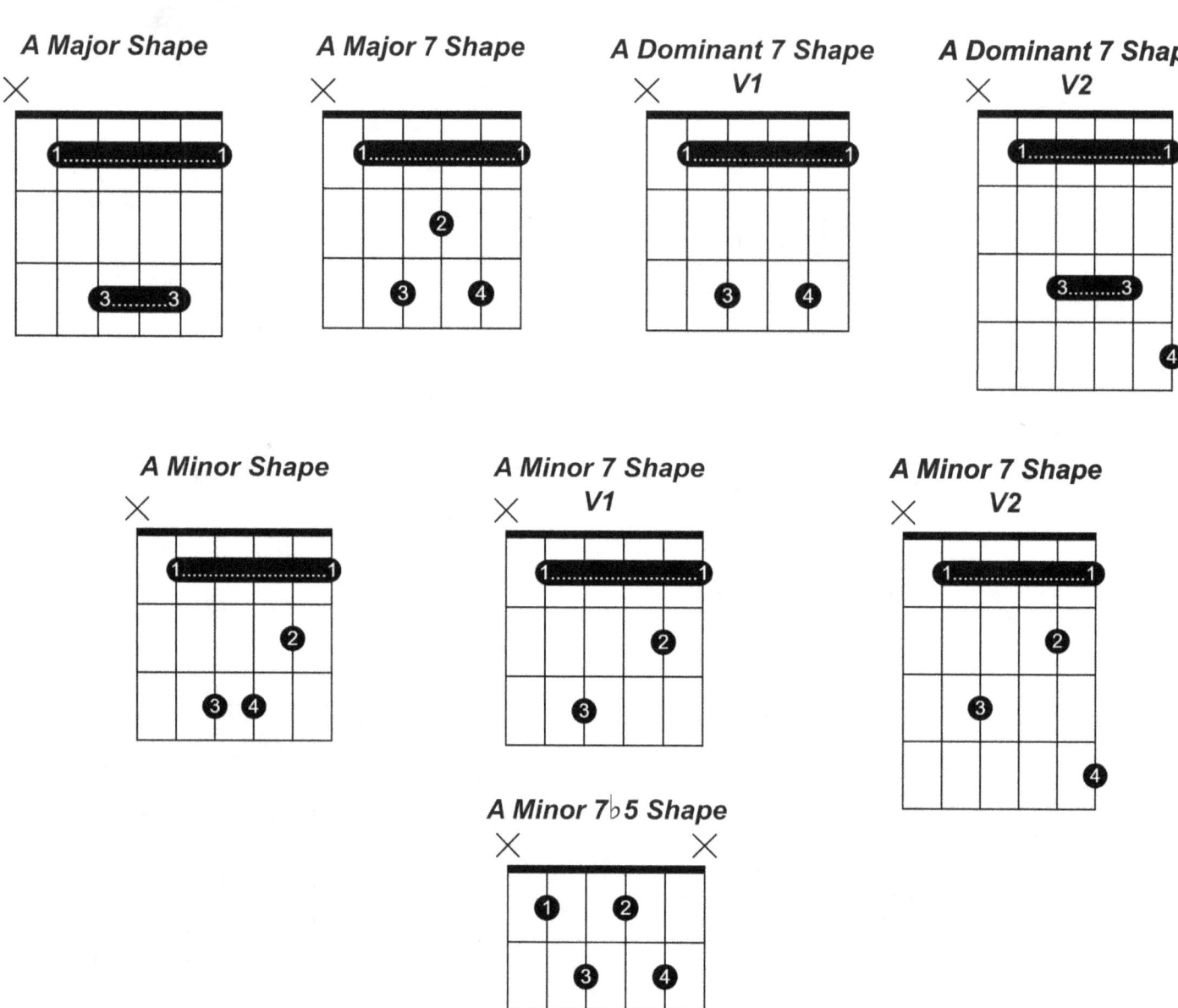

For the A shapes, find the root on the A string with your index finger and place the rest of your fingers in the shape from there. For instance, if you need a D major chord, find the D on the A string (5th fret)—this is where the index finger will barre across—and then place the rest of the shape from there. You are now playing a D major chord using the A major shape.

Helpful tip: When playing an A shape barre chord, use the tip of your index finger to lightly touch the side of your 6th string to mute it.

Simple rule: If the root is on the A string, use an A shape.

Exercise

A good way to practice barre chords is to pick a chord and play it in both E and A shapes. This exercise is not only good for practicing and solidifying barre chords in both shapes, but will also help you with note names on both the E and A strings.

Let's take a C major chord as an example.

For the E shape:
- Find a C on the E string, which is the 8th fret
- Barre across the 8th fret with your index finger
- Use the E major shape from there

For the A shape:
- Find a C on the A string, which is the 3rd fret
- Barre across the 3rd fret with your index finger
- Use the A major shape from there

These chords should sound similar, but the voicing—or order of notes in the chord—will sound different.

C major using E shape

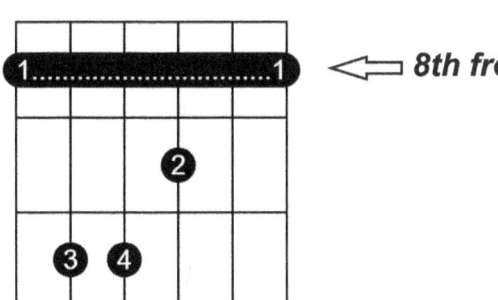 ⇐ 8th fret

C major using A shape

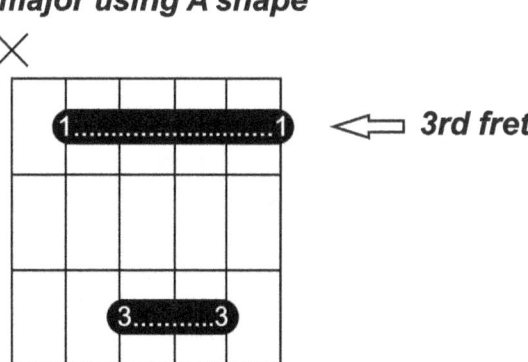 ⇐ 3rd fret

Now, try and find other matching chords using E and A shapes. Remember to try different chord types (minor, dominant, etc.).

>> *E shapes use a root on the E string*

>> *A shapes use a root on the A string*

Helpful tip: When playing a barre chord, start with the barre (your index finger). Next, put your 3rd and 4th fingers down as a pair. Lastly place your 2nd finger, if it is being used. You're putting your fingers down in the order that you will strum them.

OCTAVE PATTERNS

An *octave* is the distance from one note to the next highest note with the same name. For example, if you play a *C*, the next highest *C* is one octave above it. The same is true for any note—and you can also move backward to find the lower octave. A simple example on guitar is playing the **open E string** and then the **E at the double-dot** fret (12th fret) on that same string. That's an octave, and there are no other E's in between those two notes.

We'll learn **5 octave patterns** that connect together so you can play octaves anywhere across the fretboard. Each pattern will be assigned a number, and later, we'll use those same numbers when we get to the pentatonic scales.

Pattern 1
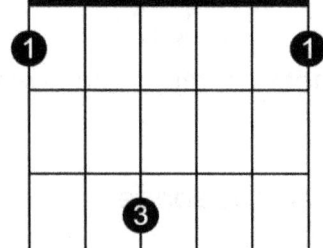

Pattern 2
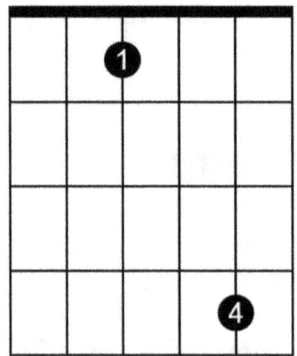

Pattern 3
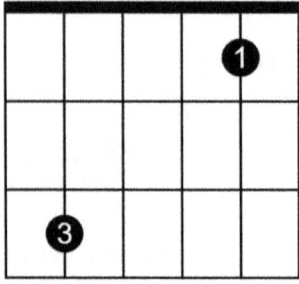

Pattern 4
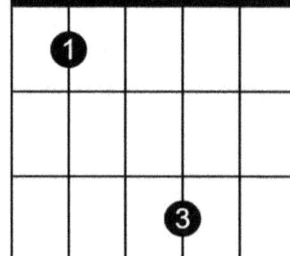

Pattern 5
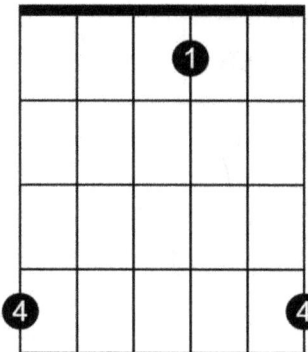

These might seem a bit random, but I will show you on the next page that there are actually only 3 patterns you need to learn to use this system!

Patterns 1 and 4 are actually the same. Put your first finger on any note on the 6th or 5th string and go up 2 strings and 2 frets. On Pattern 1, we include the 1st string because the 6th and 1st strings are the same note, just 2 octaves apart. Below is Pattern 1 without the 1st string so you can see how they are the same.

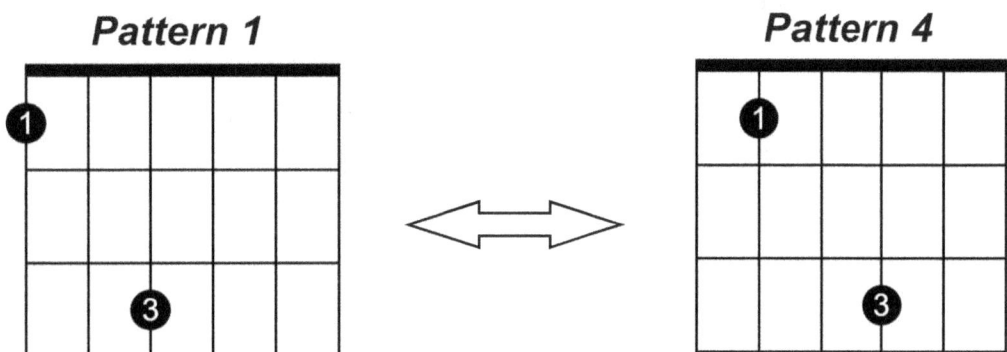

Patterns 2 and 5 are also the same. Put your first finger on any note on the 4th or 3rd string and go up 2 strings and 3 frets. On Pattern 5, we have the 6th string included because the 6th and 1st strings are the same note, just 2 octaves apart. Below is Pattern 5 without the 6th string so you can see how they are the same.

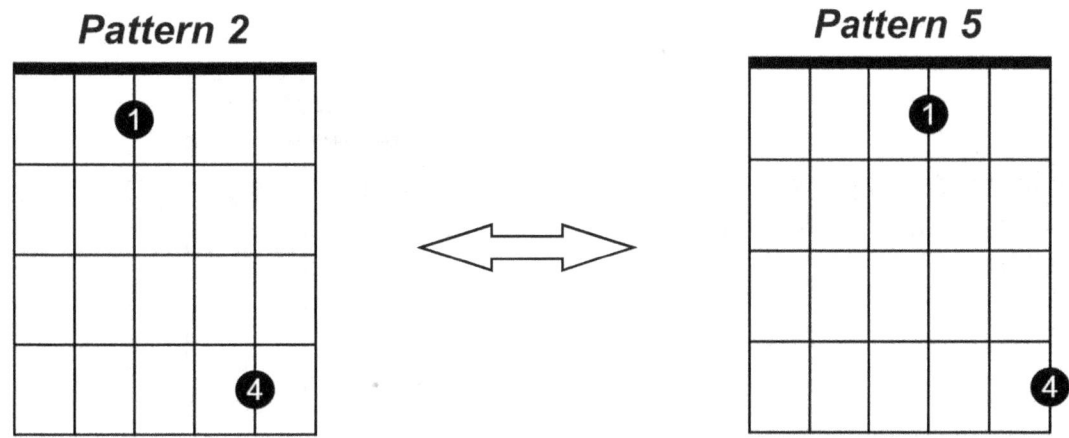

Think of Pattern 3 as an open C chord with no 2nd finger.

These patterns are useful on their own, but it is also important to be able to tie them together. We will start with Pattern 1 and go from there, but ultimately you can start from any pattern.

1. Start by playing **Pattern 1**.

Next put your 1st finger where your 3rd finger was. This will put you in Pattern 2.

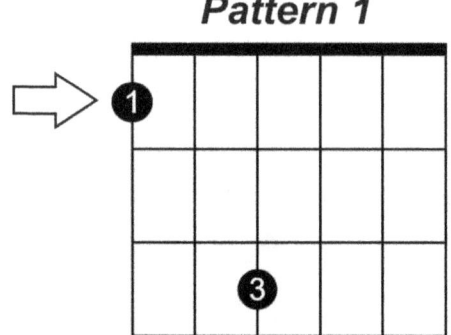

Pattern 1

2. Now play **Pattern 2**.

Next put your index finger where your 4th finger was. This will put you in Pattern 3.

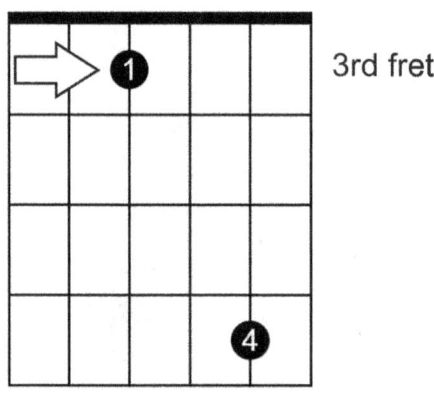

Pattern 2 — 3rd fret

3. Now play **Pattern 3**.

Next put your index finger where your 3rd finger was. This will put you in Pattern 4.

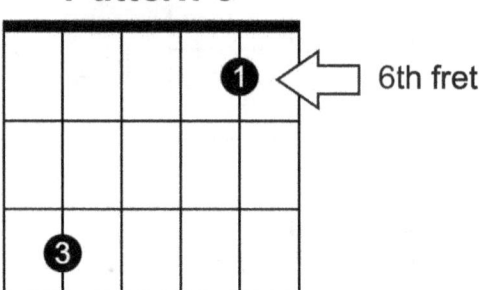

Pattern 3 — 6th fret

4. Now play **Pattern 4**.

Next put your index finger where your 3rd finger was. This will put you in Pattern 5.

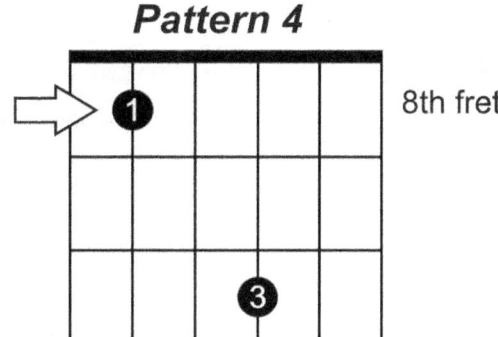

5. Now play **Pattern 5**.

Next put your index finger where your 4th finger was. This will put you in Pattern 1. (Note: Remember that the 6th and 1st strings are the same, so remember to include them in Patterns 1 and 5). You can continue this until you run out of frets.

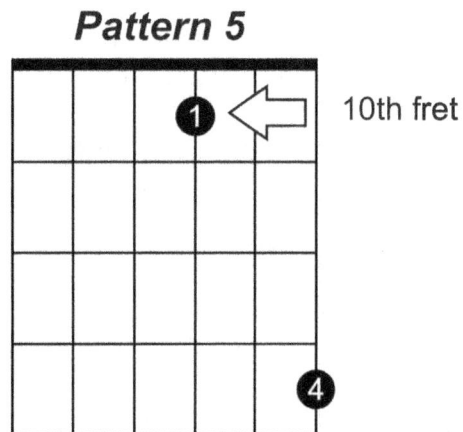

If you just did this exercise starting on the 1st fret of the E string, you just played all of the F's on your guitar. It is also important to realize that you can start from any pattern. For instance, if you wanted to play all of the C's on your guitar from the nut, you would want to start in Pattern 3, on the 1st fret of your B string. From there you would continue the patterns in order (4, 5, 1, etc.) and eventually play all of the C's on your guitar. It is also important to be able to do the patterns backward. You should practice these patterns until you can visualize them without actually playing them.

Here is a different view of all 5 patterns on the fretboard:

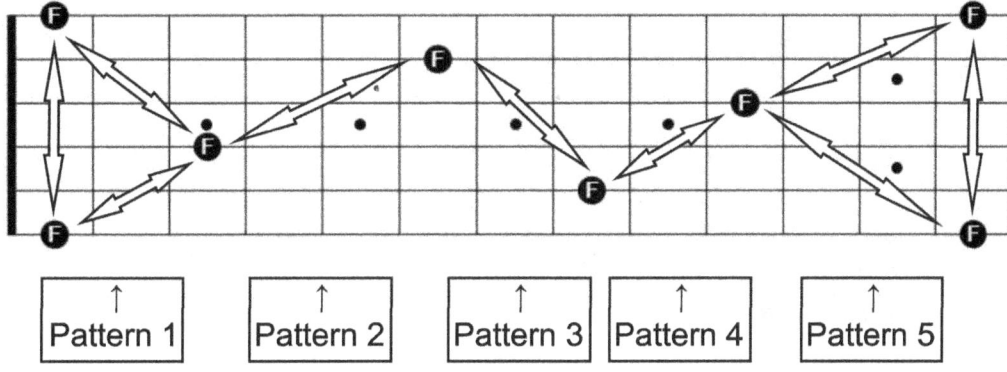

57

PENTATONIC SCALES

Pente - **Greek for 5**

Tonic - **Tone**

A *pentatonic scale* is a **5-note scale**. It is one of the oldest known scales in the world, dating back to 570 BC! The word "pentatonic" is derived from the Greek words "pente" meaning 5 and "tonic" meaning tone. It is used in all music genres and is said to have first been used in Japanese and Chinese music. On the guitar, we use this scale the most often for soloing and composing melodies.

There are 5 pentatonic patterns and all patterns use the same 5 notes. By learning all 5 patterns, you will know where to play those 5 notes all over the fretboard.

Pentatonic scales are based off of full *heptatonic*—or *7-note—scales*. Here are the the notes in a *C major scale*:

C D E F G A B

A *C major pentatonic scale* is a C major scale with the *4th* and *7th notes eliminated*:

C D E G A

Here are the the notes in a *A minor scale*:

A B C D E F G

An *A minor pentatonic scale* is an A minor scale with the *2nd and 6th notes eliminated*:

A C D E G

Notice how all of these scales use the **same notes**. You don't have to understand the relationship yet, or how to get from major to minor. But looking at it like this might help you understand how a scale can be made **major** or **minor** depending on the **starting note**.

MINOR PENTATONIC PATTERNS

You'll want to *learn all 5 of these patterns*—doing so will give you the freedom to play anywhere across the neck.

When you're starting out, it's important to use **consistent fingerings**. I've provided recommended fingerings that I believe are the most practical and useful in real playing situations.

Each pattern contains both *major and minor root notes*. This concept can feel tricky at first, but it's worth it—instead of learning 10 separate patterns, you only need to learn 5.

We just covered *octave patterns*, and we'll be using those to identify the root notes within the pentatonic patterns. The first step is to learn all the patterns starting from the **6th string**. In my experience, this is the easiest and most logical way to master all 5 pentatonic patterns.

Use the diagrams below as a *visual reference*, but be sure to follow the practice instructions on the next page so you can actually apply them.

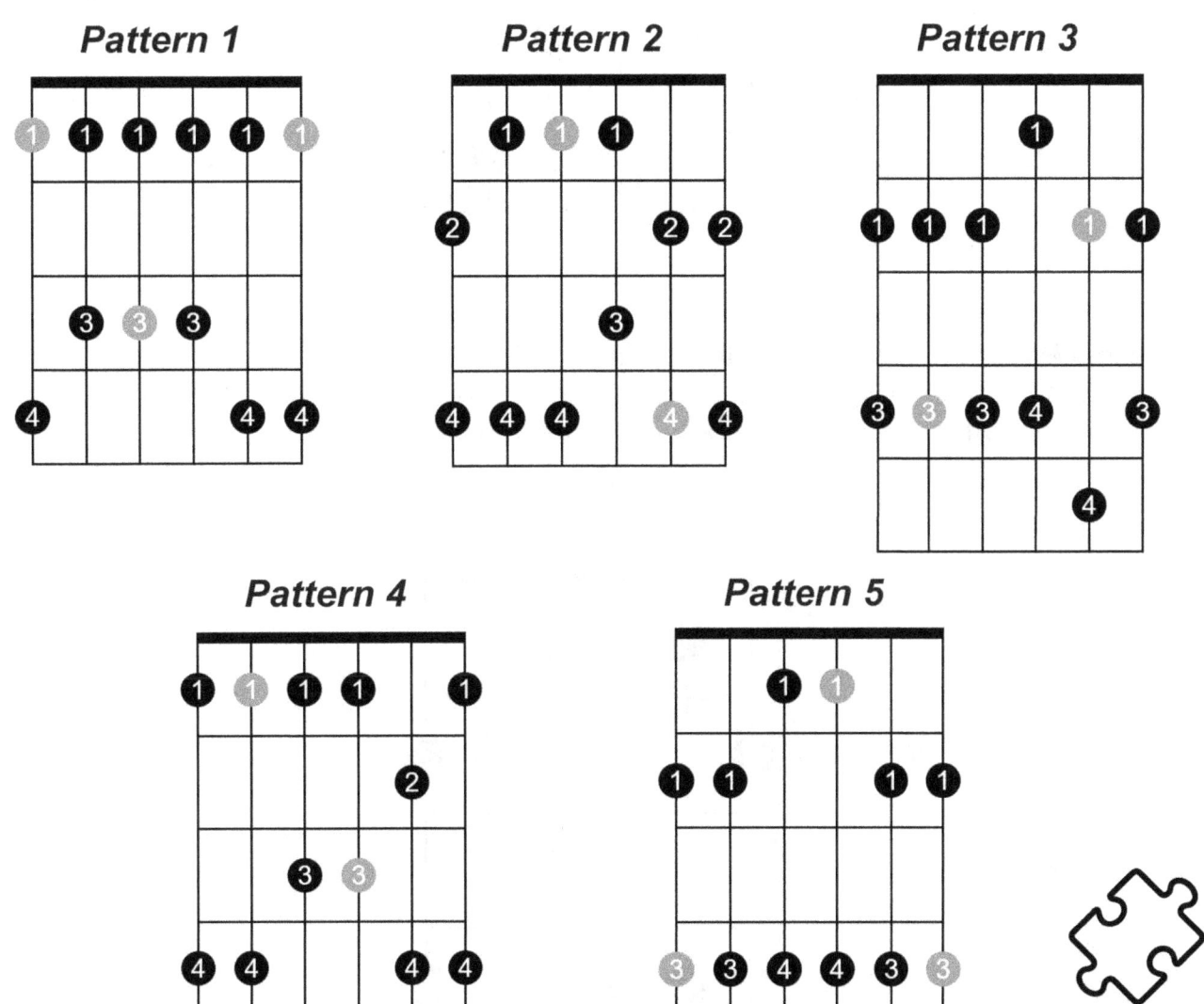

Helpful tip: The patterns fit together like puzzle pieces. The bottom of Pattern 1 is the top of Pattern 2, the bottom of Pattern 2 is the top of 3, the bottom of 3 is the top of 4, etc.

 By the way, the gray notes are the minor roots in each pattern. These are explained in the next chapter.

To play these patterns correctly in order, you must always start the next pattern on the 2nd note of the previous pattern. I walk you through that below.

Start with **Pattern 1** on the 1st fret of the 6th string.

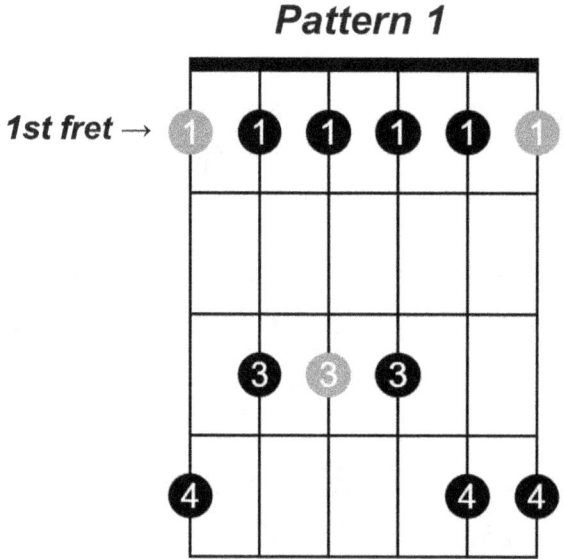

To move into **Pattern 2**, you'll start on the 2nd note of Pattern 1.
• Put your 2nd finger where your 4th finger was on the 6th string (4th fret).
• Also, notice below that the bottom of Pattern 1 is the top of Pattern 2.

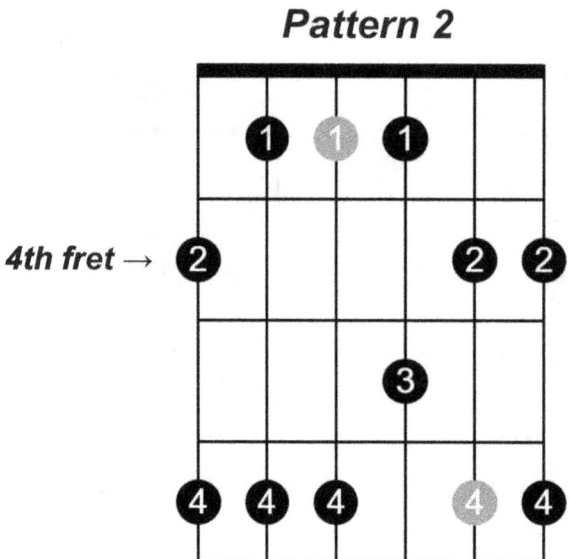

To move into **Pattern 3**, you'll start on the 2nd note of Pattern 2.
• Put your 1st finger where your 4th finger was on the 6th string (6th fret).
• Again, notice that the bottom of Pattern 2 is the top of Pattern 3.

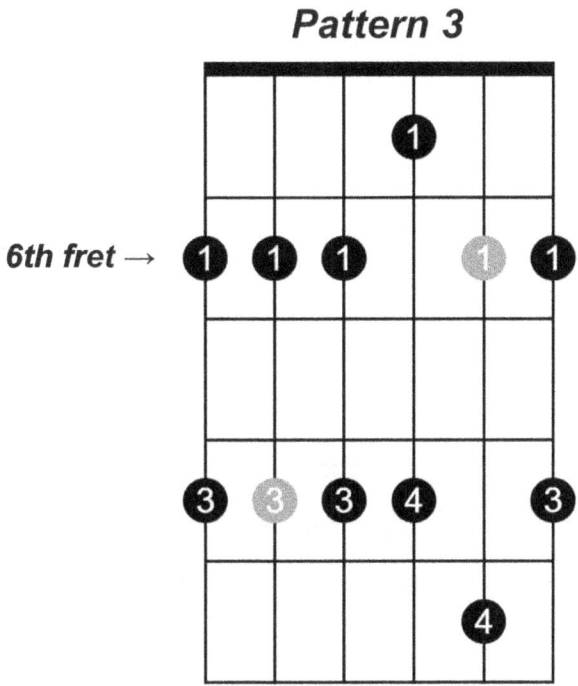

To move into **Pattern 4**, you'll start on the 2nd note of Pattern 3.
• Put your 1st finger where your 3rd finger was on the 6th string (8th fret).
• Once again, notice below that the bottom of Pattern 3 is the top of Pattern 4.

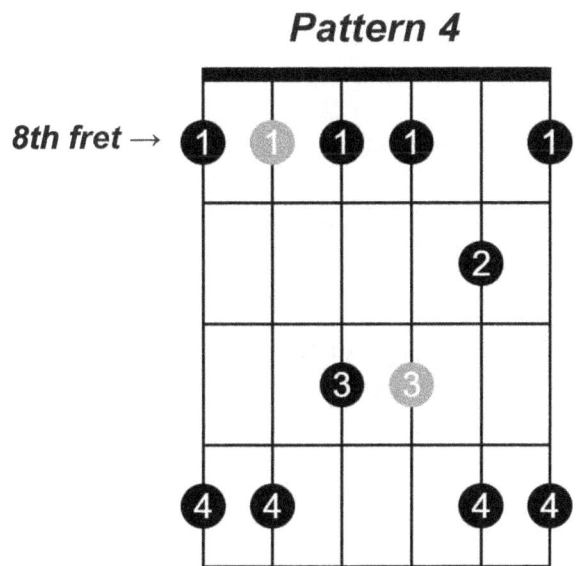

To move into **Pattern 5**, you'll start on the 2nd note of Pattern 4.
• Put your 1st finger where your 4th finger was on the 6th string (11th fret).
• Lastly, notice that the bottom of Pattern 4 is the top of Pattern 5, and the bottom of Pattern 5 is the top of Pattern 1.

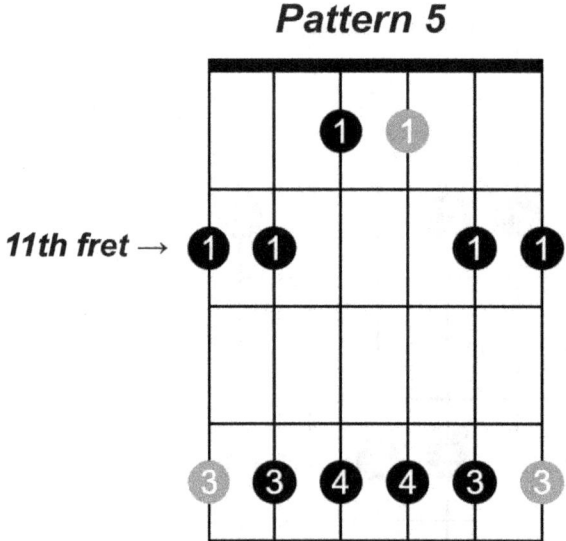

The patterns now start over. Your 3rd finger on the 6th string is on the 13th fret, which is an octave higher than where we started on that string with Pattern 1.

You just played the notes in an F minor pentatonic through all 5 pentatonic patterns. The notes that you just played were F, A♭, B♭, C, and E♭.

On the next page you'll be able to see all 5 patterns in the context of how you just played them.

Helpful tips:

• The reaches (1-3 or 1-4) will always be the same on your 6th and 1st strings in each pattern.

• You will only have two of the long reaches (1-4) in each pattern, with the exception of Patterns 1 and 4, since your 6th and 1st strings are both E's.

• Pattern 3 starts out with 1-3, 1-3, 1-3. Pattern 4 starts with 1-4, 1-4.

Here are the 5 minor pentatonic patterns in order.

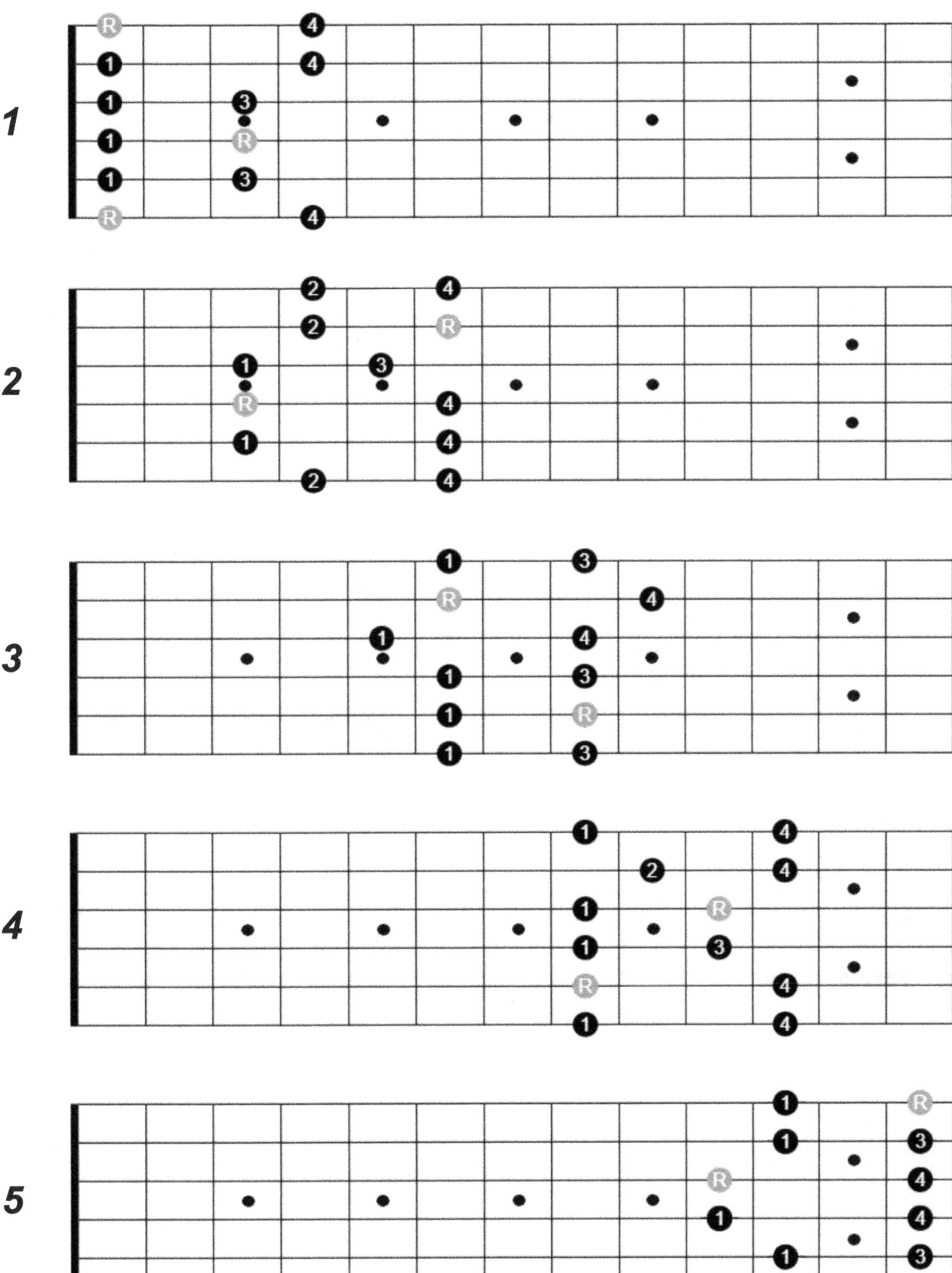

PENTATONIC EXERCISES

Exercise 1

In this exercise, you'll be playing **two strings** at a time from each pattern.

1. Start with **strings 6 and 5** in **Pattern 1**.

2. Move to **strings 6 and 5** in **Pattern 2**, then **Pattern 3**, and so on, until you reach the top at **Pattern 5**.

3. From there, descend back down through the patterns.

Once you've finished with strings 6 and 5, shift to **strings 5 and 4** in each pattern.

Continue this process with **strings 4 and 3**, then **3 and 2**, and finally **2 and 1**, until all string pairs are complete.

Strings 6 and 5:

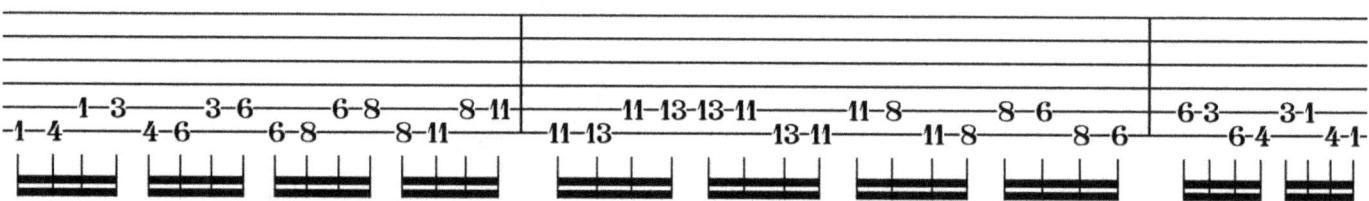

Strings 5 and 4:

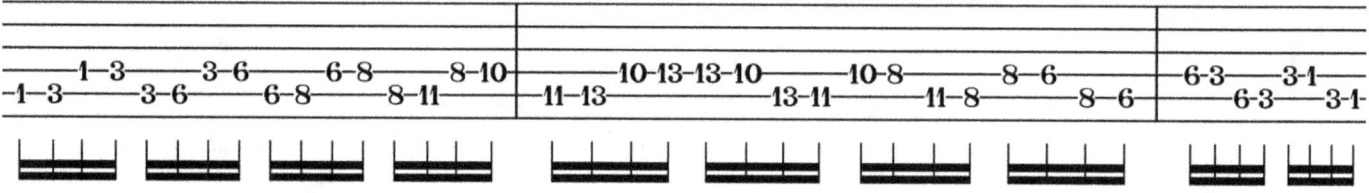

<u>Helpful tip</u>: Use a metronome when practicing these exercises. Start at a slow tempo and increase the bpm as you practice, rather than setting a fast tempo right away and trying to keep up with it.

Strings 4 and 3:

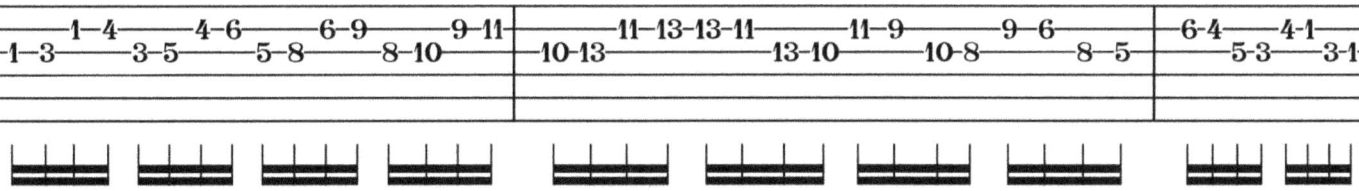

Strings 3 and 2:

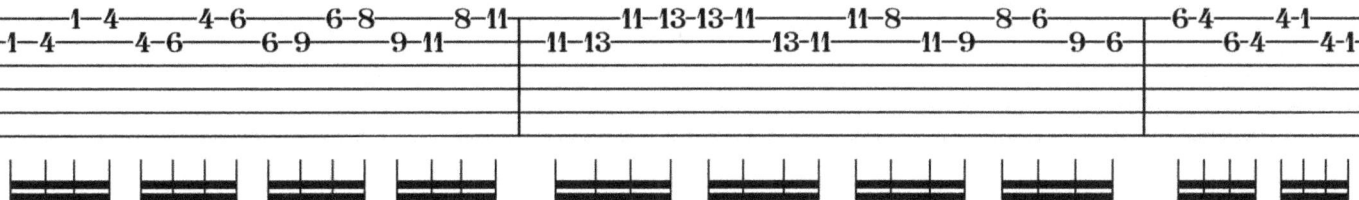

Strings 2 and 1:

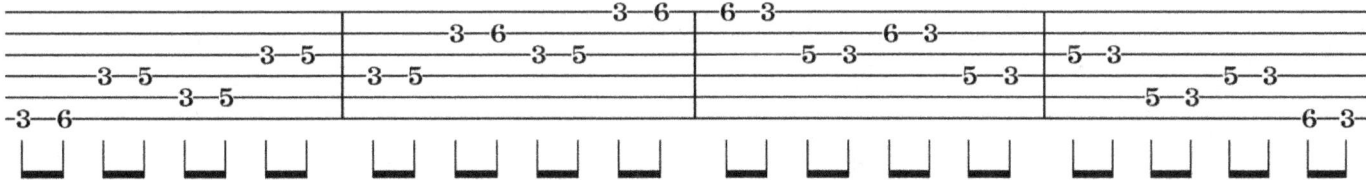

Exercise 2

In this exercise, you'll be *skipping strings within the same pattern*.

Below is **Pattern 1**, starting on the **3rd fret**. Practice the string-skipping sequence shown, and then repeat the same process in *all patterns* across the neck.

Exercise 3

In this exercise, you'll be playing **3-note sequences** from each note in the pattern.

• **Ascending**: play up 3 notes from each starting note.

• **Descending**: play down 3 notes from each starting note.

• Use a **triplet rhythm** to keep the flow even.

Below is **Pattern 1**, starting on the **3rd fret**. Be sure to practice this exercise in **all patterns** across the neck.

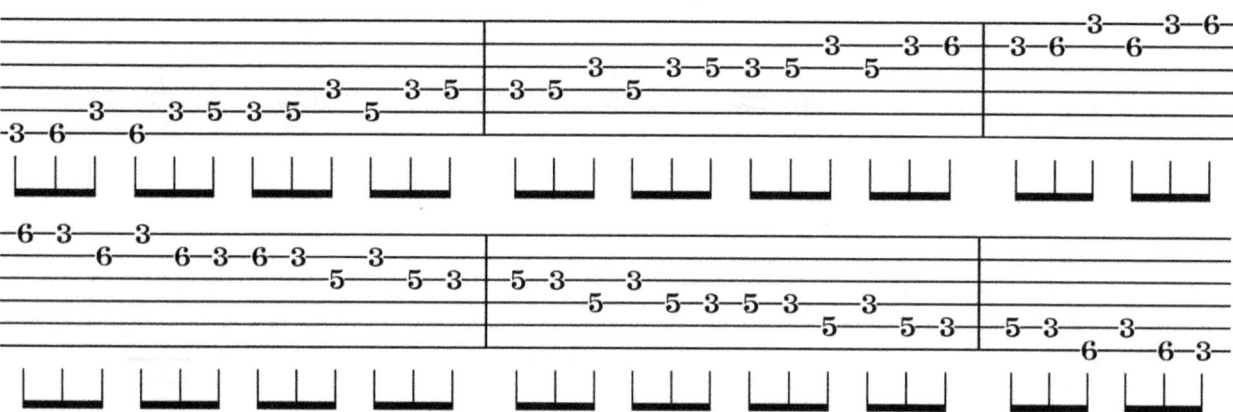

Exercise 4

In this exercise, you'll be playing **4-note sequences** from each note in the pattern.

• **Ascending**: play up 4 notes starting from each note in the pattern.

• **Descending**: play down 4 notes starting from each note in the pattern.

• Use a steady **sixteenth-note rhythm** to keep it even.

Below is **Pattern 1**, starting on the **3rd fret**. Be sure to practice this exercise in **all patterns** across the neck.

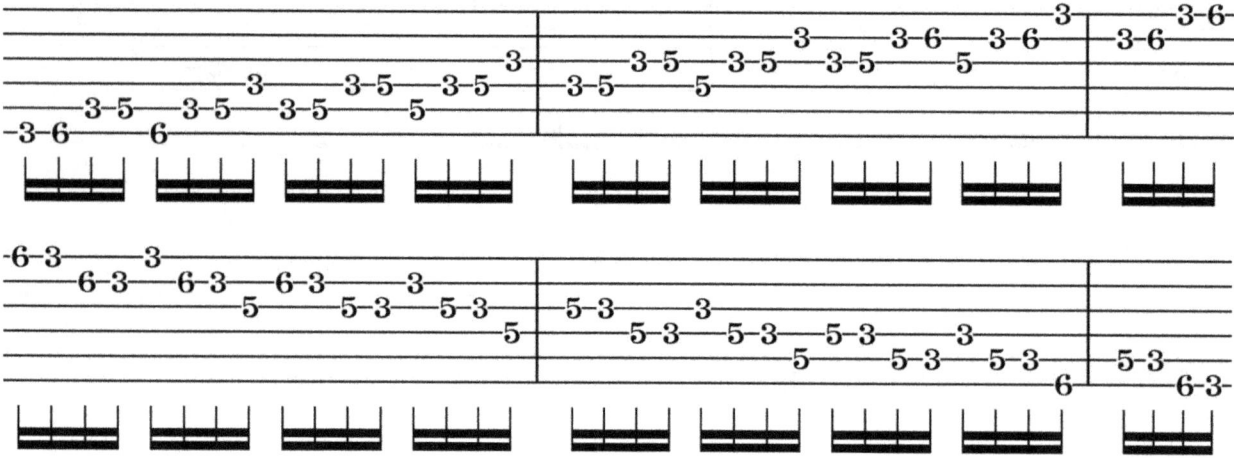

MINOR ROOT NOTES
WITHIN PENTATONIC SCALES

Pattern 1 is often called the *"minor pentatonic,"* but in reality, *every pattern contains minor root notes*. When you start a pattern from its minor root note (or notes), the sound will be minor.

The reason Pattern 1 carries the "minor pentatonic" label is because its very first note happens to be the *lowest minor root in that pattern*. In the other patterns, the minor roots are located in different places, so they aren't automatically thought of as "minor" unless you start from those roots.

By learning where the *minor root notes* are in every pattern, you'll be able to use each pattern independently to create minor-sounding solos anywhere on the neck.

You will use the octave patterns to map out the minor roots in each pattern. *Octave Pattern 1* shows you the *minor root notes in pentatonic Pattern 1*, *octave Pattern 2* shows you the *minor root notes in pentatonic Pattern 2*, and so on.

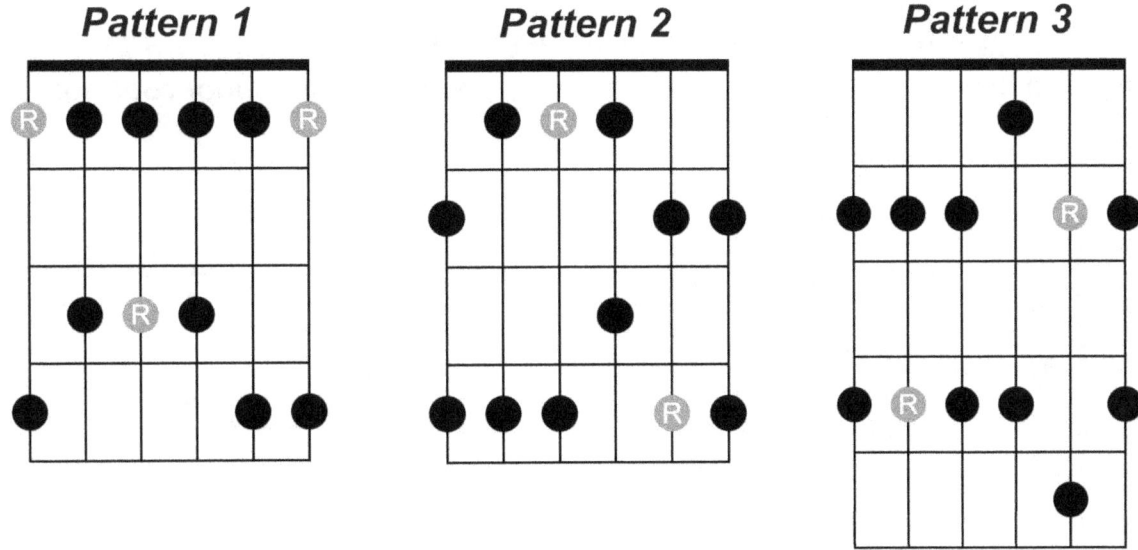

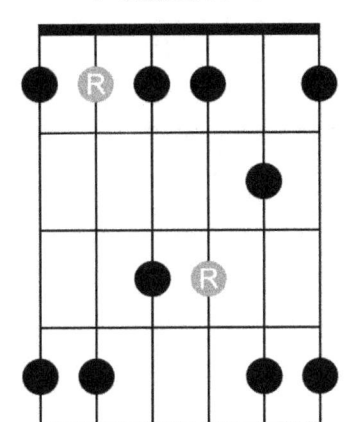

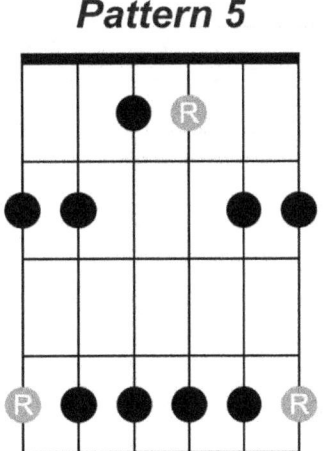

First, practice playing each pattern starting from its *lowest minor root note* with your *index finger*. Use the *first 5 notes of Pattern 1* as your template. This approach will give you the *first 5 notes of any pattern*, beginning from its lowest minor root note with your index finger.

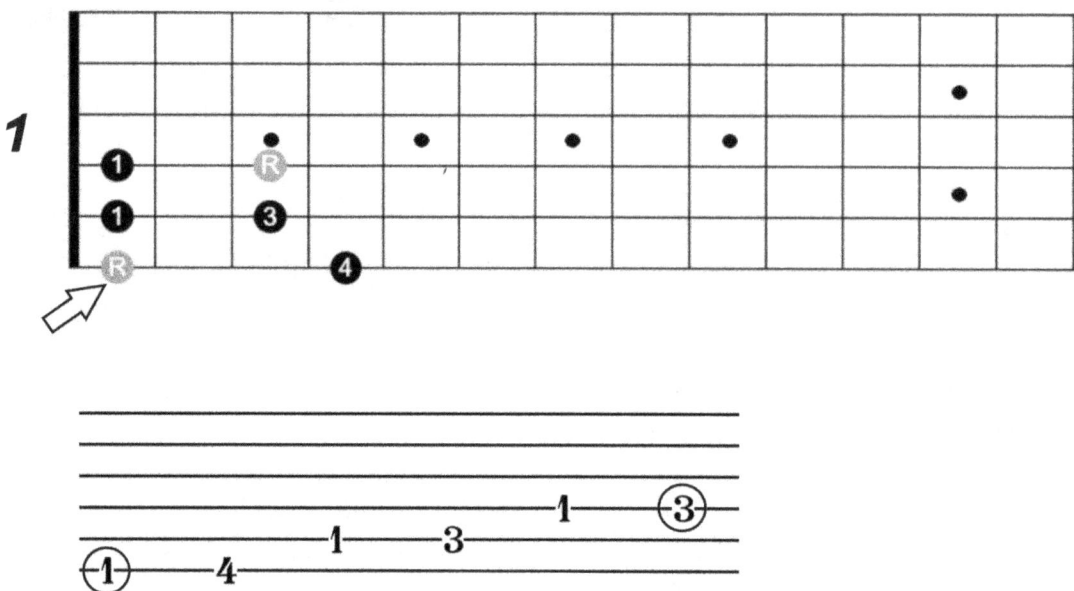

Next, continue the pattern upward until you reach the *highest note* on the *1st string*. Then, descend back down to your starting point, making sure to *recognize the minor root note*s as you pass them.

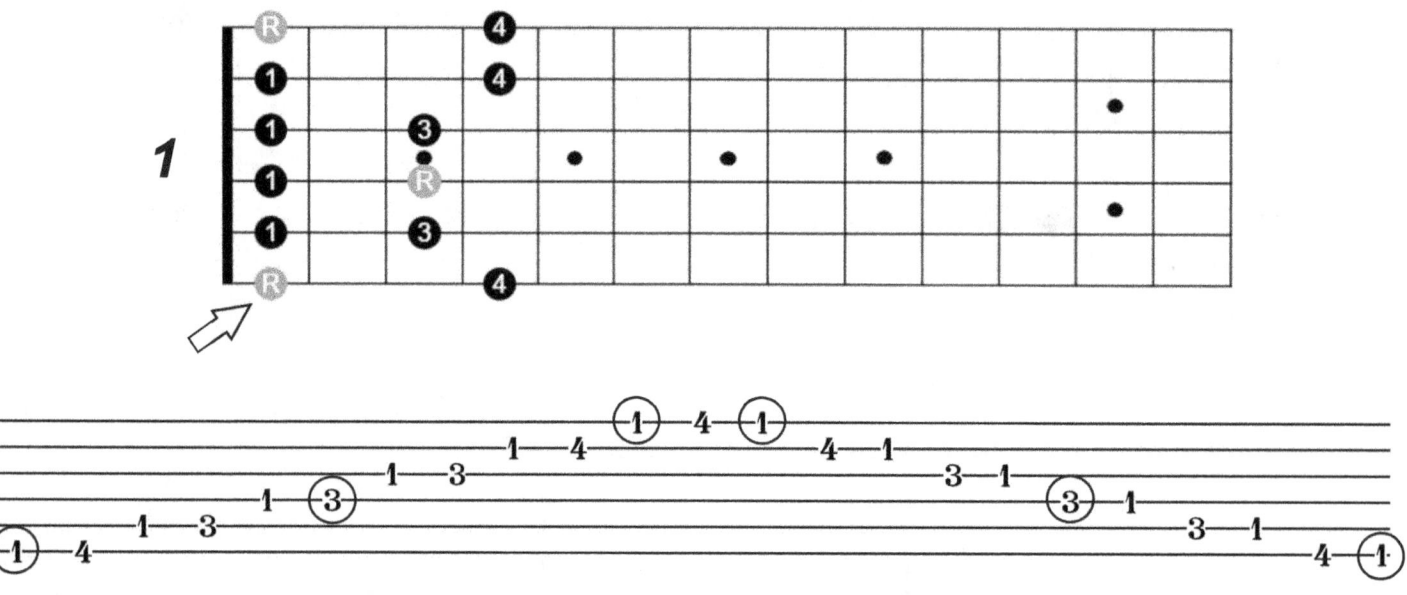

Next, take the *first 5 notes of Pattern 2*, starting from the **lowest minor root note**. You'll use the *same 5-note sequence* as in Pattern 1.

Remember: whenever you cross onto the **B string**, you'll need to shift the pattern up by **one fret** to keep the notes in key.

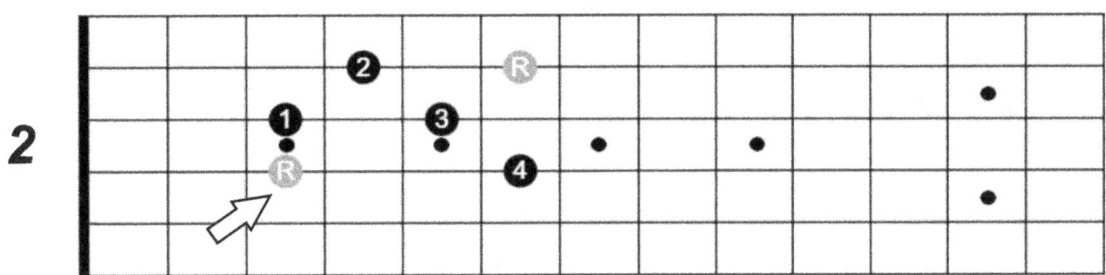

Now continue the pattern upward until you reach the **highest note** on the **1st string**. Then, descend all the way down to the **lowest note** of the pattern on the **6th string**. Finally, ascend back to your starting point, making sure to *recognize the minor root notes* as you pass them.

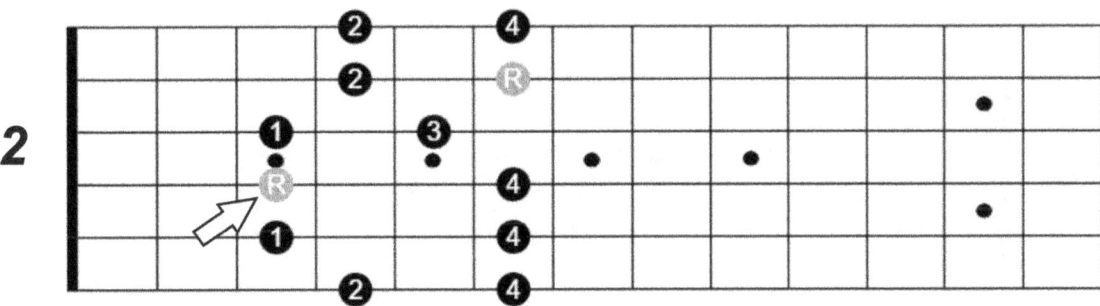

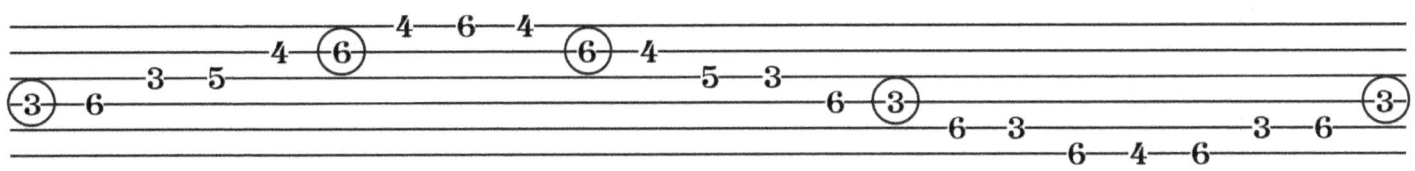

Next, take the **first 5 notes of Pattern 3**, starting from the **lowest minor root** note played with your **index finger**. As before, you'll use the same **5-note sequence** from Pattern 1.

In this pattern, the shape looks a little different because you can't play the final **1–3** interval in the usual place. Since the **1st and 6th strings are both E strings**, you'll shift that final **1–3** onto the **A string** instead.

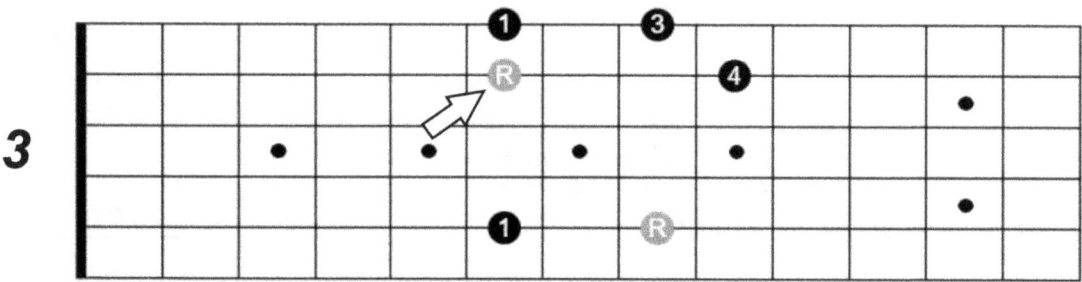

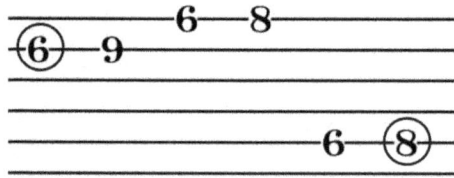

Start this pattern again and ascend all the way to the **highest note** on the **1st string**. Then, descend down to the **lowest note** of the pattern on the **6th string**. Finally, ascend back to your starting point, making sure to **identify the minor root notes** as you pass them.

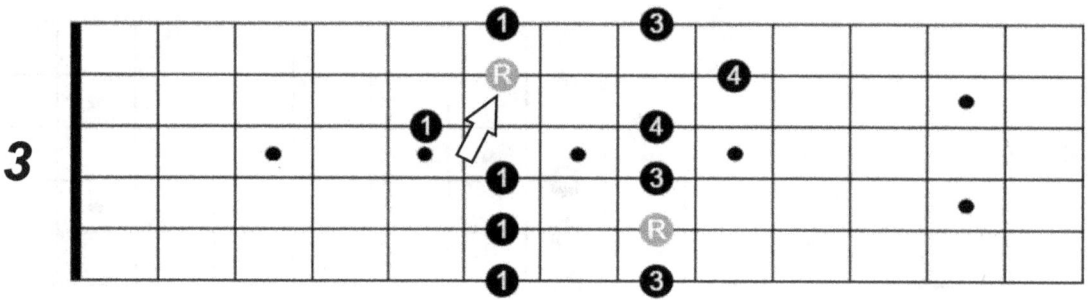

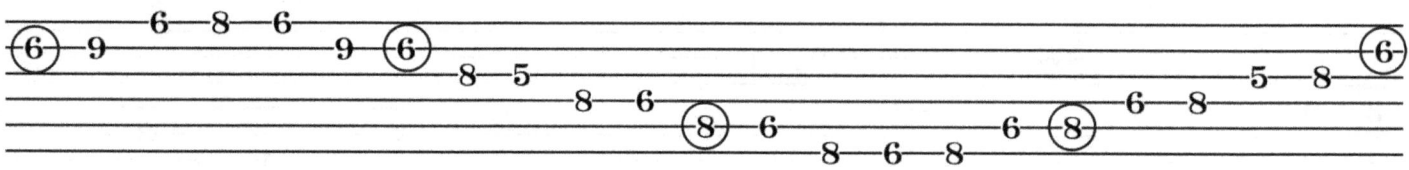

Next, take the **first 5 notes of Pattern 4**, starting from the **lowest minor root note**. You'll use the **same 5-note sequence** as in Pattern 1.

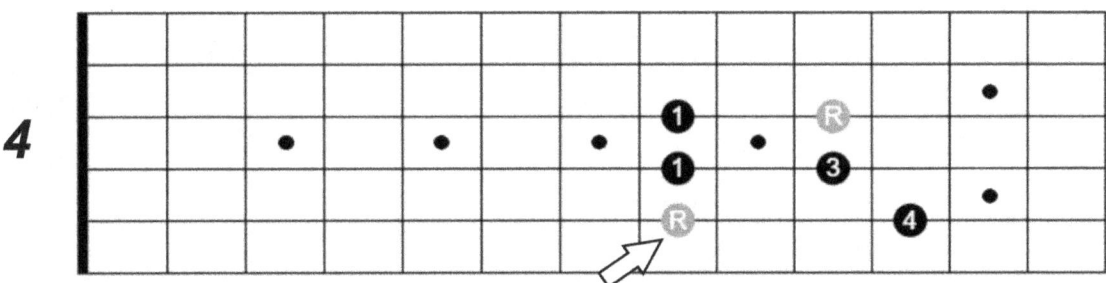

Continue the pattern all the way up to the **highest note** on the **first string**, then descend to the **lowest note** on the **6th string**. From there, ascend back to your starting point, paying attention to the **minor root notes** as you pass them

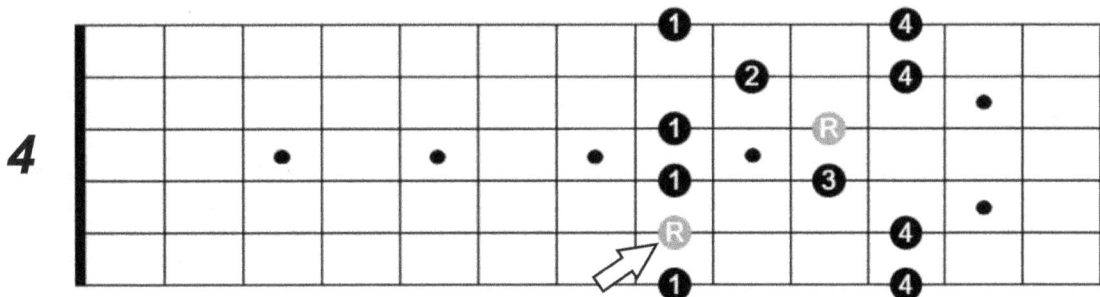

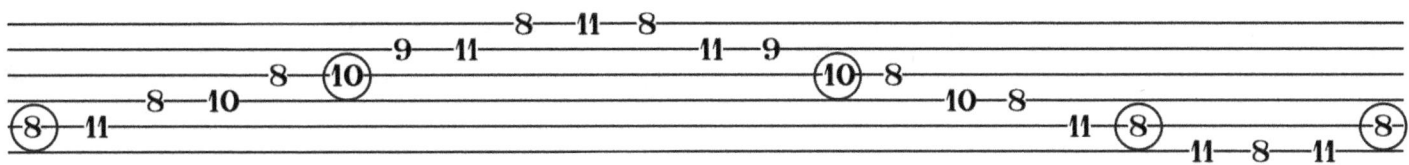

Lastly, take the first 5 notes in **Pattern 5** from the **lowest minor root** note you play with your **index finger**. Again, use the same 5-note pattern from Pattern 1. Remember, you will always need to shift the pattern one fret higher when you reach the B string.

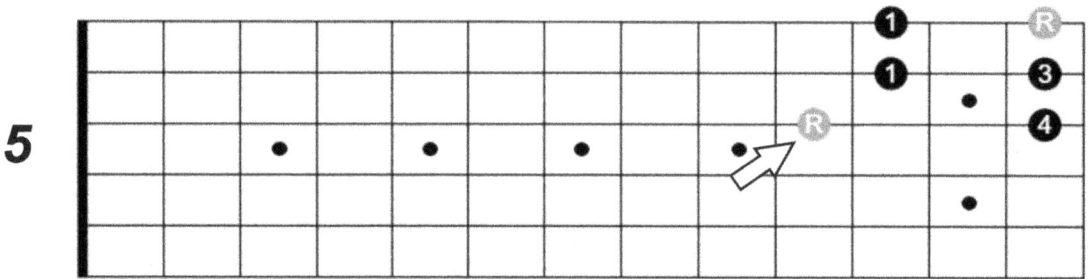

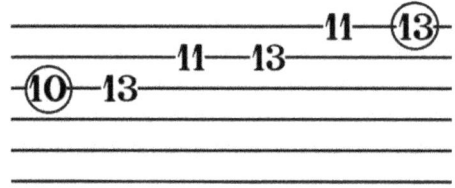

Start this pattern again and ascend all the way to the **highest note** on the **1st string**. Then, descend down to the **lowest note** of the pattern on the **6th string**. Finally, ascend back to your starting point, making sure to *identify the minor root notes* as you pass them.

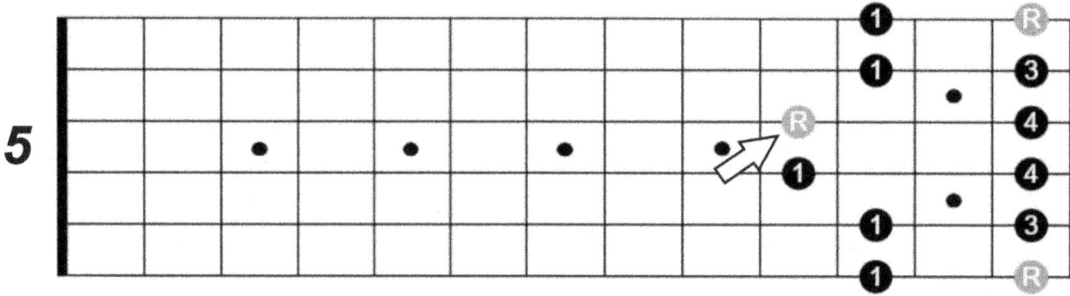

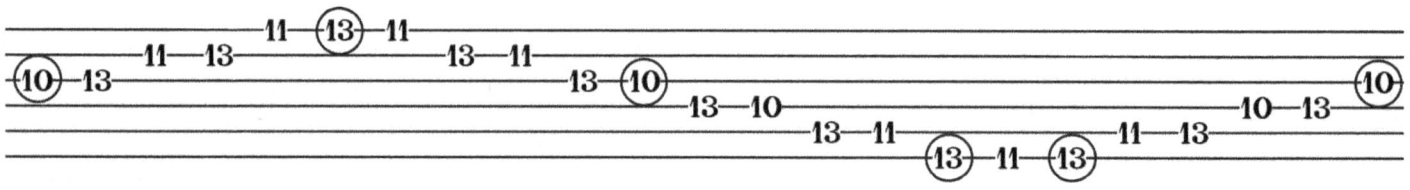

It is normal to struggle playing these patterns from the minor root notes, or any note other than the lowest note on the 6th string, which is how you originally learned them. Give it time, and use the exercises on upcoming pages to help with this.

72

 We have to shift the pattern *up 1 fret* every time we reach the **B string** because the guitar is tuned in **4ths** from the 6th string to the 1st string, except between the 3rd string *(G)* and the 2nd string *(B)*. That tuning interval is a **major 3rd**, and because of this we need to compensate by shifting the notes in the pattern on the B string **1 fret higher**.

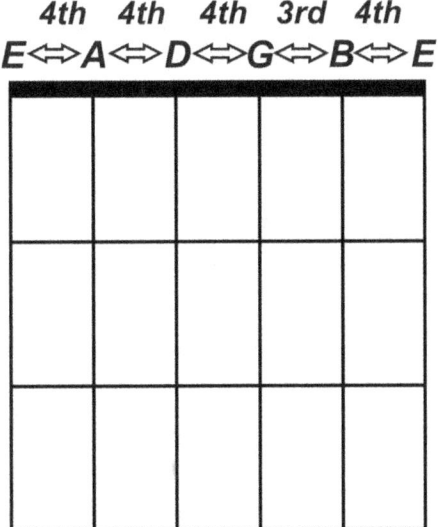

E STANDARD TUNING

The guitar is typically tuned in what's known as **E standard tuning**. As mentioned above, this tuning consists of a series of **perfect fourths** with **one major third** interval between the G and B strings.

The origins of the guitar can be traced back to 16th-century Spain, where a small, four-stringed instrument called the vihuela was commonly played.

In the early days of the guitar, tuning systems varied widely—not just between regions, but also from player to player. Many early guitars used open tunings, in which the open strings formed a complete chord when strummed without fretting. These tunings were often chosen for ease of play, though they were generally less versatile. Today, guitarists still use open tunings, typically for specific songs or stylistic effects.

By the early 19th century, a variation of E standard tuning had become the norm, with the strings typically tuned to E, A, D, F# (or G), B, and E.

Over time, the guitar evolved into the familiar 6-string instrument we know today, with E standard becoming the most common tuning system.

Next, we will learn to move from pattern to pattern using the minor root notes as connectors.

• We will focus on starting each pattern with our *index finger* on the *lowest minor root* in each pattern. Use the first 5 notes from Pattern 1, which will bring you from the lowest minor root note to the next highest minor root note, which is an octave.

• Once you make it to the octave with your 3rd finger, replace it with your index finger. You are now in Pattern 2, just like the original octave patterns.

• You will continue this 5-note pattern throughout.

• Just remember that whenever you hit the **B string**, you need to **shift the pattern up 1 fret** due to the tuning of the guitar. Also, the pattern gets broken up and transferred in Pattern 3, as seen in the previous exercise.

Play **Pattern 1** until you reach the octave:

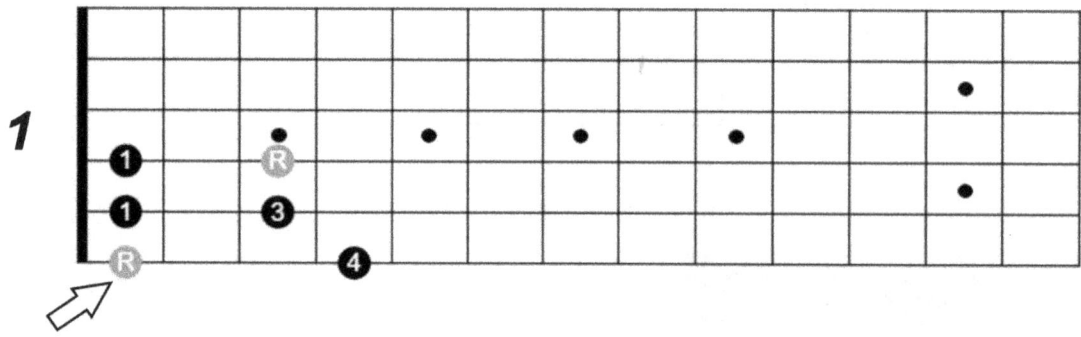

Replace your 3rd finger with your 1st and play **Pattern 2** until you reach the octave:

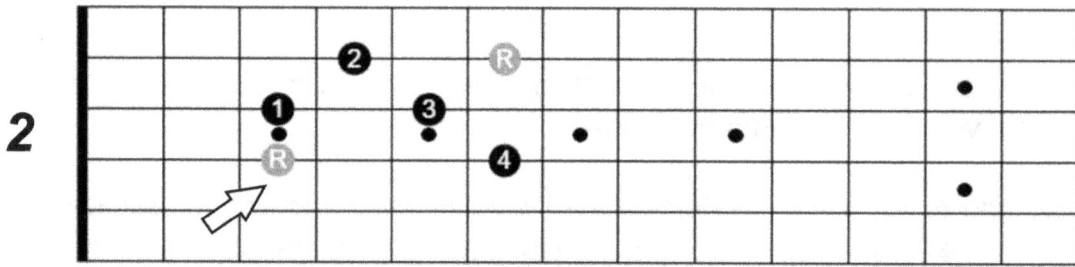

Replace your 4th finger with your 1st and play **Pattern 3** until you reach the octave:

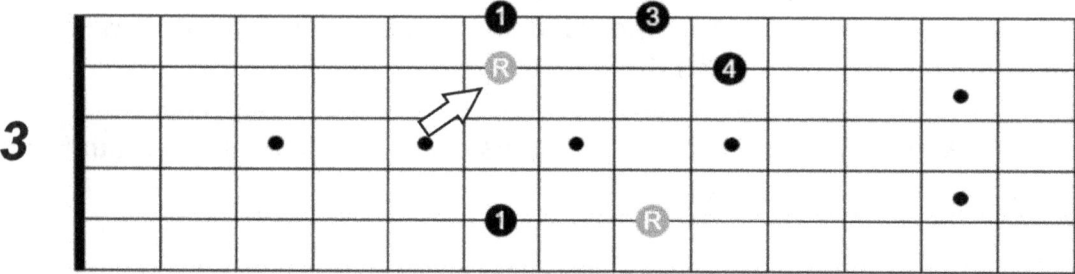

Replace your 3rd finger with your 1st and play **Pattern 4** until you reach the octave:

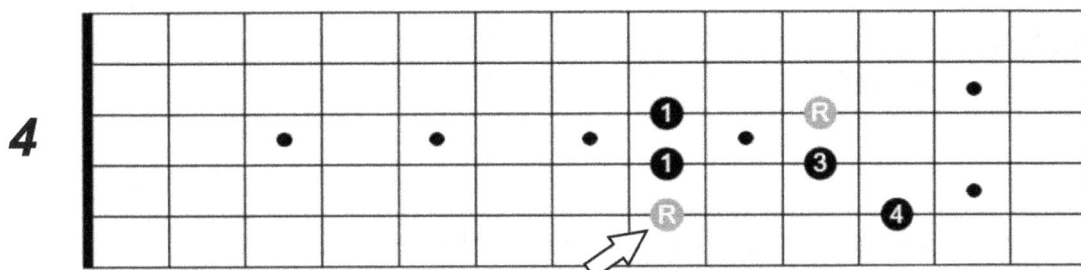

Replace your 3rd finger with your 1st and play **Pattern 5** until you reach the octave:

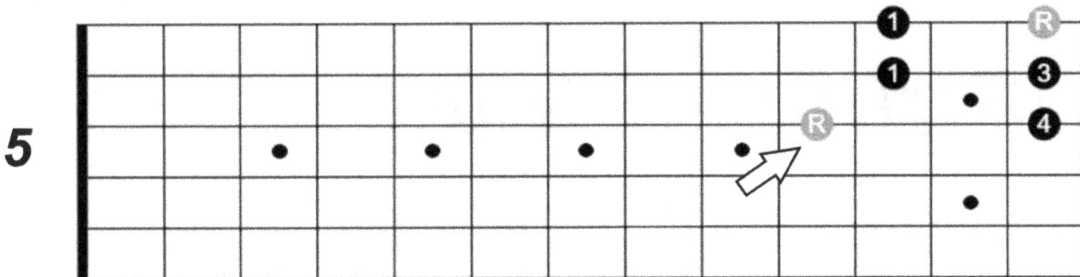

Once you make it to the top of Pattern 5, you can transfer that root to the same fret of the 6th string and start over with Pattern 1. This is the full fretboard view:

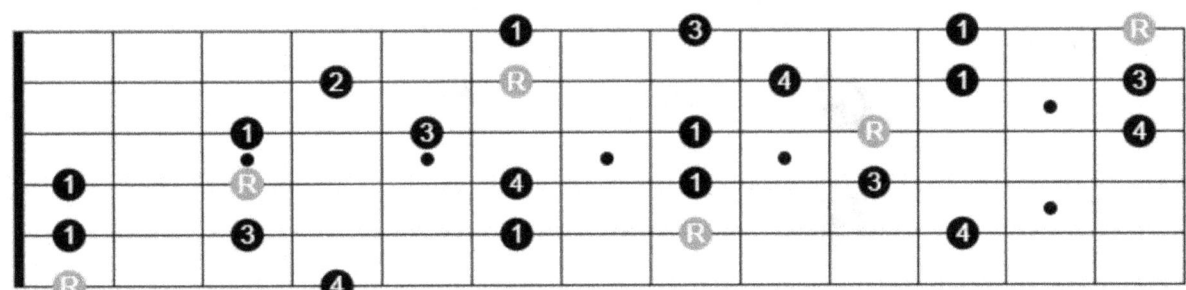

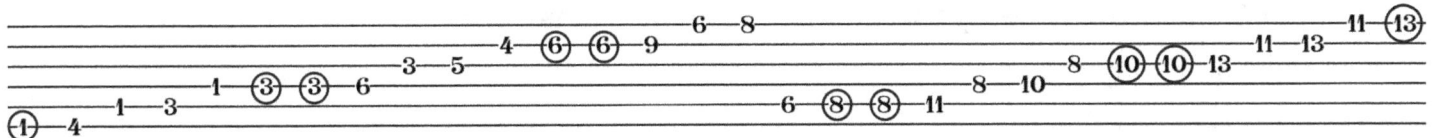

You should be able to move fluidly through the patterns—and also feel comfortable starting anywhere on the neck. Most guitarists naturally gravitate toward starting with Pattern 1, but with a bit of memorization, you can start confidently in any pattern. The string assignments for each pattern are on the next page.

Each pattern is *tied to a specific string*.

If you memorize the starting points from the *minor root note* with your index finger—along with the matching string assignments—you'll always know which pattern to play.

For example:

• Minor root note on the *E (6th) string* with your index finger → always play *Pattern 1*

• Minor root note on the *A (5th) string* with your index finger → always play *Pattern 4*

The same logic applies for every string–pattern pairing. Once you learn the system, finding the right pattern becomes automatic.

String   Pattern

E → 1

A → 4

D → 2

G → 5

B → 3

An easy way to remember these assignments is to count *1 through 5*, starting on the **6th string** and *skipping a string* to get to each number. Use the charts below.

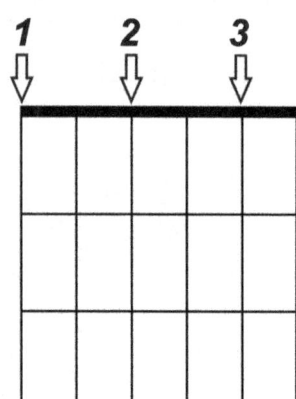 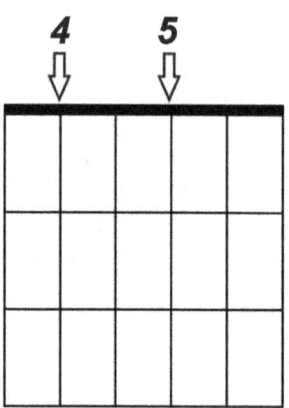

To execute these *starting points* efficiently, you will either need to know the *note names* on each *string* or be able to *visualize* and quickly connect the *octave patterns*.

Exercise

Let's say you want to play a solo in **A minor**. Using this system, all you need to do is find an A on any string with your index finger and you'll be ready to play the notes in the correct pattern. A good way to practice this is to improvise using each pattern, going in order of the patterns.

• Find an **A** with your index finger on the **E string** (5th fret) and use **Pattern 1**

• Find an **A** with your index finger on the **D string** (7th fret) and use **Pattern 2**

• Find an **A** with your index finger on the **B string** (10th fret) and use **Pattern 3**

• Find an **A** with your index finger on the **A string** (12th fret) and use **Pattern 4**

• Find an **A** with your index finger on the **G string** (2nd or 14th fret) and use **Pattern 5**

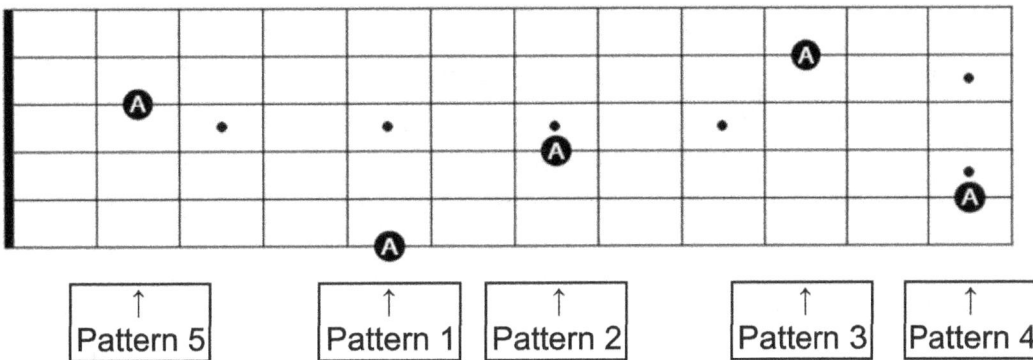

Now, we'll do the same thing using **D minor**, but move in order of the strings, starting on the 6th string, then the 5th string, then the 4th, etc.

• Find a **D** with your index finger on the **E string** (10th fret) and use **Pattern 1**

• Find a **D** with your index finger on the **A string** (5th fret) and use **Pattern 4**

• Find a **D** with your index finger on the **D string** (12th fret) and use **Pattern 2**

• Find a **D** with your index finger on the **G string** (7th fret) and use **Pattern 5**

• Find a **D** with your index finger on the **B string** (3rd fret) and use **Pattern 3**

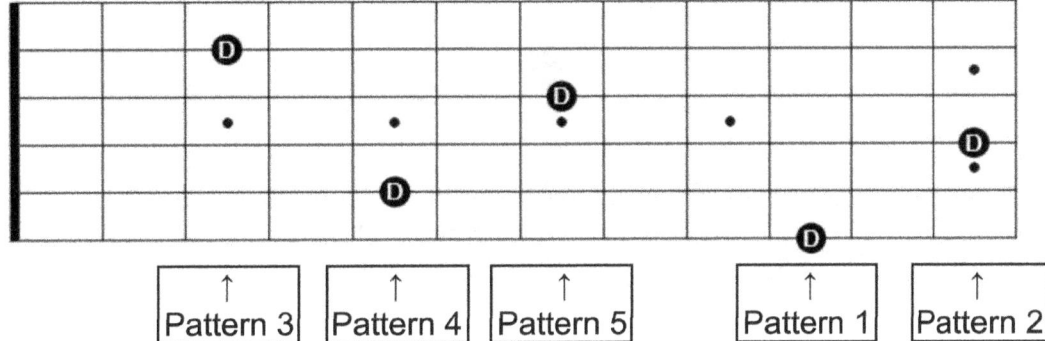

Now we will look at playing each pattern from its **lowest minor root note** you play with your **3rd or 4th finger**, depending on the pattern. Start each pattern from the ↗.

Play **Pattern 1** starting at the **3rd finger minor root note**. Ascend until you reach the **highest note** on the **1st string**, then descend until you hit the **lowest note** on the **6th string**, then ascend back to where you started.

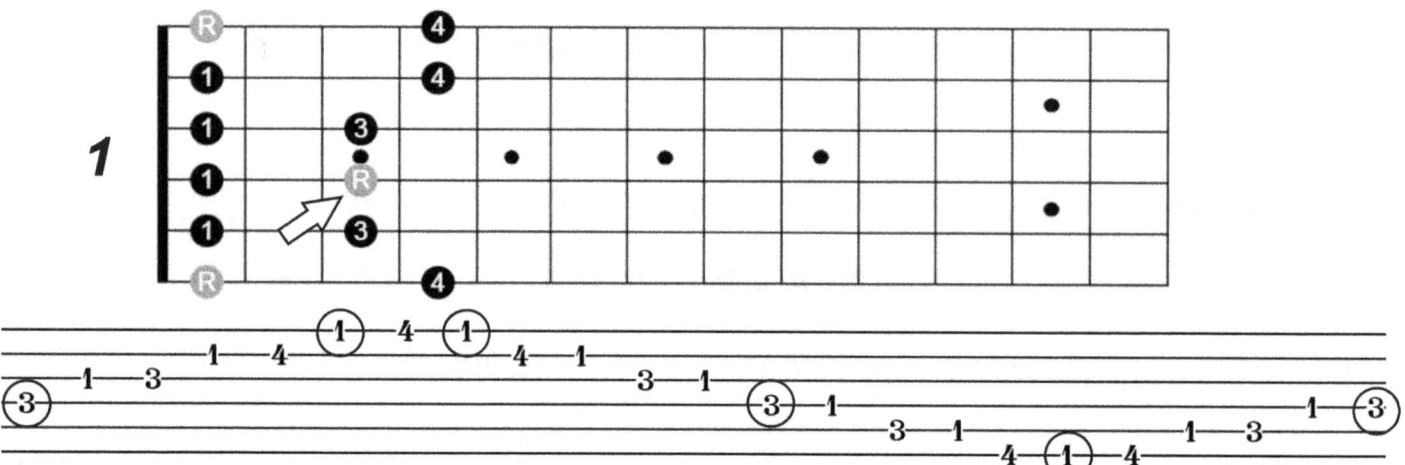

Play **Pattern 2** starting at the **4th finger minor root note**. Ascend until you reach the **highest note** in the pattern on the **1st string**, then descend until you hit the **lowest note** in the pattern on the **6th string**, then ascend back to where you started.

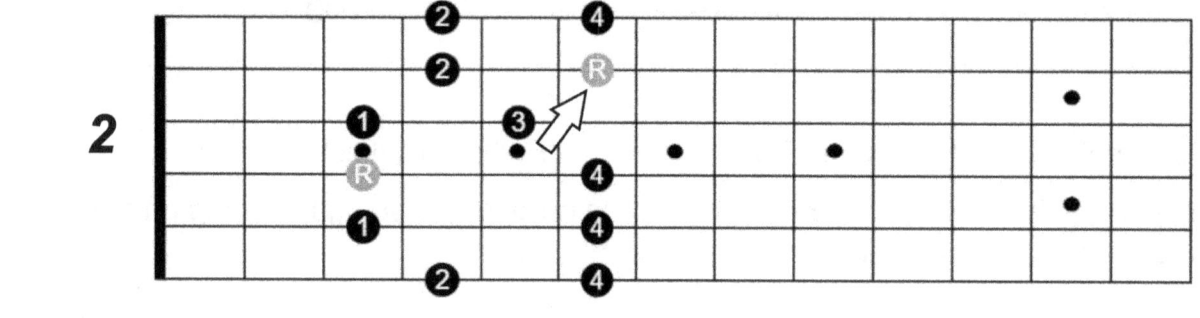

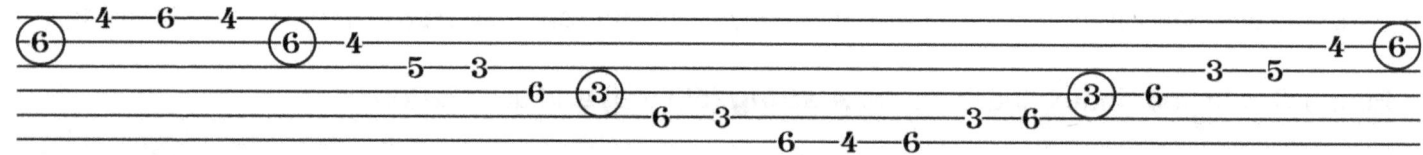

Play **Pattern 3** starting at the **3rd finger minor root note**. Ascend until you reach the **highest note** in the pattern on the **1st string**, then descend until you hit the **lowest note** in the pattern on the **6th string**, then ascend back to where you started.

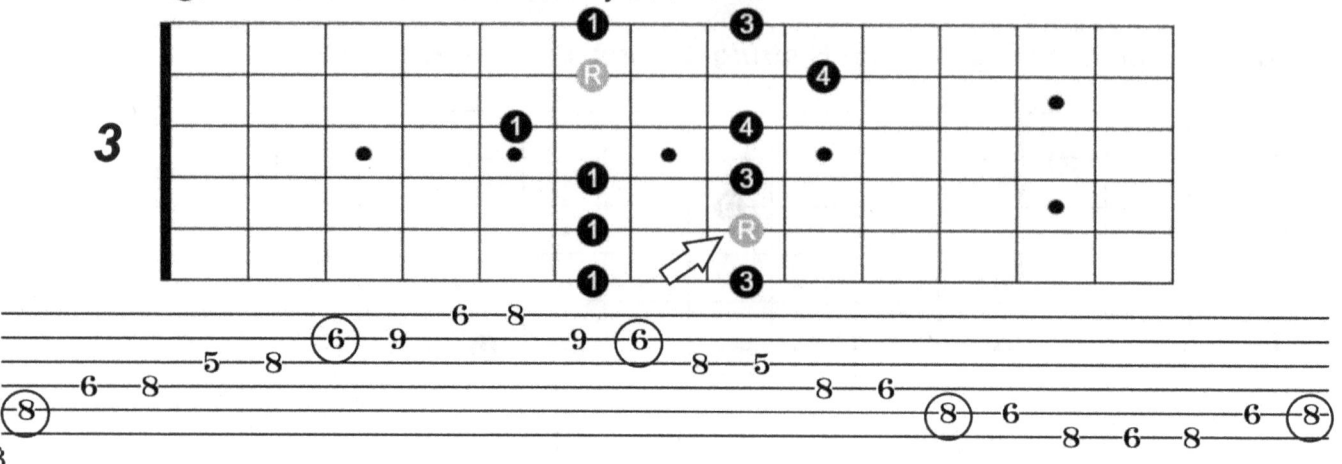

Play **Pattern 4** starting at the **3rd finger minor root note**. Ascend until you reach the **highest note** on the **1st string**, then descend until you hit the **lowest note** on the **6th string**, then ascend back to where you started.

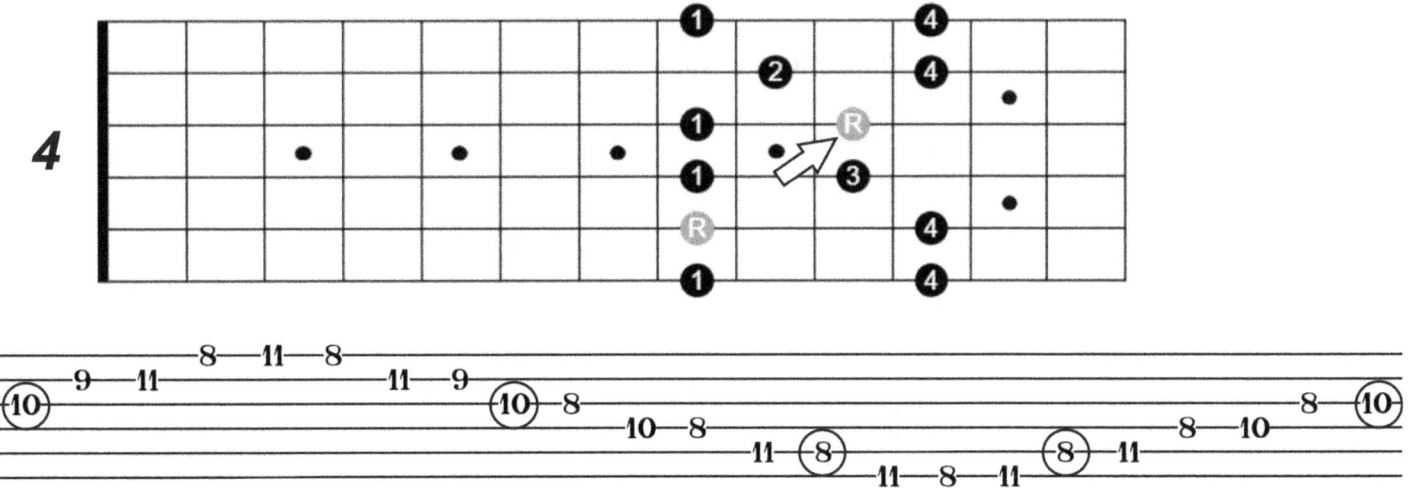

Play **Pattern 5** starting at the **3rd finger minor root note**. Ascend until you reach the **highest note** on the **1st string**, then descend until you hit the **lowest note** on the **6th string**, then ascend back to where you started.

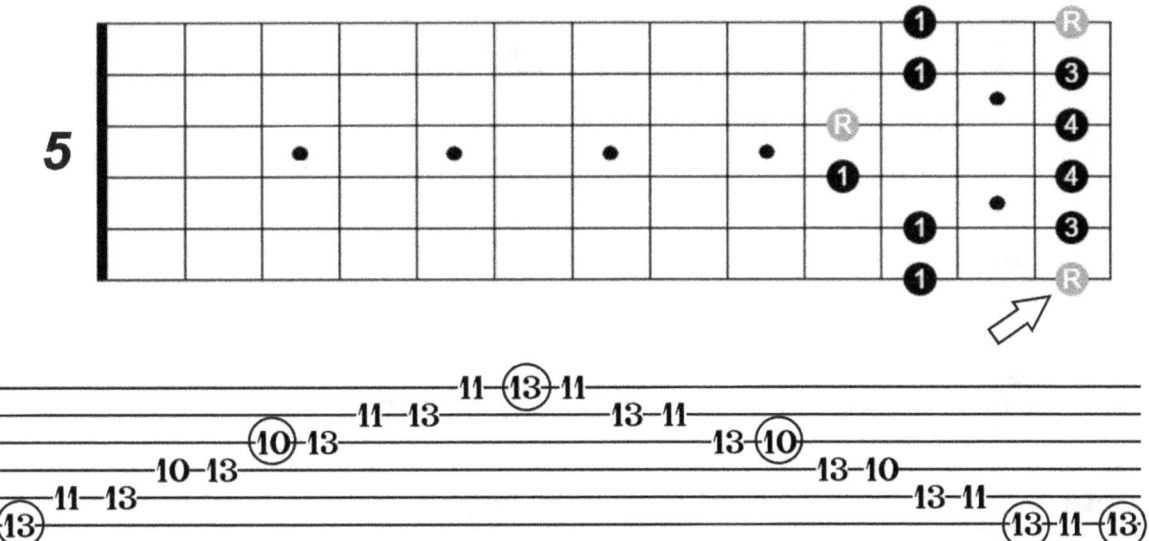

On the next page, you will learn string assignments for these root notes.

When you find a *minor root note* with your *index finger*, you can determine the pattern using the *String–Pattern Assignment Chart* below.

But there's more—each root note position can give you **2 possible patterns**:

• *Index finger on the root* → Use the pattern in the chart below.

• *3rd finger on the root* (4th finger for Pattern 2) → Use the pattern that is one number lower than the index finger pattern (Pattern 1 loops back to Pattern 5).

Example:

• If you find *A* with your *index finger* on the 6th string → *Pattern 1*

• If you play that same *A* with your *3rd finger* on the 6th string → *Pattern 5*

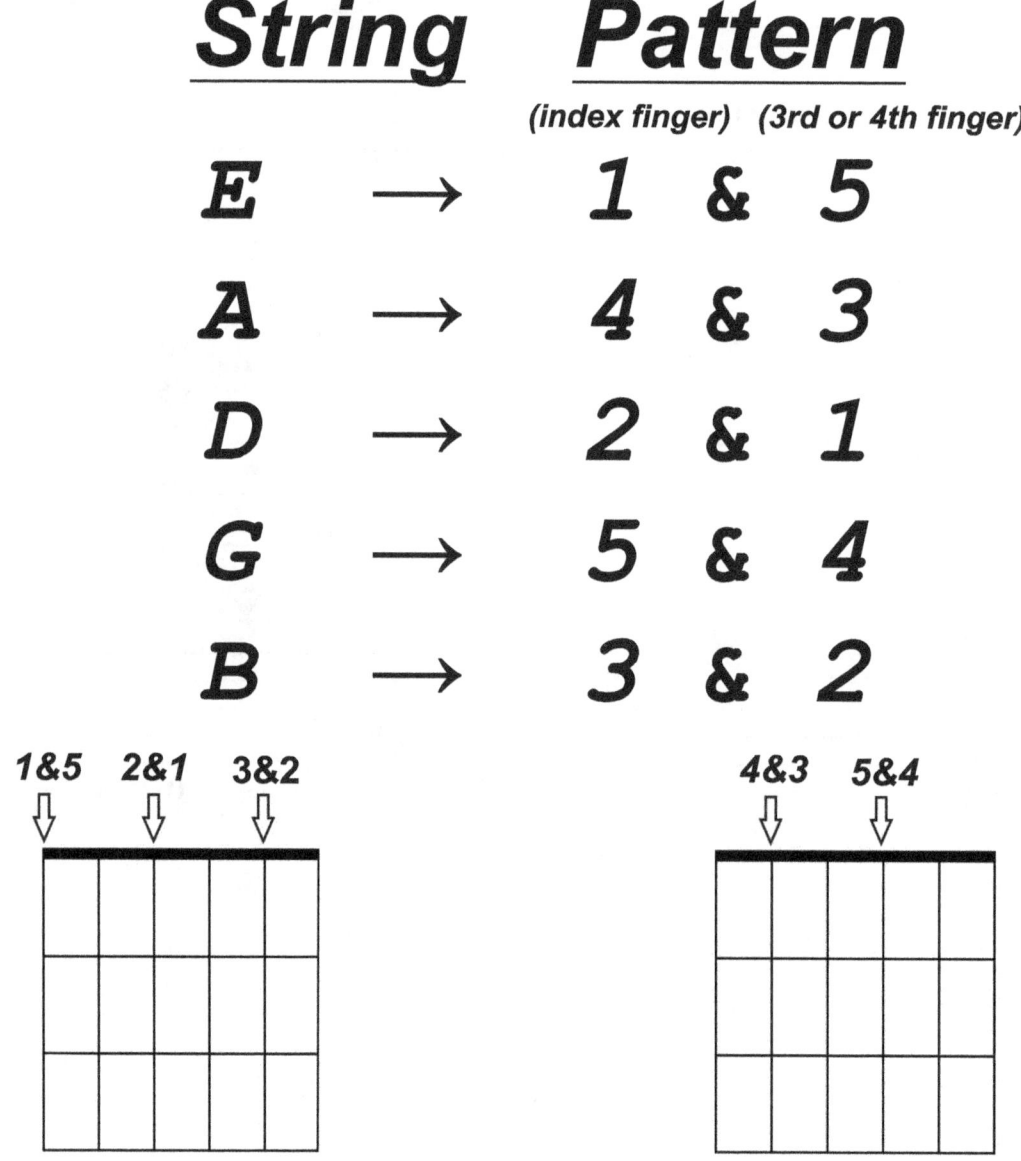

Continue to the next page for fretboard diagrams of the patterns that share the same minor root note.

80

Now, let's take a look at how **2 patterns share the same minor root note**. The large arrow is pointing to the shared minor root note. (Patterns 1 and 5 share two minor root notes.)

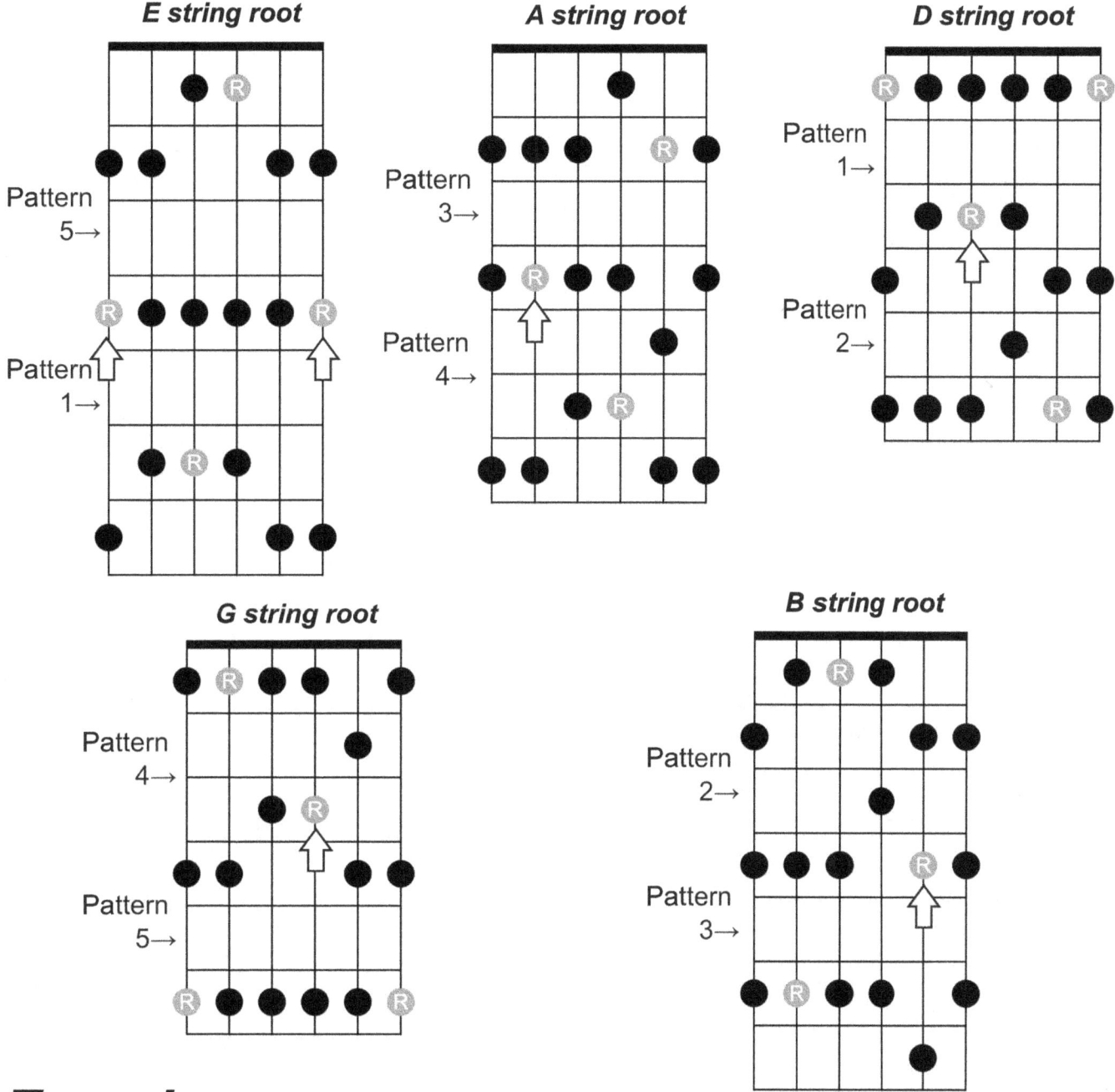

Exercise

Practice these groupings to get **comfortable going back and forth within the grouping** using the shared minor root note(s) as anchors.
- Start with **Pattern 1** on an **A** (5th fret of E string).
- Play from the **lowest root note** of Pattern 1 to the **highest root note** (5th fret of 1st string).
- **Shift your hand back 2 frets** and you are now in Pattern 5.
- **Descend Pattern 5** until you reach the **lowest root note** (5th fret of 6th string).
- **Shift** back into **Pattern 1**.
- Practice all 5 patterns this way, treating the **shared minor root note** as a **shift point** between the two patterns.

Exercise

Fill in the charts below with the minor pentatonic patterns. Be sure to acknowledge the minor roots.

Pattern 1
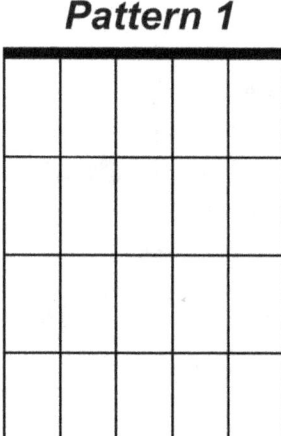

Pattern 2

Pattern 3
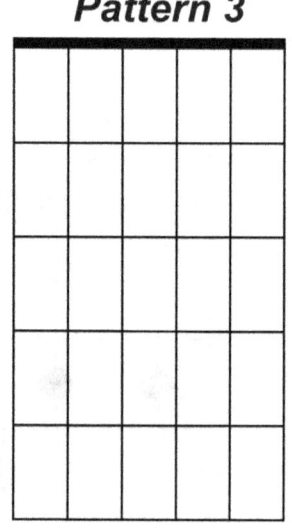

Pattern 4
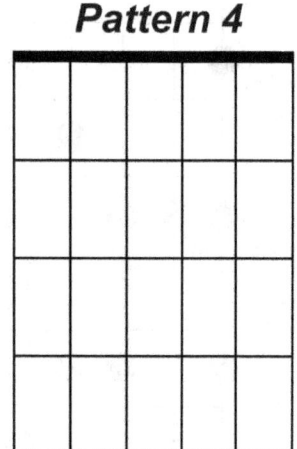

Pattern 5
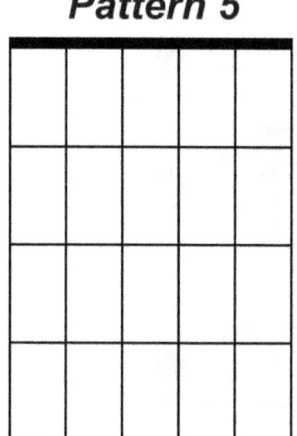

MINOR PENTATONIC LEAD PATTERNS

Lead patterns are *1-octave, 5-note patterns* that can be linked together to flow smoothly across the fretboard. You can start them from *any string and any fret*—the pattern of intervals will always stay the same.

Just Remember:

• When you cross from the **G string to the B string**, shift the pattern **1 fret higher** to stay in key.

• Your **3rd finger will always land on a root note**.

The most important thing as you learn these is to stay aware of **which of the 5 pentatonic patterns** you're in as you connect lead patterns—this will keep your playing anchored in the scale.

How to Practice Them:

1. Start each lead pattern at the root note ®.

2. Follow the sequence in the diagram, moving in the direction of the arrows (→).

3. Work both ascending and descending to build muscle memory.

Tab is provided below each pattern for clarity.

Minor pentatonic lead pattern from the **6th (E) string**.
• Starts in pentatonic **Pattern 5**, then shifts to **Pattern 1**.

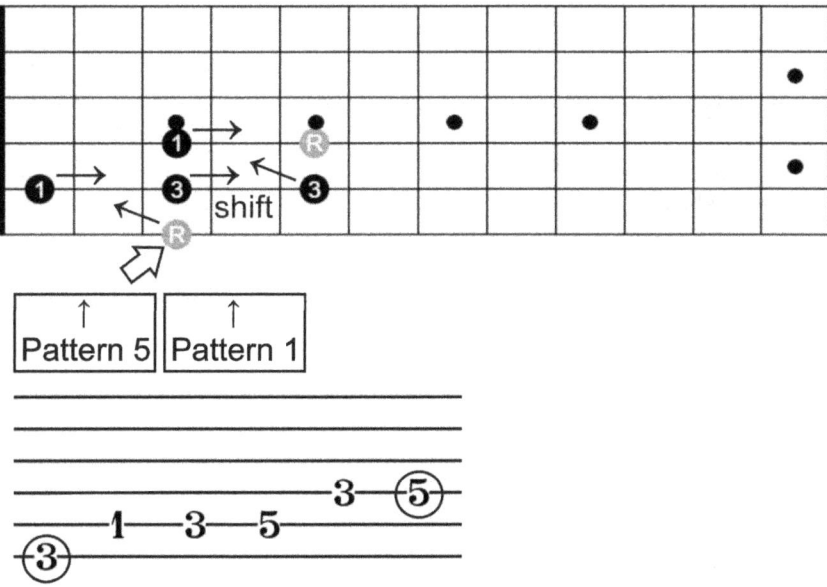

83

Minor pentatonic lead pattern from the *4th (D) string*.
• Starts in pentatonic *Pattern 1*, then shifts to *Pattern 2*.

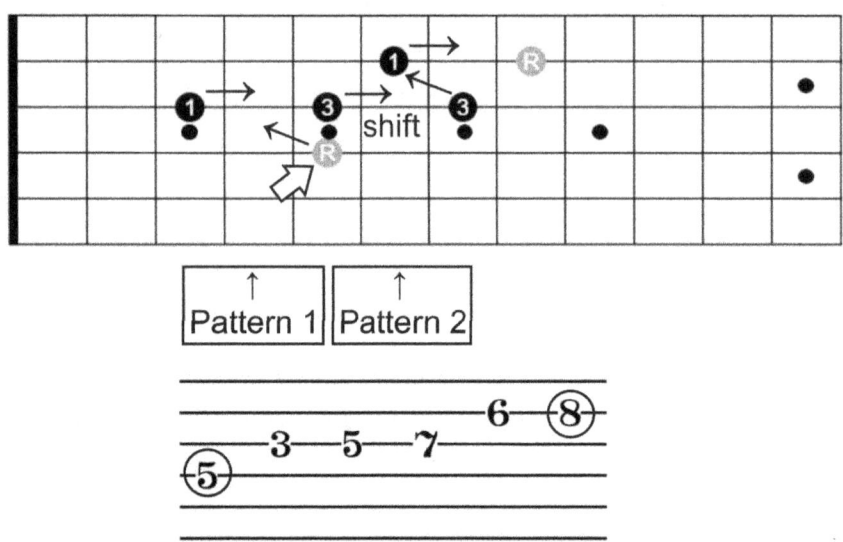

Minor pentatonic lead pattern from the *2nd (B) string*.
• Starts in pentatonic *Pattern 2*, then shifts to *Pattern 3*.

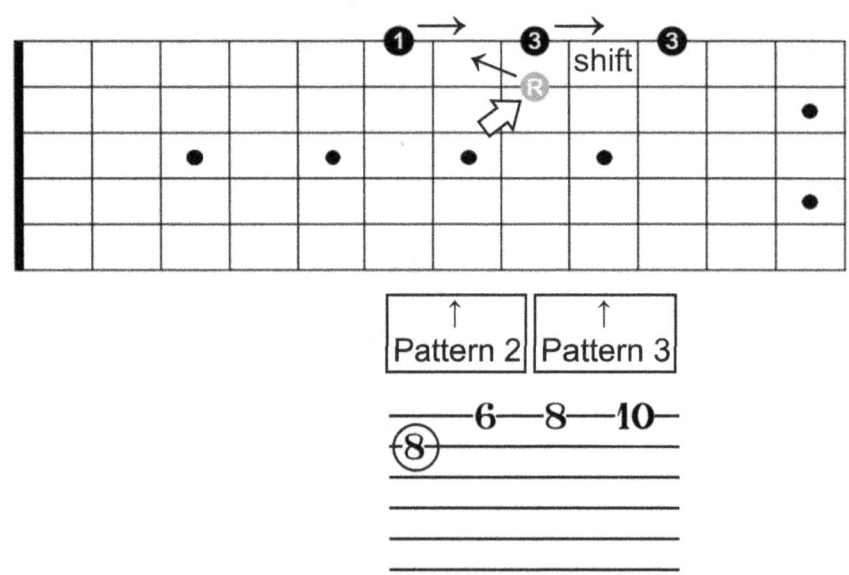

Below shows the **_first 3 lead patterns_** put together.
• Starts in pentatonic **Pattern 5** and ends in pentatonic **Pattern 3**.

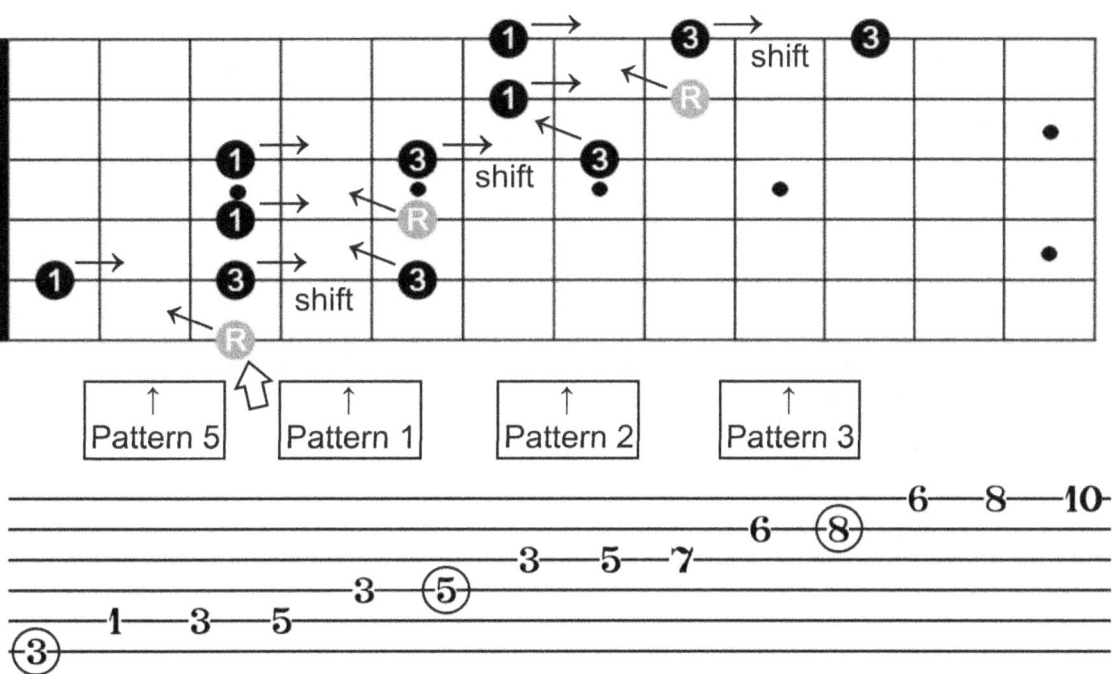

Minor pentatonic lead pattern from the **A (5th) string**.
• Starts in pentatonic **Pattern 3**, then shifts to **Pattern 4**.

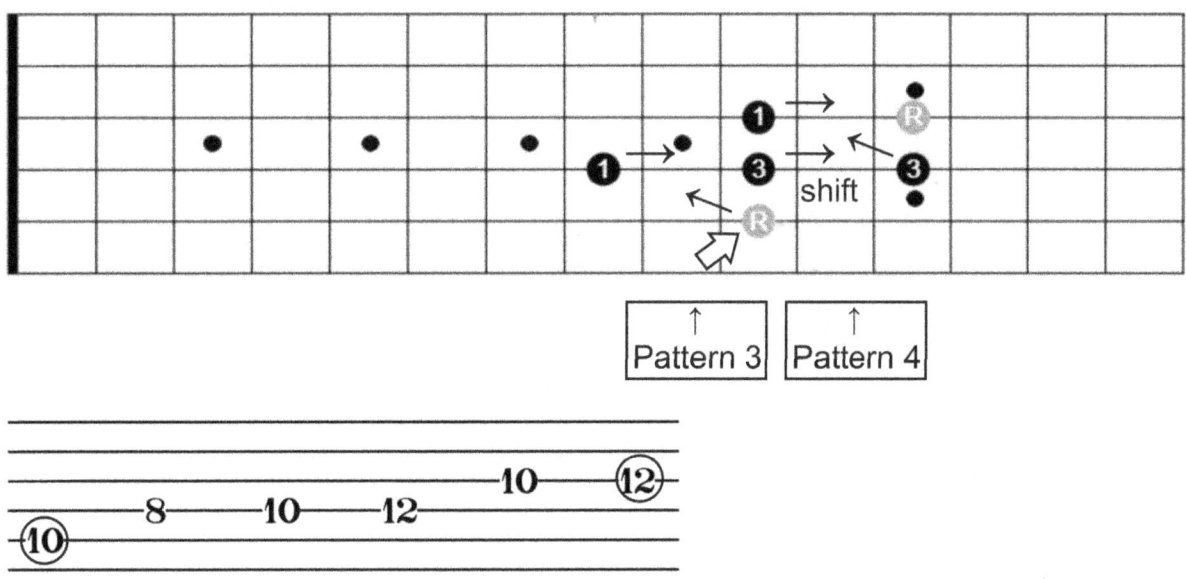

Minor pentatonic lead pattern from the **G (3rd) string**.
• Starts in pentatonic **Pattern 4**, then shifts to **Pattern 5**.

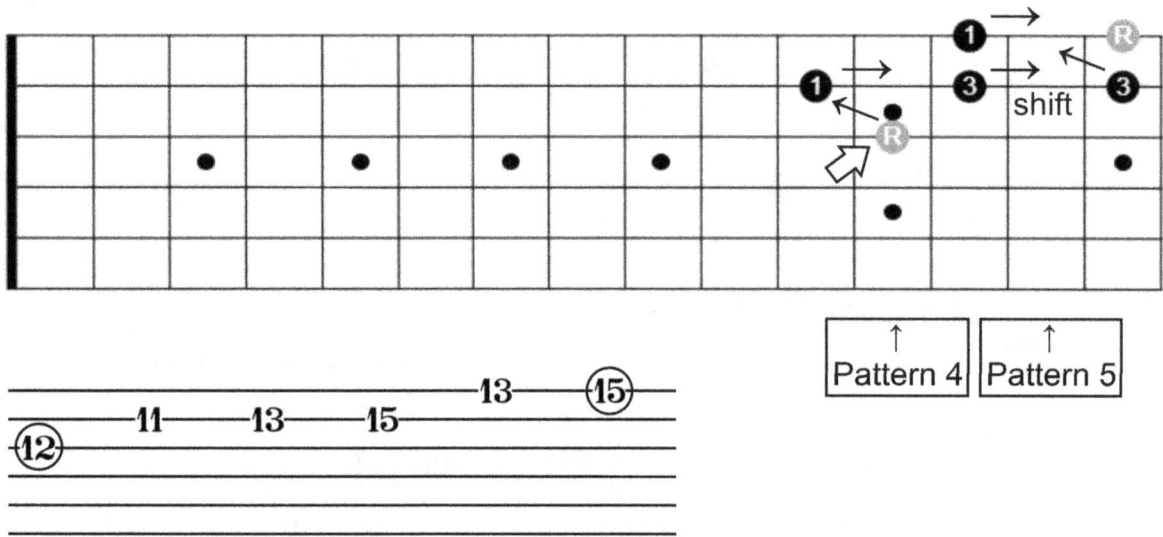

Below shows the **previous 2 patterns put together**.
• Starts in pentatonic **Pattern 3**, and ends in pentatonic **Pattern 5**.

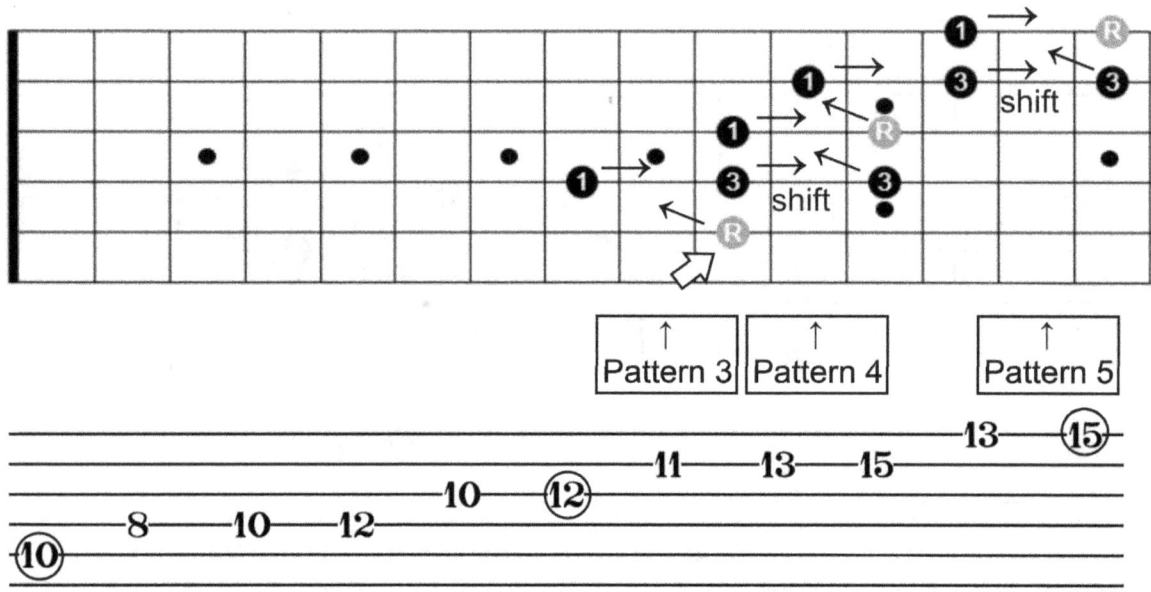

Exercise

Practice these minor pentatonic lead patterns individually and then connect them for the full lead patterns. By thinking about which minor pentatonic pattern number you are currently in as you play the lead pattern, you will have access to all of the notes in the numbered pentatonic pattern as well.

Both full minor pentatonic lead patterns:

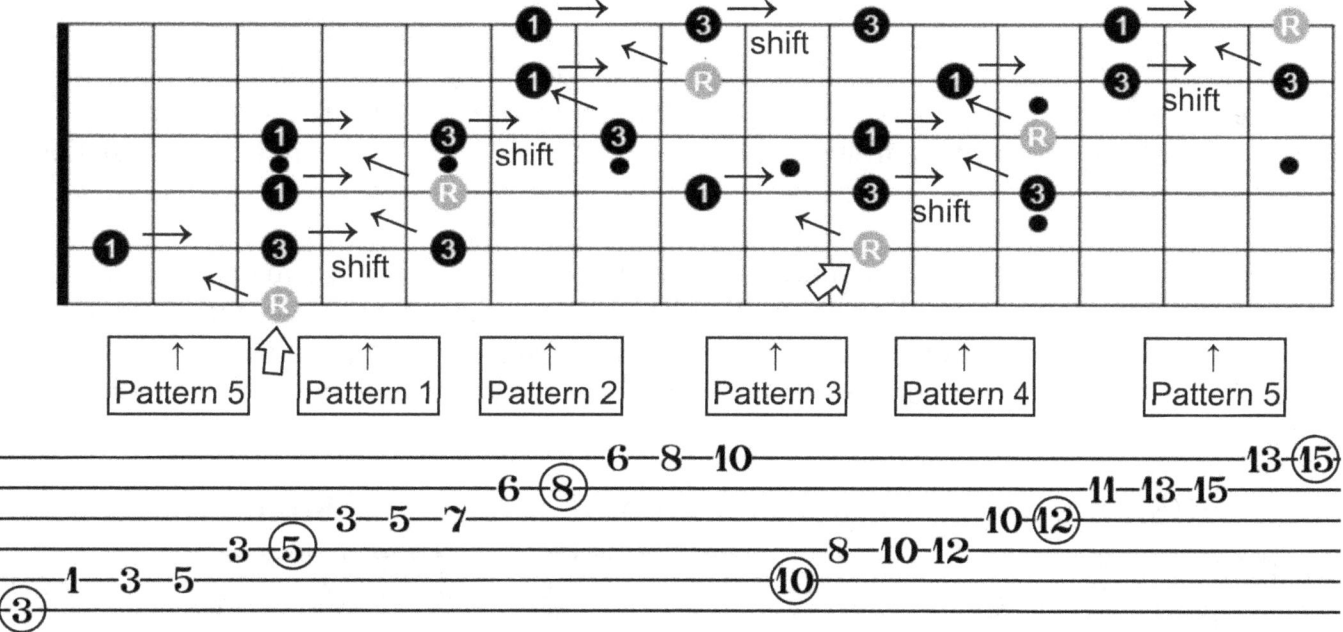

These 2 patterns don't connect. If you take the 1st lead pattern you learned, that will bring you to the ***top*** of minor pentatonic **Pattern 3**. To connect them, **walk down** the notes from the top of pentatonic **Pattern 3** until you hit the **minor root** note on the **A string**, then continue with the next lead pattern. Both lead patterns with the Pattern 3 walkdown connector:

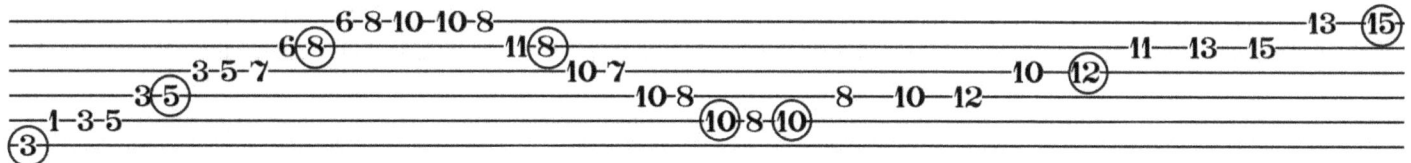

Summary

At this point, you should start getting comfortable with:

- Playing all 5 pentatonic patterns
- Playing a minor pentatonic scale from each string
- Tying the pentatonic scales together using minor root notes
- Using minor lead patterns within multiple pentatonic patterns

It will take time to be fluid at this. I would recommend using blues backing tracks to practice. Let's say you have a "***blues in G***" backing track. To solo you should use a ***G minor pentatonic***. First, find a ***G*** on ***any string***, then use whichever ***patterns*** that are ***assigned to that string*** as your starting point.

CAGED

The **CAGED system** is a way of organizing the guitar fretboard into **5 chord shapes**. These shapes are named after the open chords they come from: **C, A, G, E, and D**. By using these shapes, guitarists can map out the fretboard, locate chord inversions, and connect major scales and pentatonic scales.

We'll begin by looking at the **5 chord shapes** themselves. This process involves turning open chords (chords that use open strings) into **barre chords**, which are movable up and down the neck. You've already learned the **A** and **E** shapes. Some of the remaining shapes may be tricky to play in their complete form, but don't worry—you won't need to master the full chord shape to take advantage of the system.

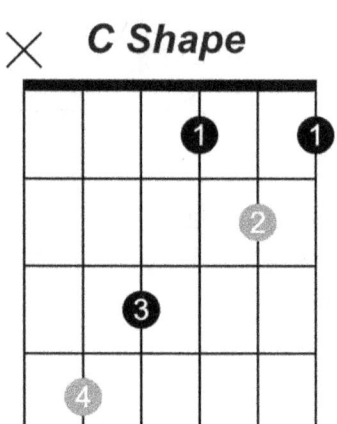
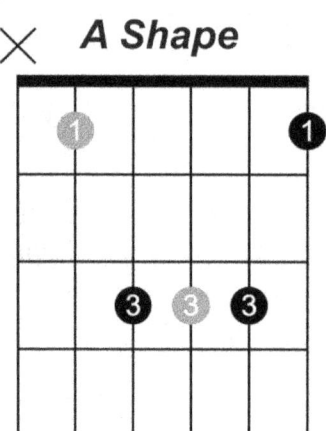
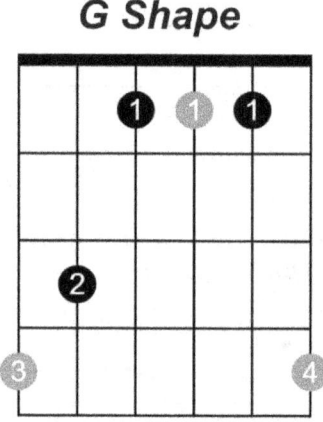
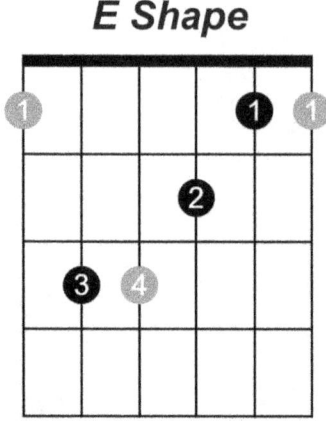
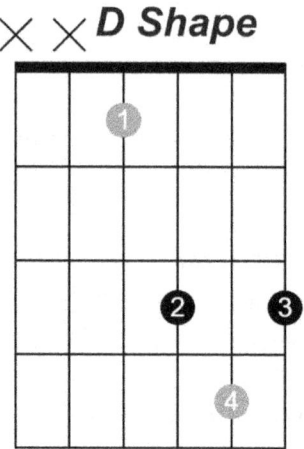

You can also refer to these chord shapes as "forms."

For this exercise, we'll play the five shapes in order: **C–A–G–E–D**. We'll connect them using **octave patterns**, which outline the **root notes** (shown in gray) within each chord shape.

We'll begin with the **C shape** starting on the 4th fret. Place your **pinky** on the 4th fret—this positions the shape so you're playing a **C# chord** using the **C shape** while following **octave Pattern 3**.

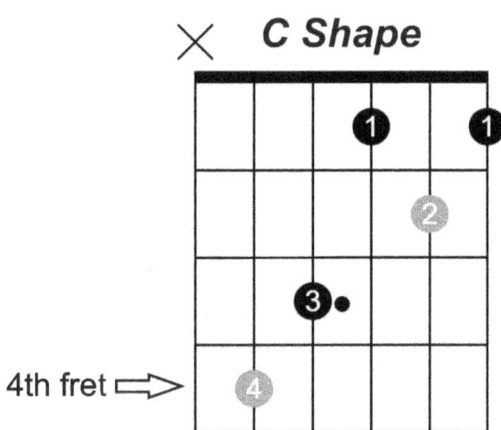

Next we move to the **A shape**. Use your pinky root and replace it with your **index finger**. You will now use the **A shape** from the 4th fret and use **octave Pattern 4**. This is also a **C# chord**.

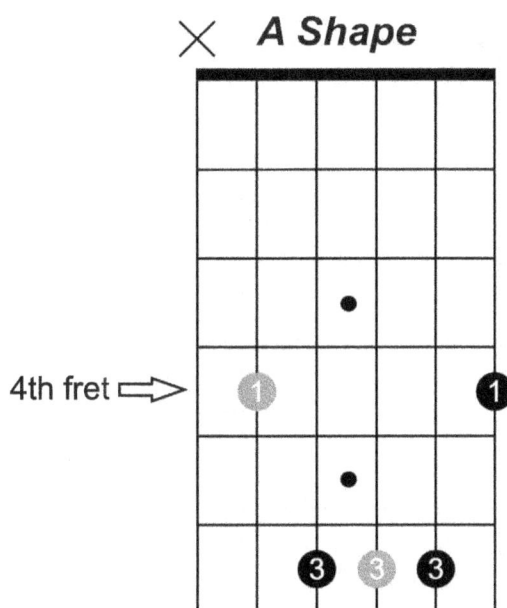

Next we move to the **G shape**. Use your 3rd finger root and replace it with your **index finger**. You will now use the **G shape** from the 9th fret, using **octave Pattern 5**. This is also a **C# chord**.

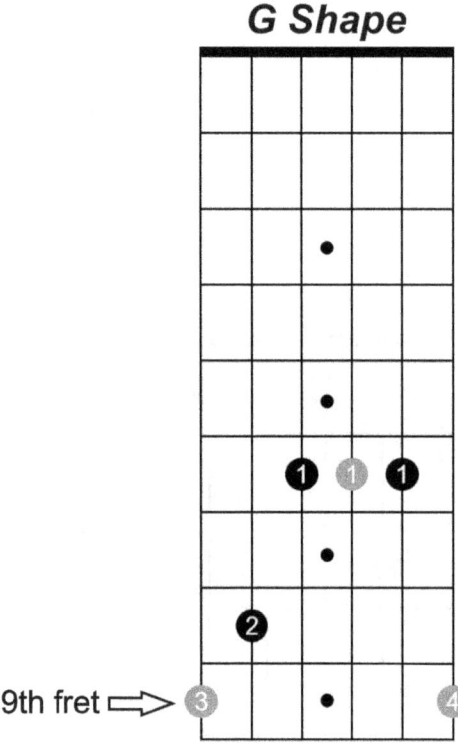

Next we move to the **E shape**. Use your 3rd finger root and replace it with your **index finger**. You will now use the **E shape** from the 9th fret, using **octave Pattern 1**. This is also a **C# chord**.

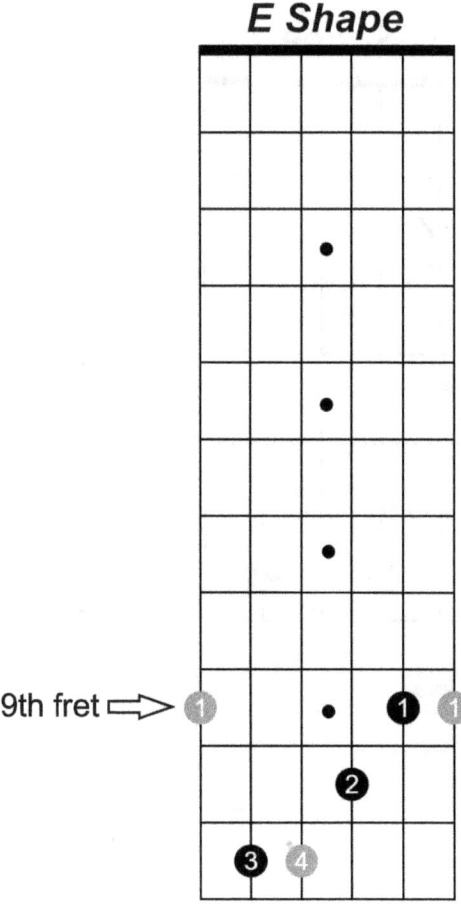

Next we move to the **D shape**. Use your 4th finger root and replace it with your **index finger**. You will now use the **D shape** from the 11th fret, and **octave Pattern 2**. This is also a **C# chord**.

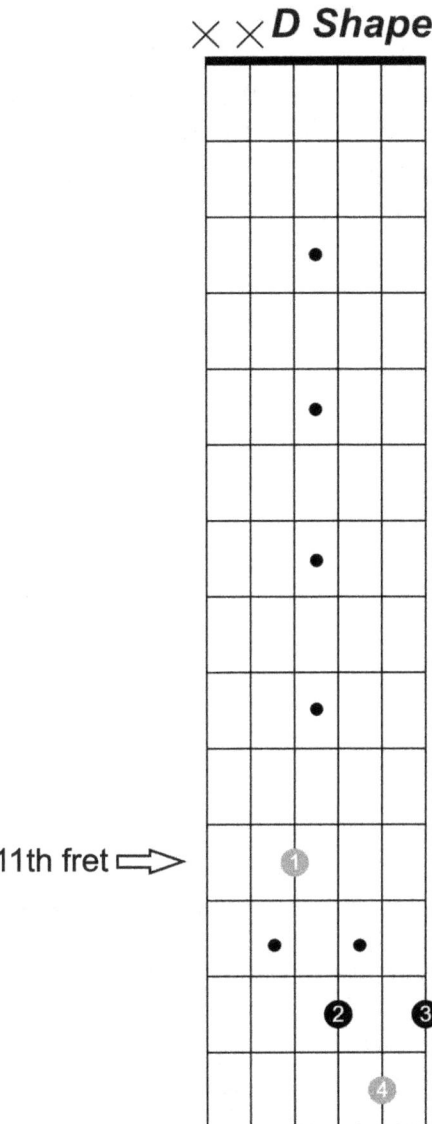

11th fret ⇨

From here, you will **start over** again with the **C shape**. Notice how the bottom on the D shape is the top of the C shape.

> By doing these **5 shapes** in order, you just played **5 different versions** of a **C# chord**. This system will work for **any chord** and you can **start with any shape**. If you start with the A shape, it still follows the same order: AGEDC. If you start with the G shape it looks like this: GEDCA. **Wherever you start, you're always following the word CAGED.**

Exercise

A great way to practice moving through the different **shapes** is to start with any of the open **C, A, G, E, or D chords** and work your way through the rest of the shapes from there. If you start on the open **A chord**, the next chord is the **G shape**, then the **E shape**, and so on. If you start on the open **D chord**, the next chord is the **C shape**, then the **A shape**, etc. Again, it will always follow the word **CAGED**. Use the **octave patterns** to map out the **root notes**, and start to assign the **octave pattern numbers** to each chord:

- *C = 3*
- *A = 4*
- *G = 5*
- *E = 1*
- *D = 2*

Another way to use the CAGED system is to build chords from root notes located on the **E, A,** and **D** strings.

In this approach, you rely less on octave patterns and more on your **memorized note names**—especially on the **E** and **A** strings.

When Applied this Way:

• The **E string** has **2 shapes** that share this root.

• The **A string** also has **2 shapes** that share this root.

• The **D string** has **1 shape** based on its root.

By thinking in terms of these string-based root notes, you can quickly form any of the five CAGED shapes without having to track all the octave patterns.

Let's say you want to play a **D chord**. Start by finding a **D** on the **E string (10th fret)**. From there you can play either the **G shape** or **E shape**.

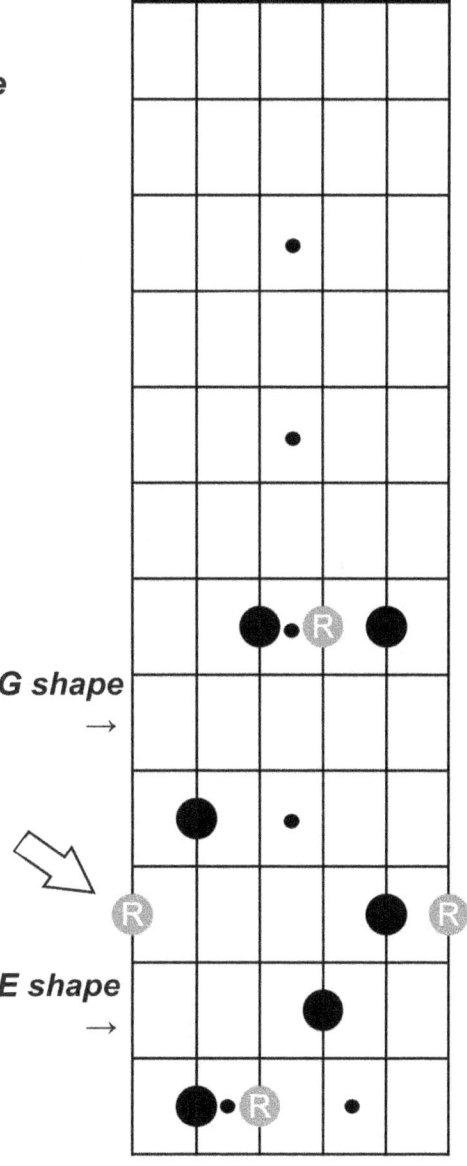

Next, find a **D** on the **A string (5th fret)**. From there you can play either the **C shape** or **A shape**.

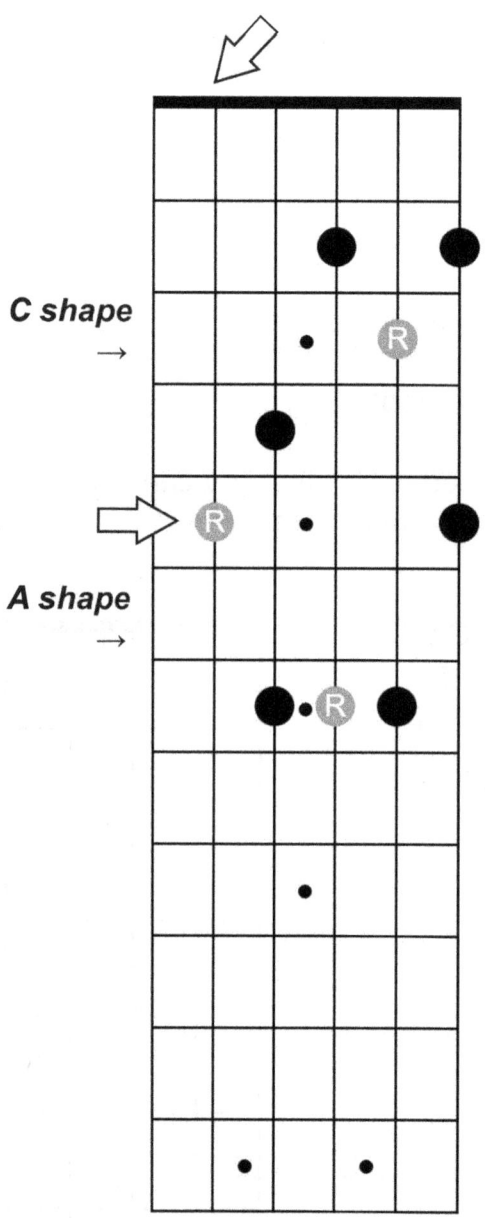

For the *D shape*, find a *D* on the *D string (12th fret)*.

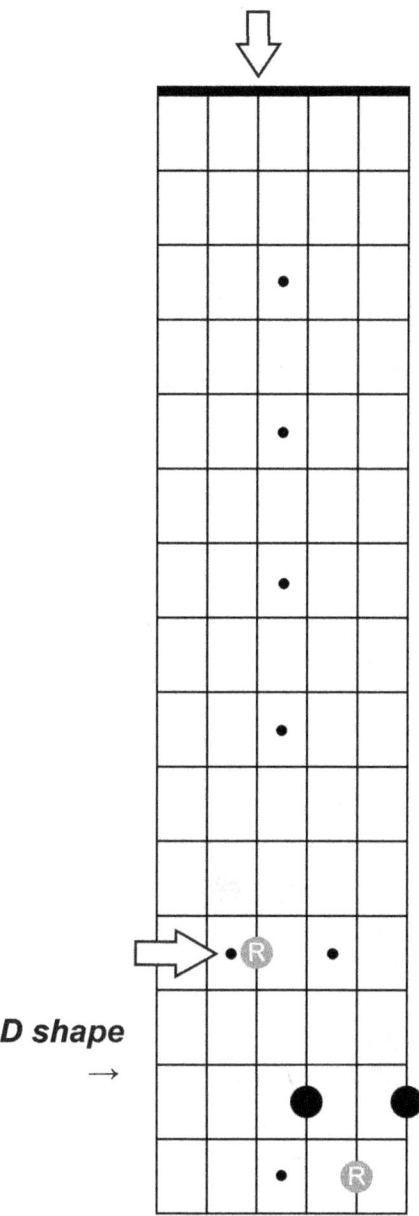

D shape
→

Ultimately, this method is the way that you will probably use the CAGED system for chords: by finding a note and playing a chord from there, rather than just playing all 5 shapes in a row.

MAJOR PENTATONIC PATTERNS

As mentioned earlier, the *minor* and *major* pentatonic patterns use the same shapes. This means you already know the major pentatonic patterns—you just need to identify the *major root notes* within each of the five patterns.

We'll use the **CAGED system** and *octave patterns* to locate these major root notes.

For numbering, we'll follow the same logic we used for the minor pentatonics:

• *Minor Pattern 2* will now be labeled *Major Pattern 1*, because its first note is the lowest *major root* in that shape.

• The other patterns will be renumbered accordingly, but remember: any pattern is only "major" if you start on one of its major root notes.

First, we'll look at how each of the **CAGED chords** are inside of the *5 pentatonic patterns*. The gray letters represent the chord found in each pattern, not the note names:

Pattern 1 - E shape
Octave Pattern 1

Pattern 2 - D shape
Octave Pattern 2

Pattern 3 - C shape
Octave Pattern 3

Pattern 4 - A shape
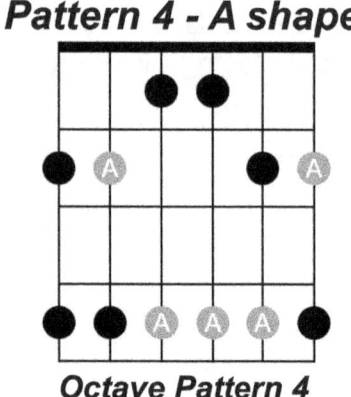
Octave Pattern 4

Pattern 5 - G shape
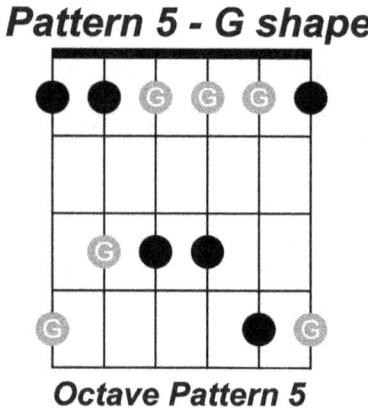
Octave Pattern 5

Next, we'll take a look at the specific major roots found within each pattern.

MAJOR ROOTS WITHIN PENTATONIC PATTERNS

The *root note* of a chord is its letter name and its lowest note. For example, the root of a G chord is **G**.

When you place **CAGED chord shapes** over the pentatonic scale patterns, the chord shape's root becomes the *lowest major root note* in that pentatonic pattern.

Remember: the *numbered octave patterns* still apply here.

Pattern 1 - E shape
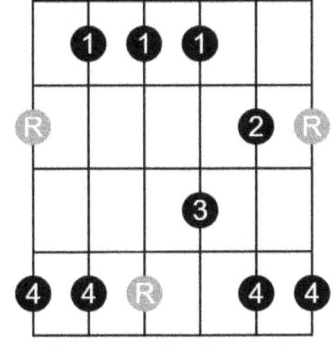
Octave Pattern 1

Pattern 2 - D shape
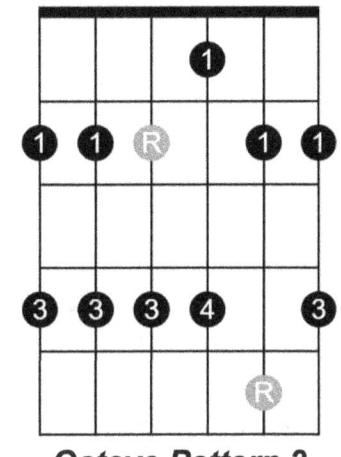
Octave Pattern 2

Pattern 3 - C shape
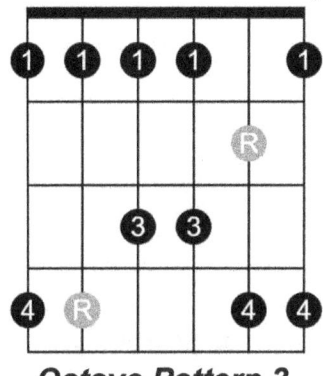
Octave Pattern 3

Pattern 4 - A shape
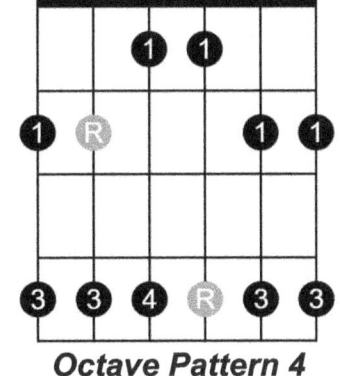
Octave Pattern 4

Pattern 5 - G shape
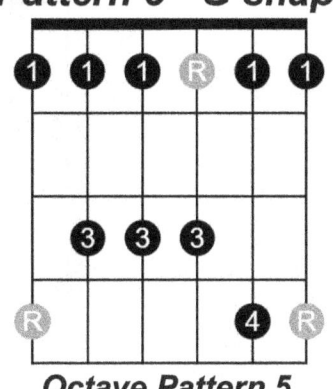
Octave Pattern 5

The CAGED chords are laid over the patterns on the next page. This will show you not only how the chord fits on top of each pattern, but will help you find those major root notes.

The *gray notes* in each pattern represent the chord notes.

Practice Tip:

1. Play the chord shape.

2. Starting from the **lowest root note** in the chord, play through the pentatonic pattern:

- From the lowest root up to the highest note in the pattern

- Back down to the lowest note in the pattern

- Finish by returning to the *major root*

This ensures you're playing the pattern as a *major pentatonic*.

Pattern 1 - E shape

Pattern 1 - E shape:

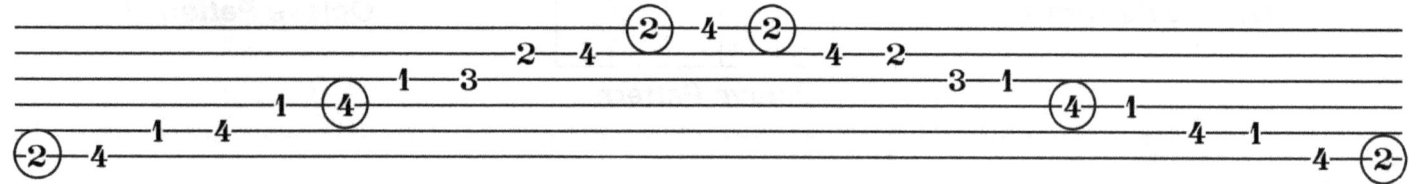

Pattern 2 - D shape

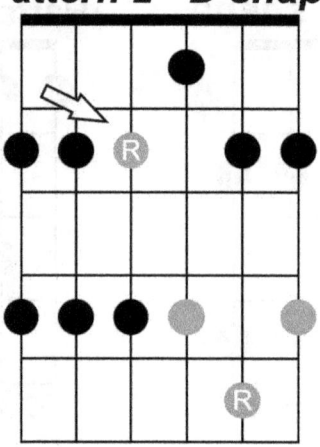

Pattern 2 - D shape:

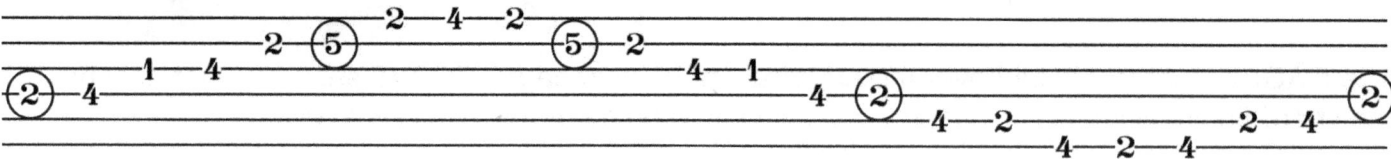

Pattern 3 - C shape

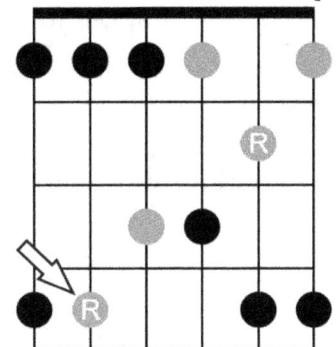

Pattern 3 - C shape:

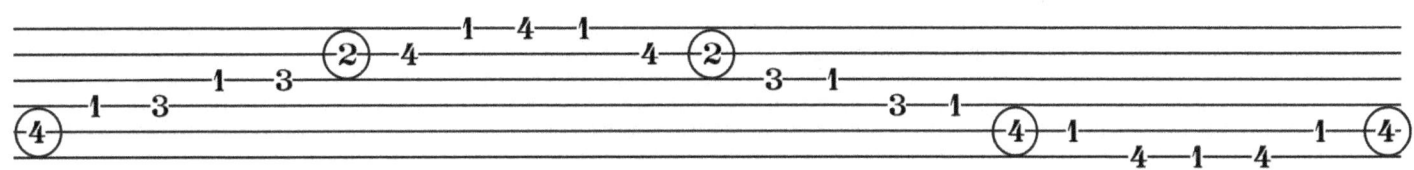

Pattern 4 - A shape

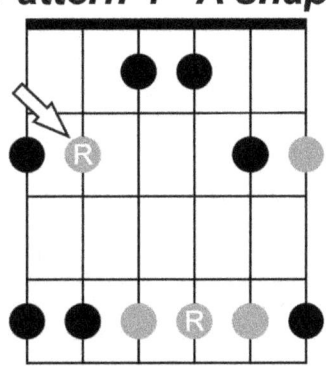

Pattern 4 - A shape:

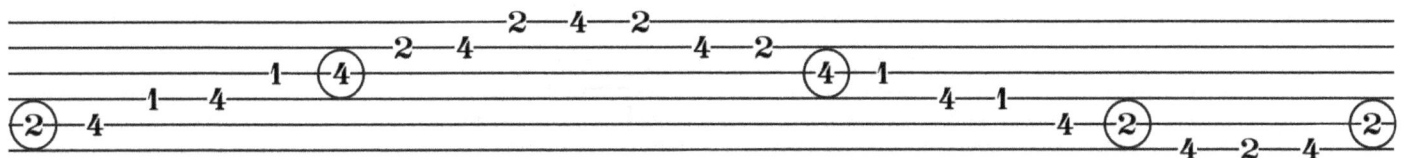

Pattern 5 - G shape

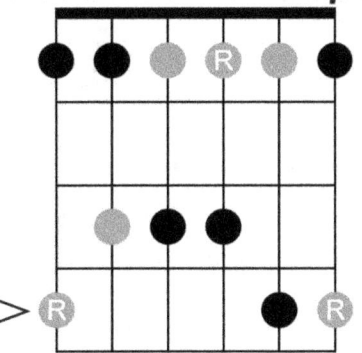

Pattern 5 - G shape:

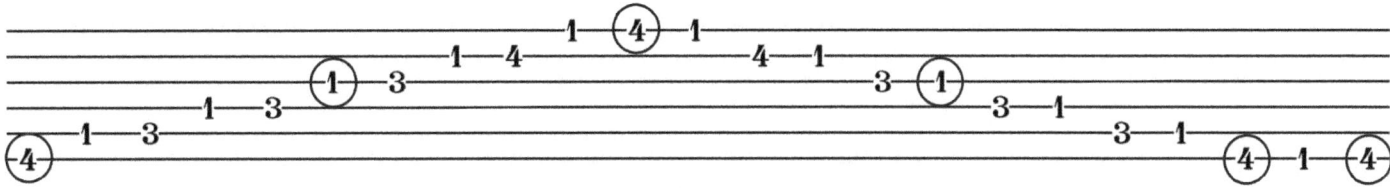

You'll want to be able to move smoothly from one pattern to the next—just like we did with the minor pentatonic patterns—but starting in different spots for each pattern.

Below is one approach for working through the patterns:

• **Start in Pattern 1** and use that as the model for the 5-note sequence.

• We are still applying the **5 octave patterns** here.

• For each pattern (except Pattern 5), start with your **2nd finger** from the ⇨ pointing to the Ⓡ.

• For **Pattern 5**, start with your **index finger** instead.

Pattern 1
E shape

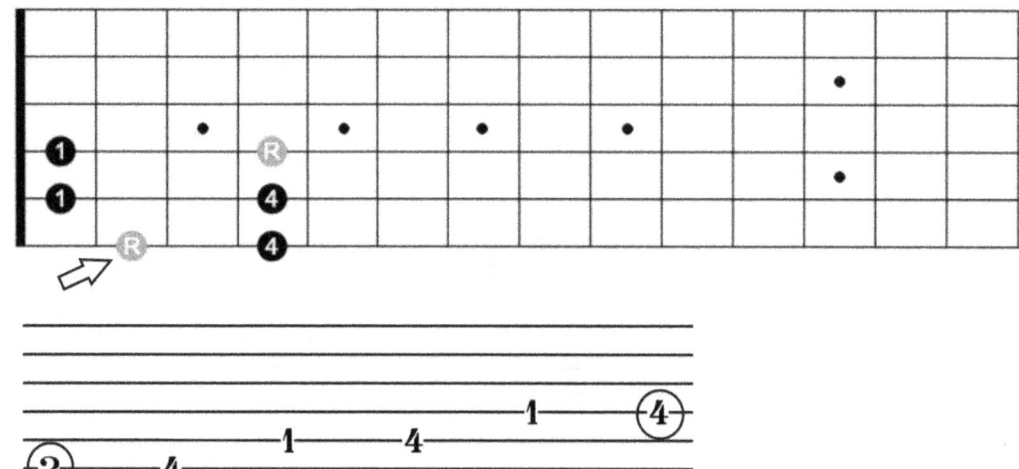

Pattern 2
D shape

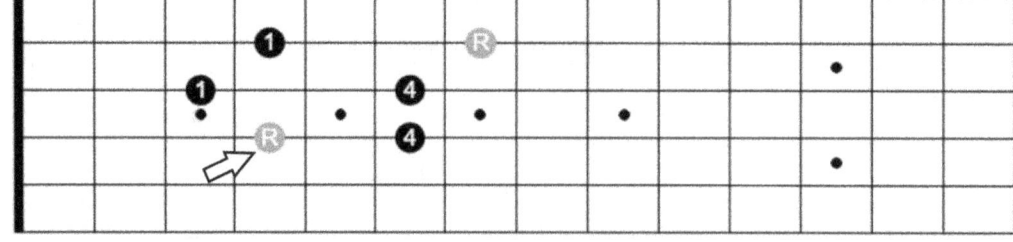

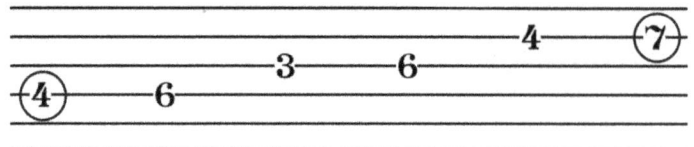

Pattern 3
C shape

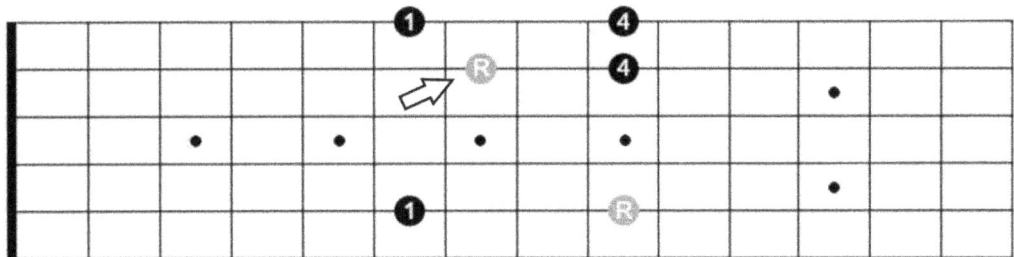

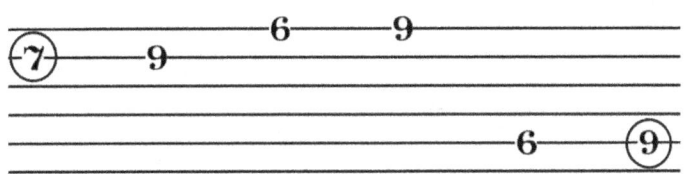

Pattern 4
A shape

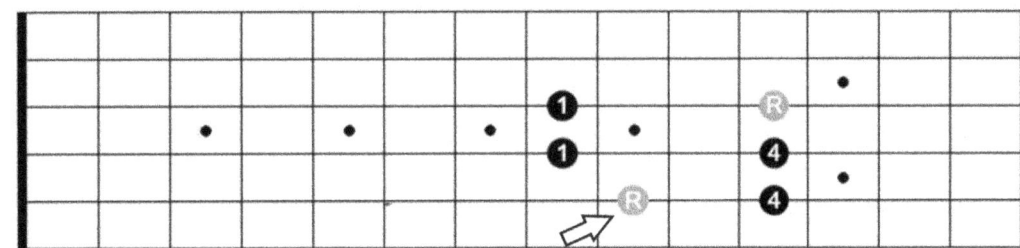

Pattern 5
G shape

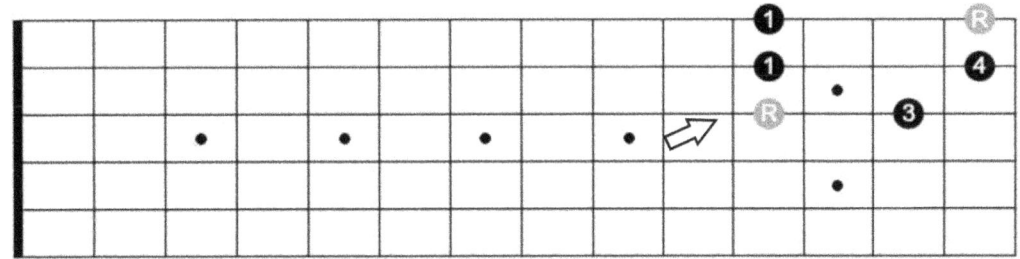

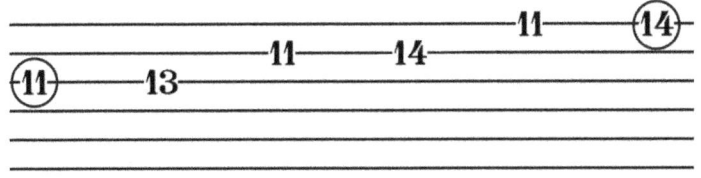

Here are all 5 patterns with a walkdown connector in Pattern 3:

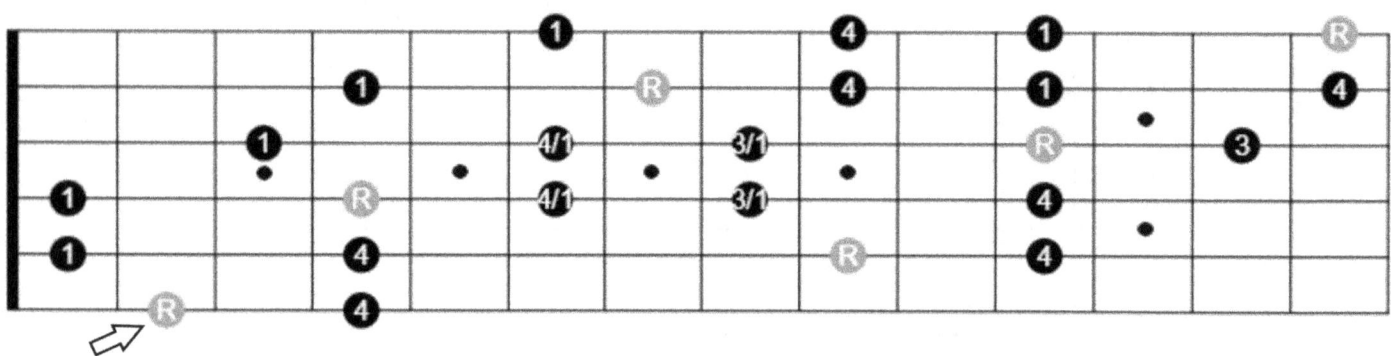
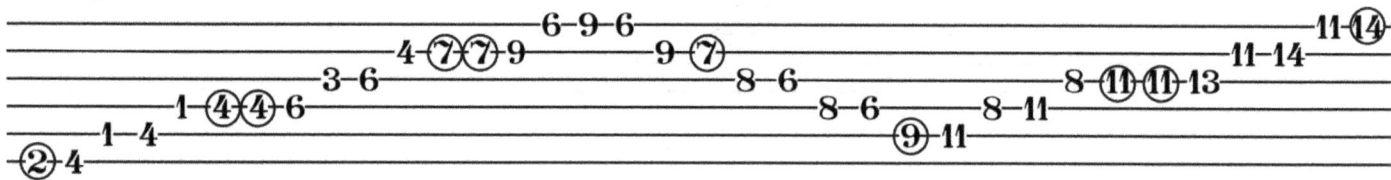

You can also start the major pentatonic scales from your **4th finger**.

For these, we'll use **Pattern 5** as the template and transfer that to the other patterns.

You'll start each of these patterns *from the* ⇨ *pointing to the* Ⓡ.

Play to the highest note in the pattern, then down to the lowest note in the pattern, and finally return to the *root* you started on.

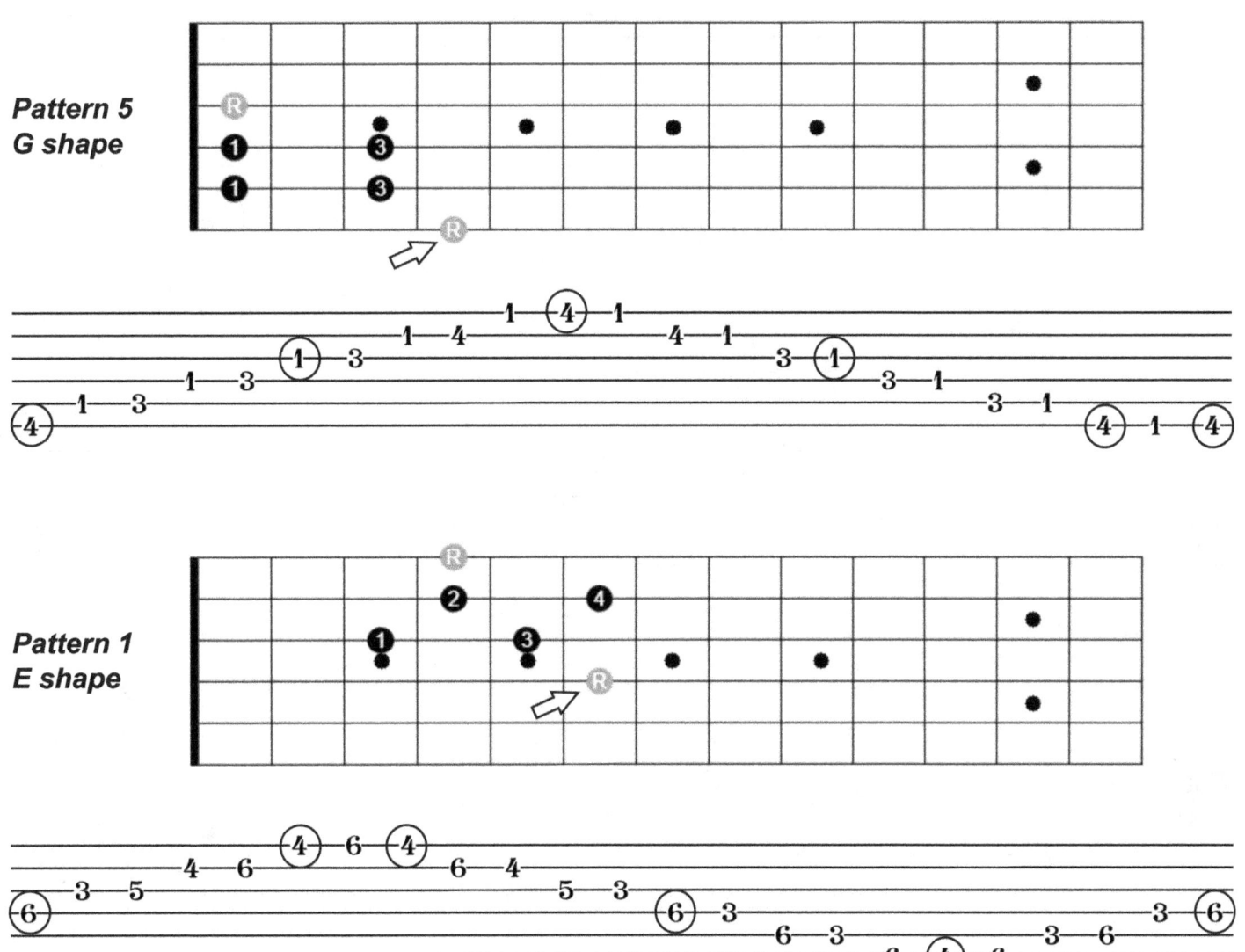

Pattern 2
D shape

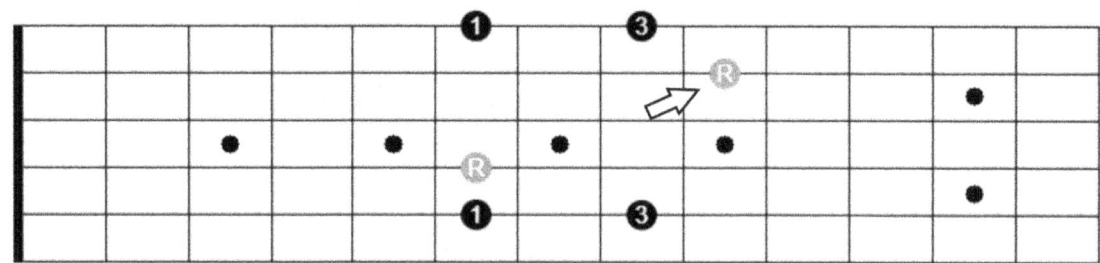

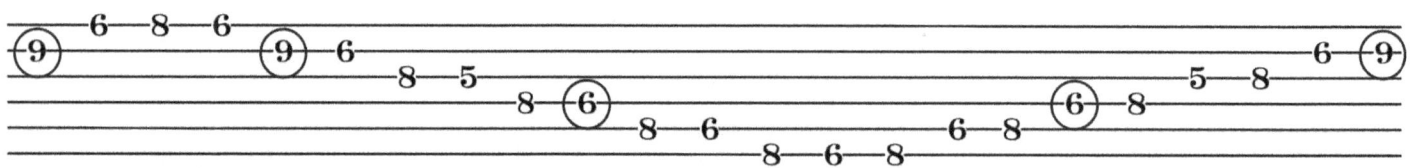

Pattern 3
C shape

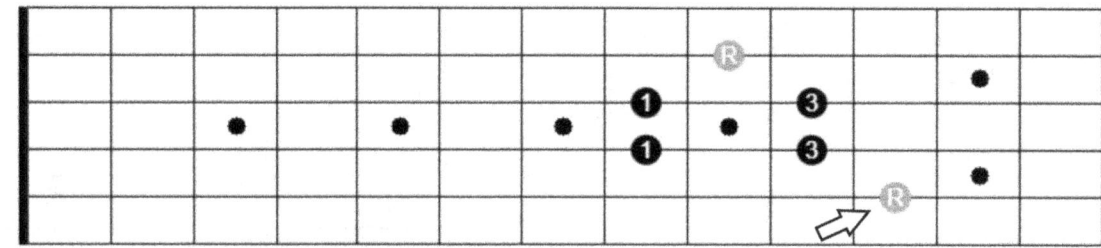

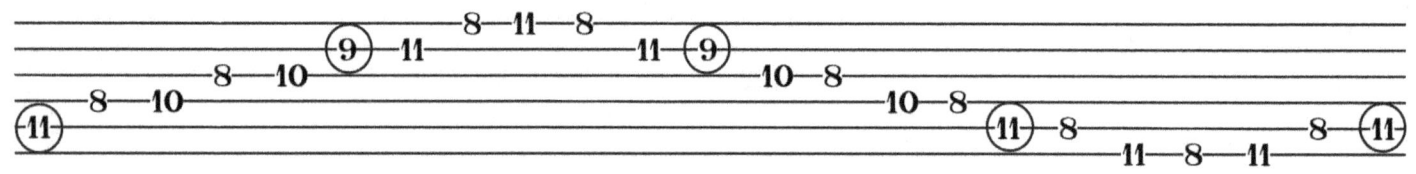

Pattern 4
A shape

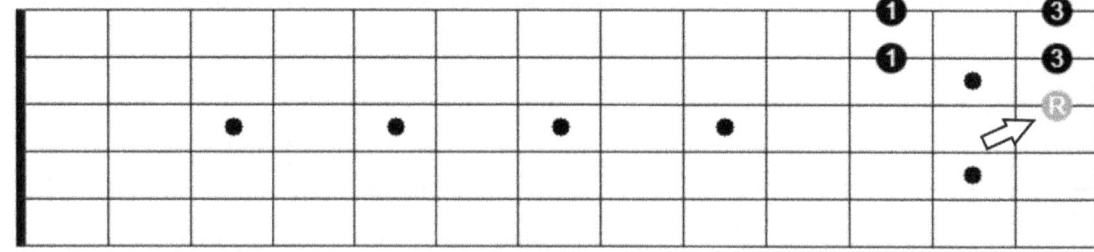

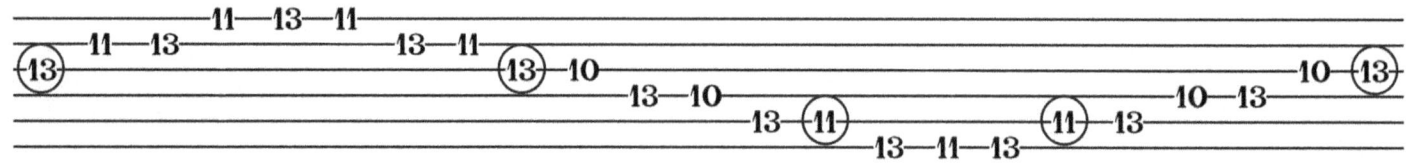

Each pattern is *tied to a specific string*.

If you memorize both the *starting points* (from the major root note with your middle finger) *and* the *string assignments*, you will always know which pattern to play.

For example:

• If you find a major root note with your middle finger on the *E string*, you will *always* use *Pattern 1*.

• If you find a major root note with your middle finger on the *A string*, you will *always* use *Pattern 4*.

This system applies to all of your string-pattern assignments, ensuring consistent navigation of the fretboard.

String   Pattern

E → 1 (E shape)

A → 4 (A shape)

D → 2 (D shape)

G → 5 (G shape)

B → 3 (C shape)

An easy way to remember these assignments is to count *1 through 5*, starting on the *6th string* and *skipping a string* to get to each number. Use the charts below.

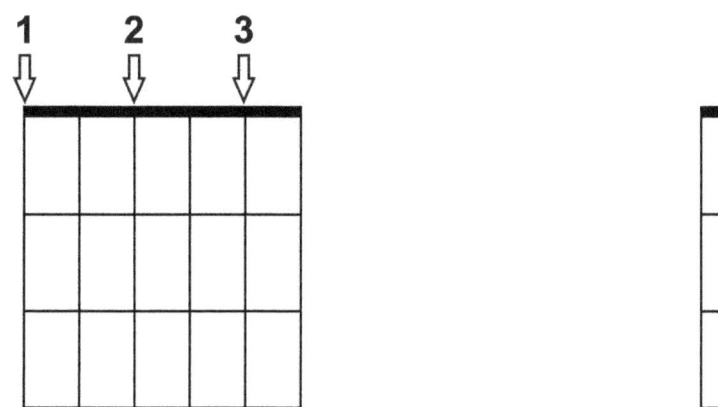

To execute these starting points efficiently, you will either need to know the note names on each string or be able to visualize and quickly connect the octave patterns.

Here, we are looking at **2 patterns with a shared major root note**. The large arrows point to the shared major root note that connects both patterns.

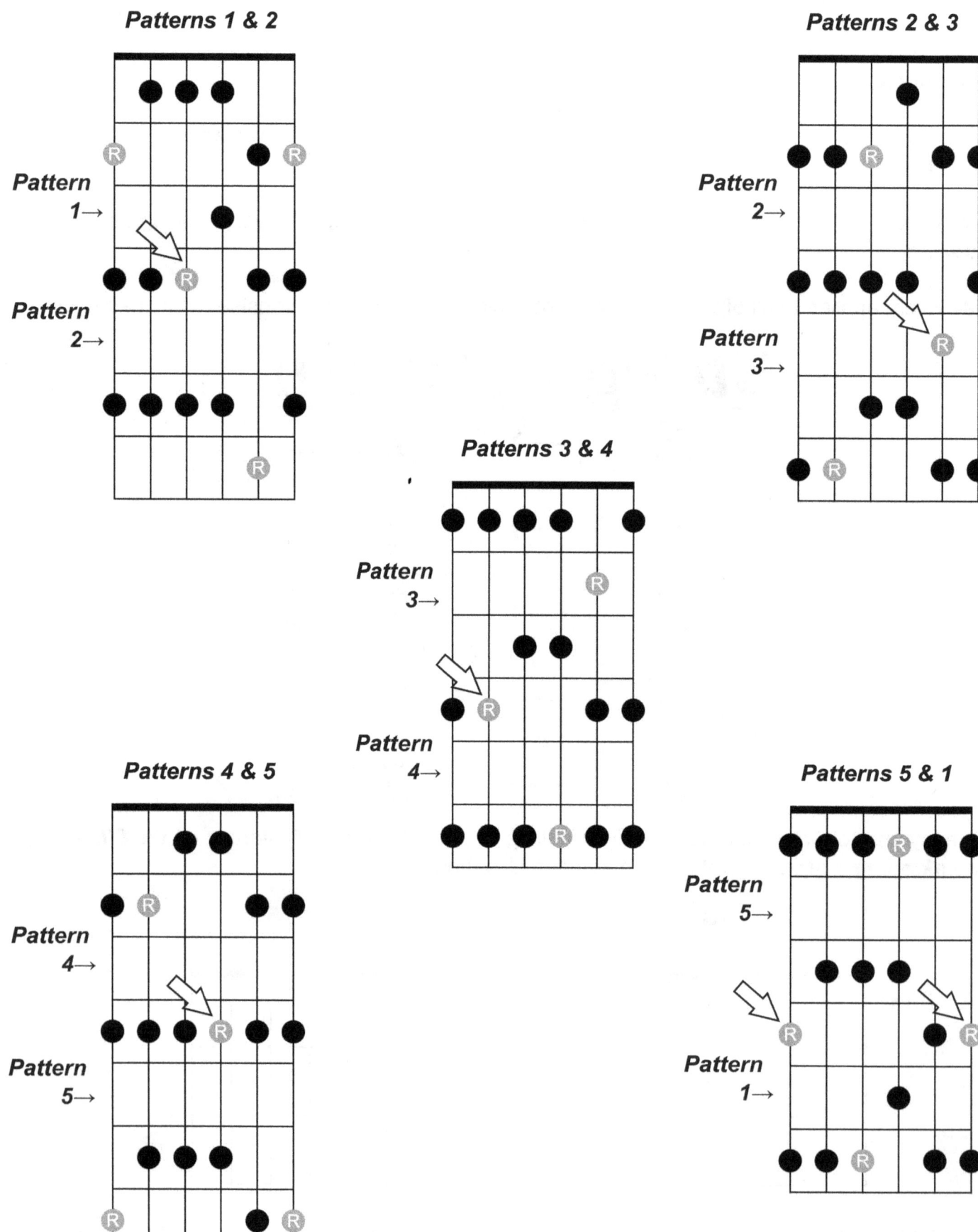

106

Below is a list of *major pentatonic scales* along with their *string assignments*. You'll notice these assignments are *identical* to those used for the minor pentatonics.

As you memorize each pattern on its assigned string, try to visualize the **CAGED chord shape** that corresponds to it. This mental connection will strengthen your ability to link scale patterns to chord positions, making the fretboard easier to navigate.

String	Pattern
E →	**1**(E shape) & **5**(G shape)
A →	**4**(A shape) & **3**(C shape)
D →	**2**(D shape) & **1**(E shape)
G →	**5**(G shape) & **4**(A shape)
B →	**3**(C shape) & **2**(D shape)

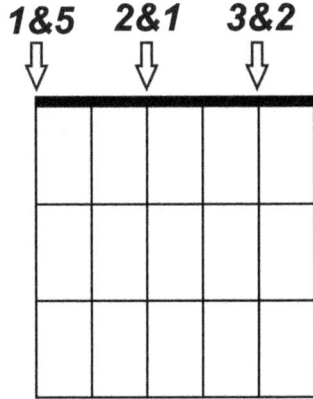
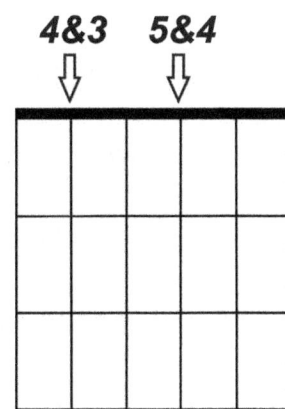

Let's say you want to play a solo in **C major**. Using this system, all you need to do is find a C note on **any string**:

- E string – 8th fret

- A string – 3rd fret

- D string – 10th fret

- G string – 5th fret

- B string – 13th fret

Once you've found your root note, use the **pattern assigned to that string** and you'll instantly be playing the correct notes for C major.

Another big advantage of knowing these scales is that you can easily add notes between or during chords. Remember, the two most common barre chord shapes are the **E shape** and **A shape**.

- If you're playing an **E major shape** barre chord, use **major Pattern 1** over that chord.

- If you're playing an **A major shape** barre chord, use **major Pattern 4**.

This approach keeps your soloing and chord playing tightly connected, so you can move seamlessly between rhythm and lead.

Exercise

- Strum 2 beats of an A chord using the E shape (5th fret of E string).

- Use the next 2 beats to improvise using major Pattern 1 (from the 5th fret).

- Next, strum 2 beats of a D chord using the A shape (5th fret of A string).

- Use the next 2 beats to improvise using Pattern 4 (from the 5th fret).

Exercise

Fill in the charts below with the major pentatonic patterns; be sure to acknowledge the major root notes in each pattern.

Pattern 1
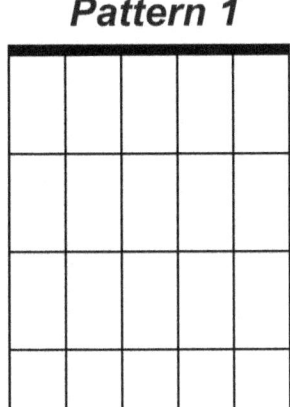

Pattern 2
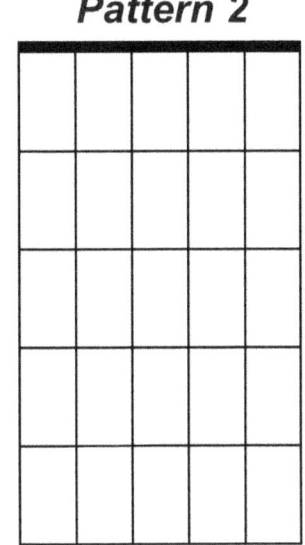

Pattern 3
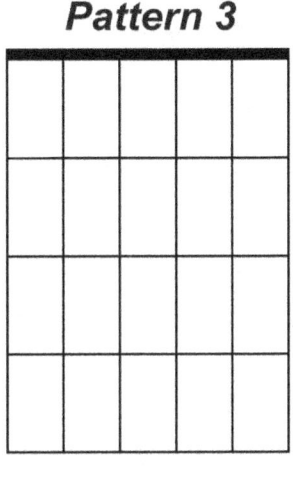

Pattern 4
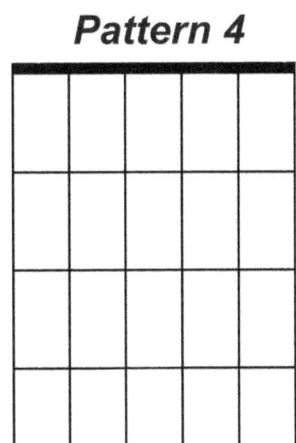

Pattern 5
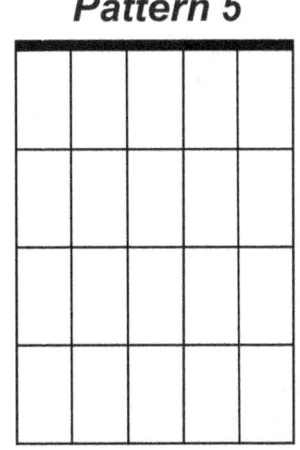

MAJOR PENTATONIC LEAD PATTERNS

Using **lead patterns** is a great way to connect the pentatonic patterns. These are **1-octave, 5-note** patterns that can be linked together across the fretboard. You can start them from **any string** and **any fret**, and the pattern itself will always remain the same.

Just Remember:

• Whenever you cross to the **B string**, shift the pattern **one fret higher**.

• The key to mastering these is knowing **which of the 5 pentatonic patterns** you're in as you move through the lead patterns.

For All of These Shapes:

• Your **1st finger** will always be on an Ⓡ.

• Start at the ⇨, then follow the →.

• The tablature for each lead pattern is listed below.

Major pentatonic lead pattern starting on the **E string**.
• Start in **Pattern 1** and shift into **Pattern 2**.

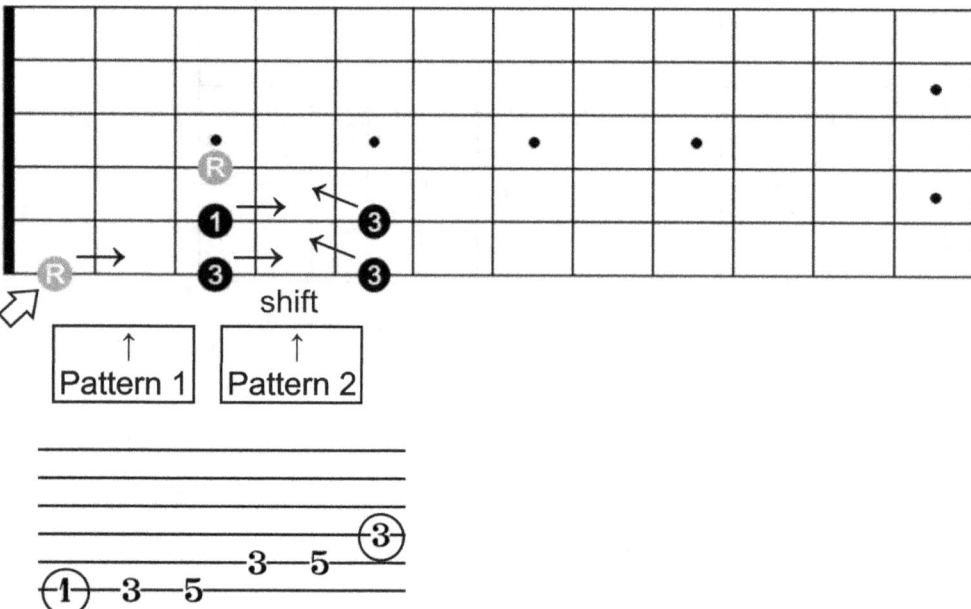

Major pentatonic lead pattern starting on the **D string**.
• Start in **Pattern 2** and shift into **Pattern 3**.

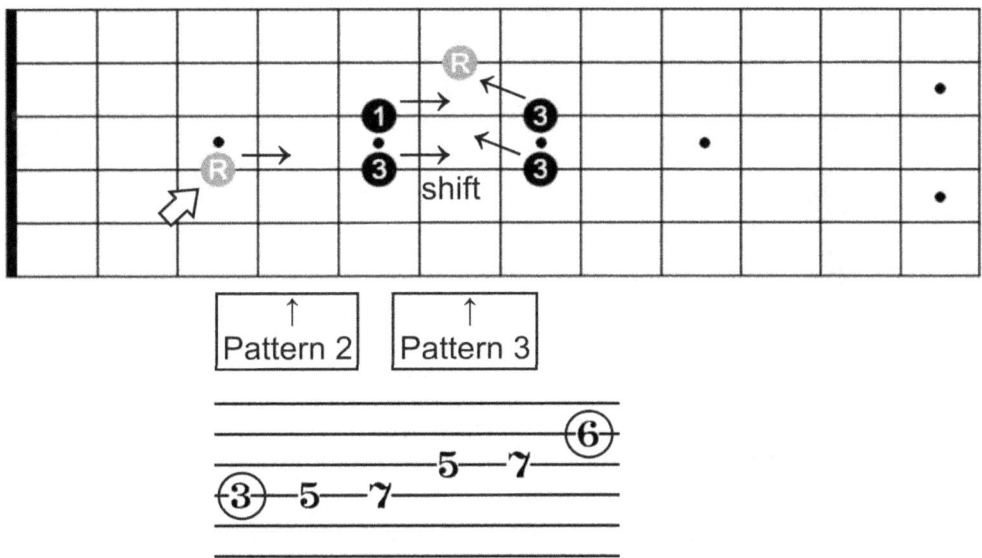

Major pentatonic lead pattern starting on the **B string**.
• Start in **Pattern 3** and shift into **Pattern 4**.

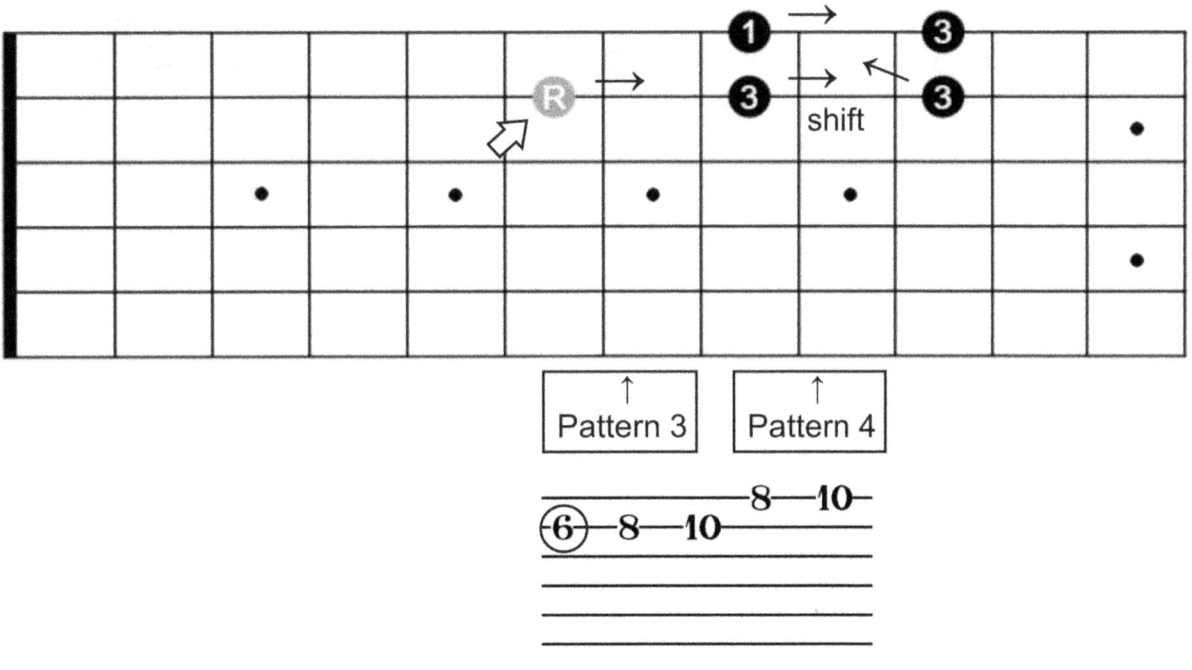

111

All *3 lead patterns* put together.
• Starting in *Pattern 1* and ending in *Pattern 4*.

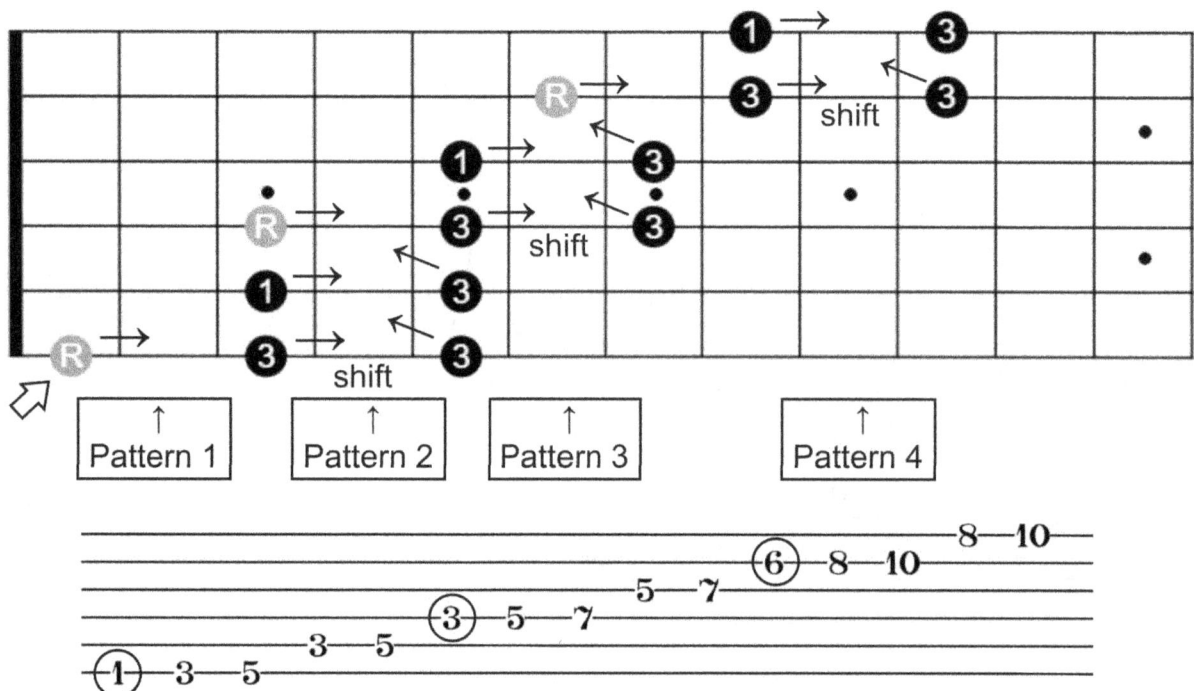

Exercise

Practice moving smoothly up and down through the entire lead pattern. As you play, **keep track of which pentatonic pattern you're in** at any given point. This way, you're not limited to just the lead pattern itself—you'll also have full access to the notes from the **numbered pentatonic patterns** as you pass through them.

We'll continue to connect **3 small patterns** into **1 larger pattern** and then connect the **2 larger patterns**.

Major pentatonic lead pattern starting on the **_A string_**.
• Start in **Pattern 4** and shift into **Pattern 5**.

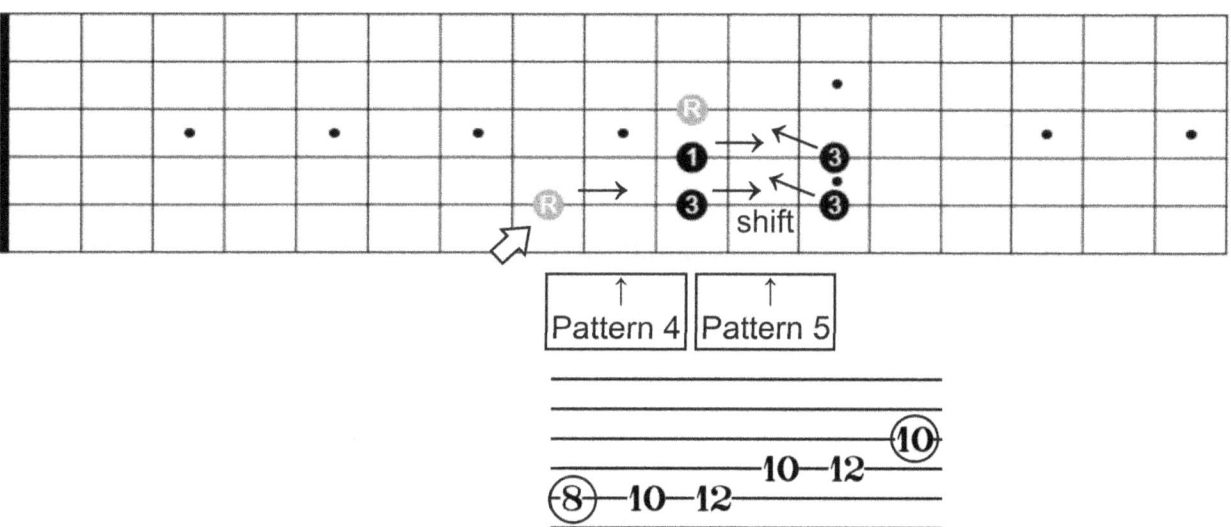

Major pentatonic lead pattern starting on the **_G string_**.
• Start in **Pattern 5** and shift into **Pattern 1**.

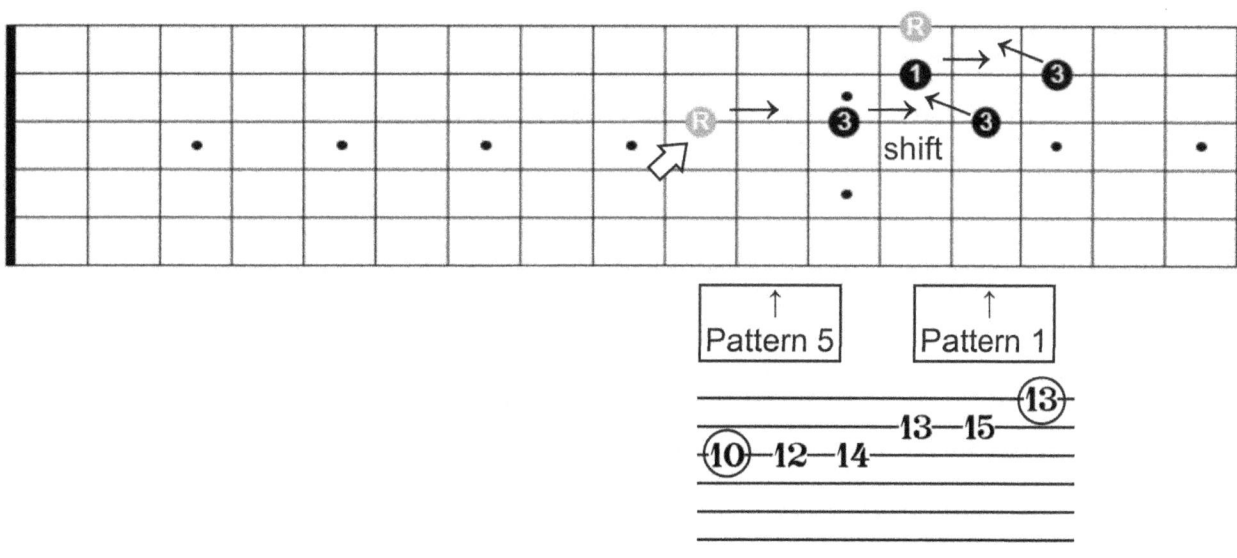

113

Major pentatonic lead pattern starting on the **E string**.
• Start in **Pattern 1** and shift into **Pattern 2**.

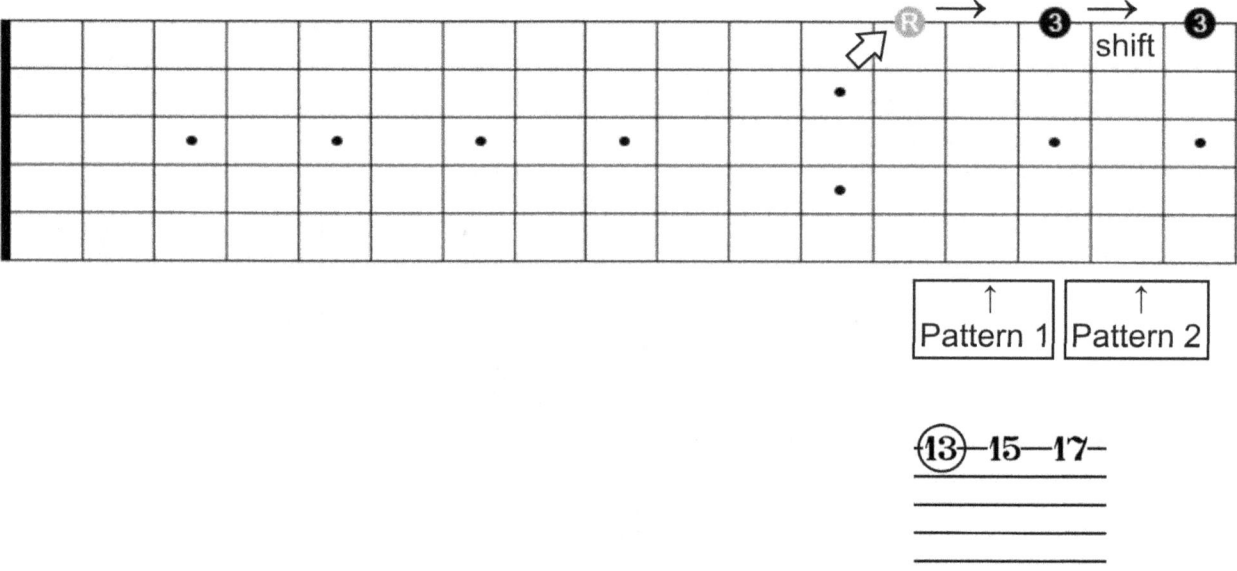

All 3 lead patterns put together.
• Starting in **Pattern 4** and ending in **Pattern 2**.

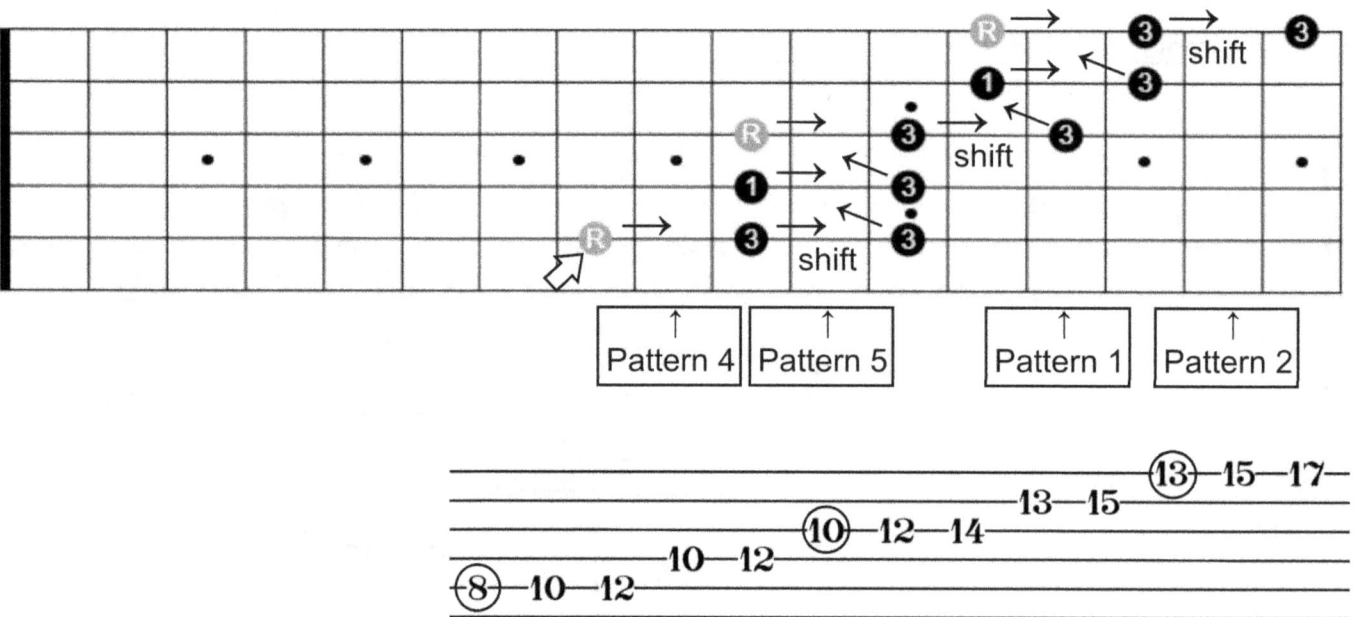

Next, we'll look at the *two large patterns* on the fretboard. These patterns don't connect directly. To link them, you'll use transitions through other pentatonic patterns:

• **From the first large pattern**: Walk down the notes in **Pattern 4** until you reach the *root note on the A string*, then continue into **Pattern 5**.

• **From the second large pattern**: Walk down **Pattern 2** until you reach the *root note on the D string*, then shift into **Pattern 3**.

Once you're comfortable with these lead patterns, you'll be able to move freely up and down the fretboard. Practice starting in different spots, and—just like with the earlier patterns—work on clearly visualizing them across the neck.

<u>*Both full major lead patterns:*</u>

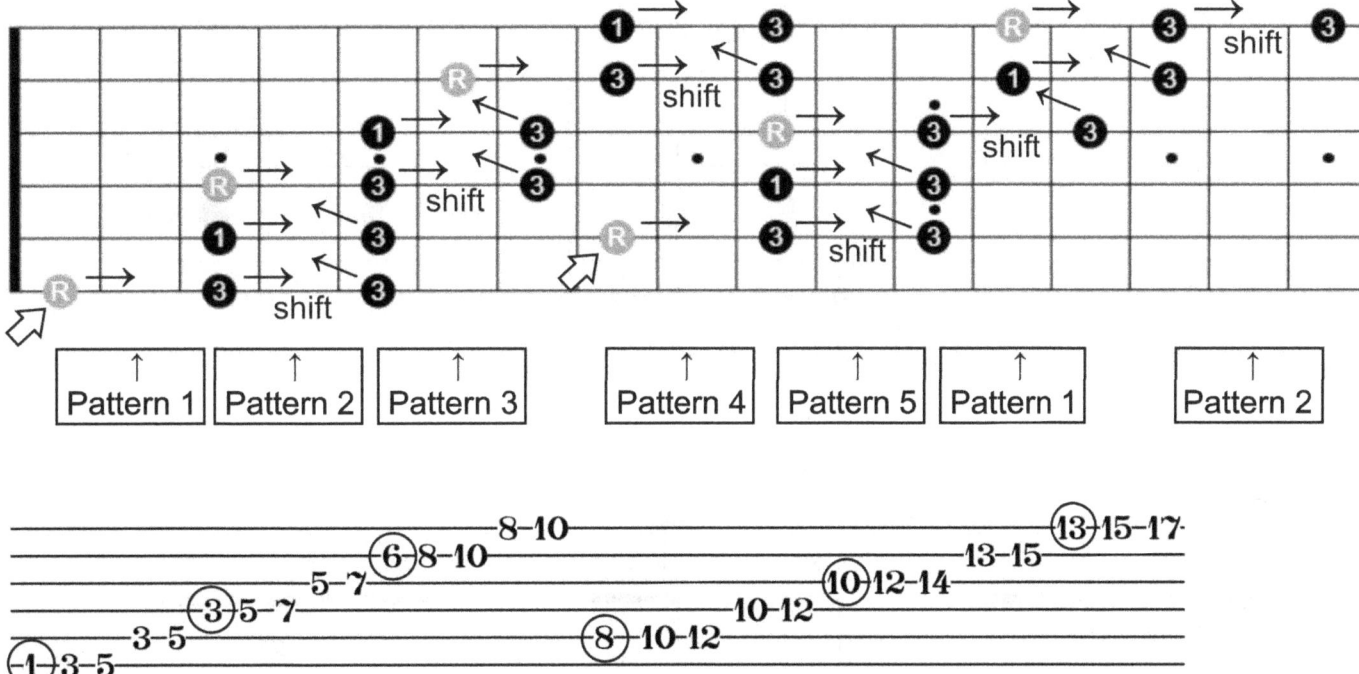

Both full major lead patterns with the **Pattern 4 connector**:

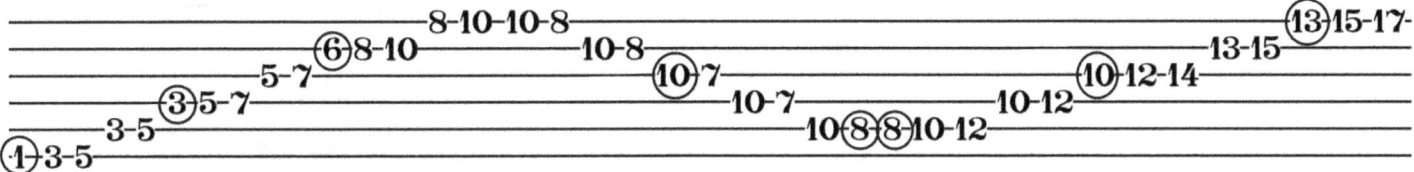

MAJOR VS MINOR PENTATONIC SUMMARY WITH OCTAVE PATTERNS

Octave Pattern 1 outlines the ***minor roots in minor pentatonic Pattern 1***, and outlines the ***major roots in major pentatonic Pattern 1***.

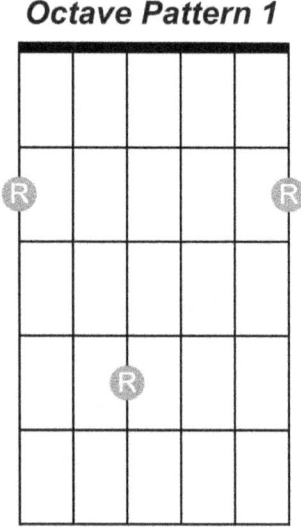
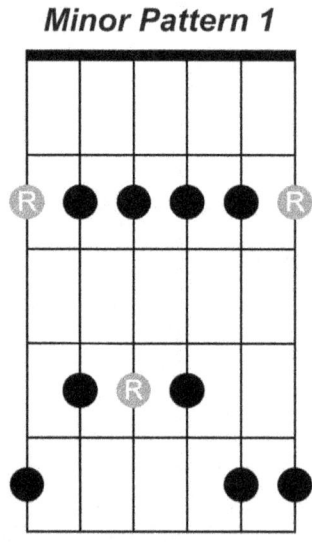
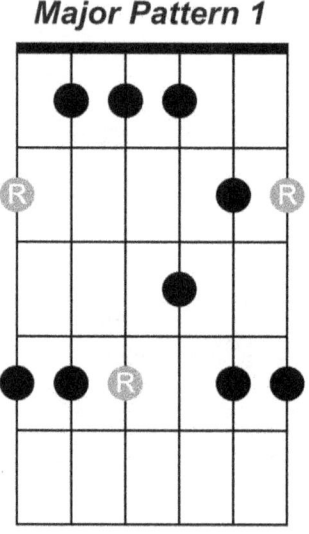

Octave Pattern 2 outlines the ***minor roots in minor pentatonic Pattern 2***, and outlines the ***major roots in major pentatonic Pattern 2***.

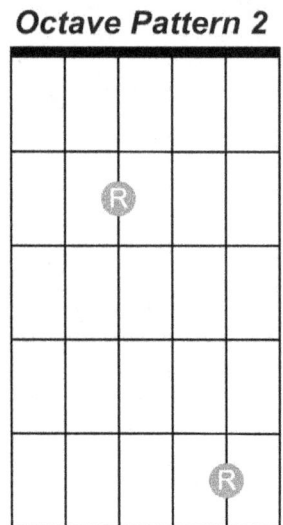
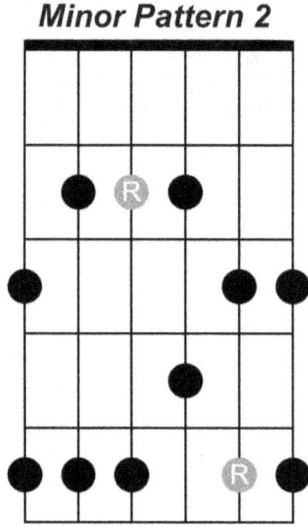
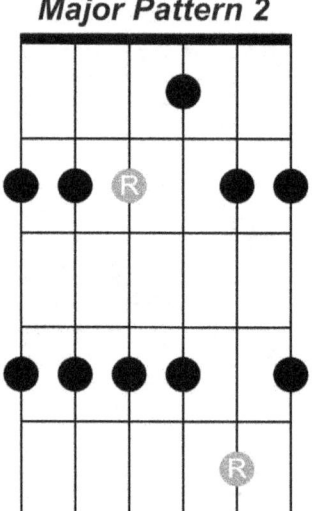

Octave Pattern 3 outlines the *minor roots in minor pentatonic Pattern 3*, and outlines the *major roots in major pentatonic Pattern 3*.

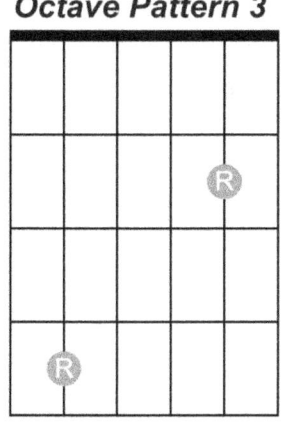
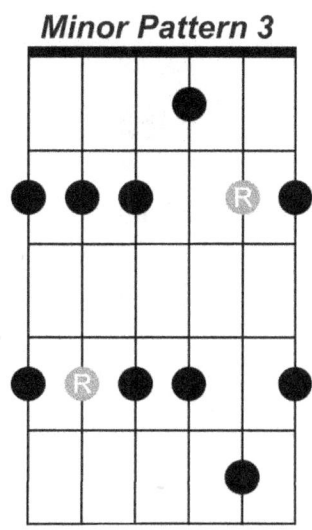
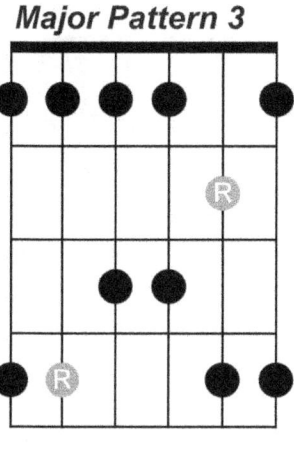

Octave Pattern 4 outlines the *minor roots in minor pentatonic Pattern 4*, and outlines the *major roots in major pentatonic Pattern 4*.

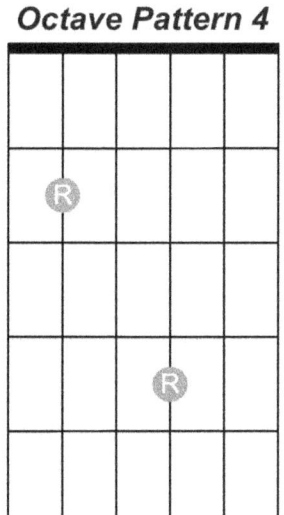
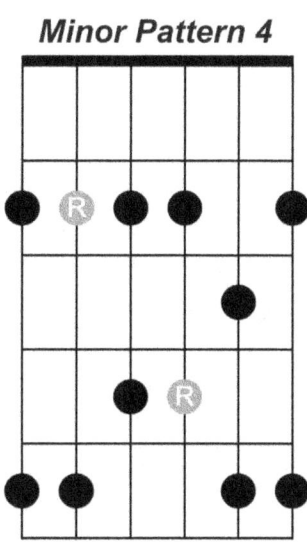
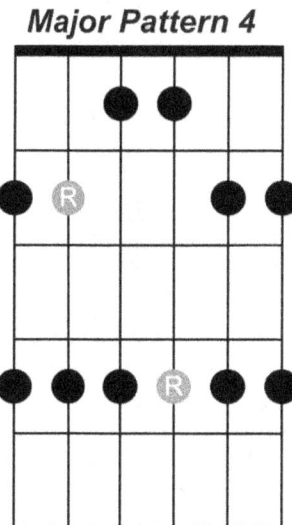

Octave Pattern 5 outlines the *minor roots in minor pentatonic Pattern 5*, and outlines the *major roots in major pentatonic Pattern 5*.

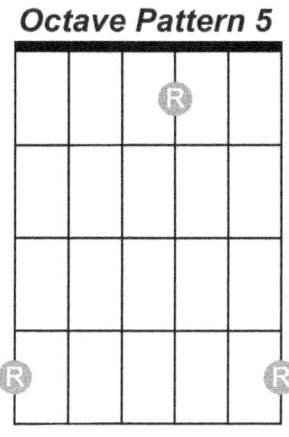
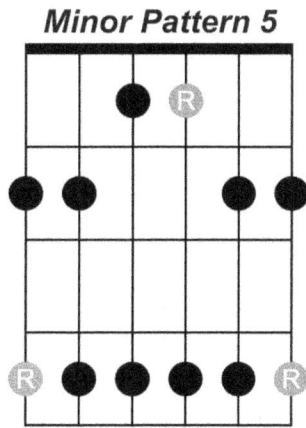
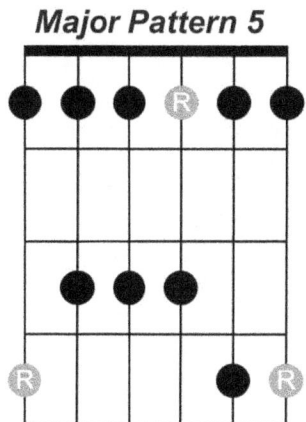

MINOR VS MAJOR
PENTATONIC EXERCISES

On each string, play a **G minor** and **G major pentatonic** from the **same starting point** using the **same shape**. You will always slide your hand back **3 frets** to get from minor to major.

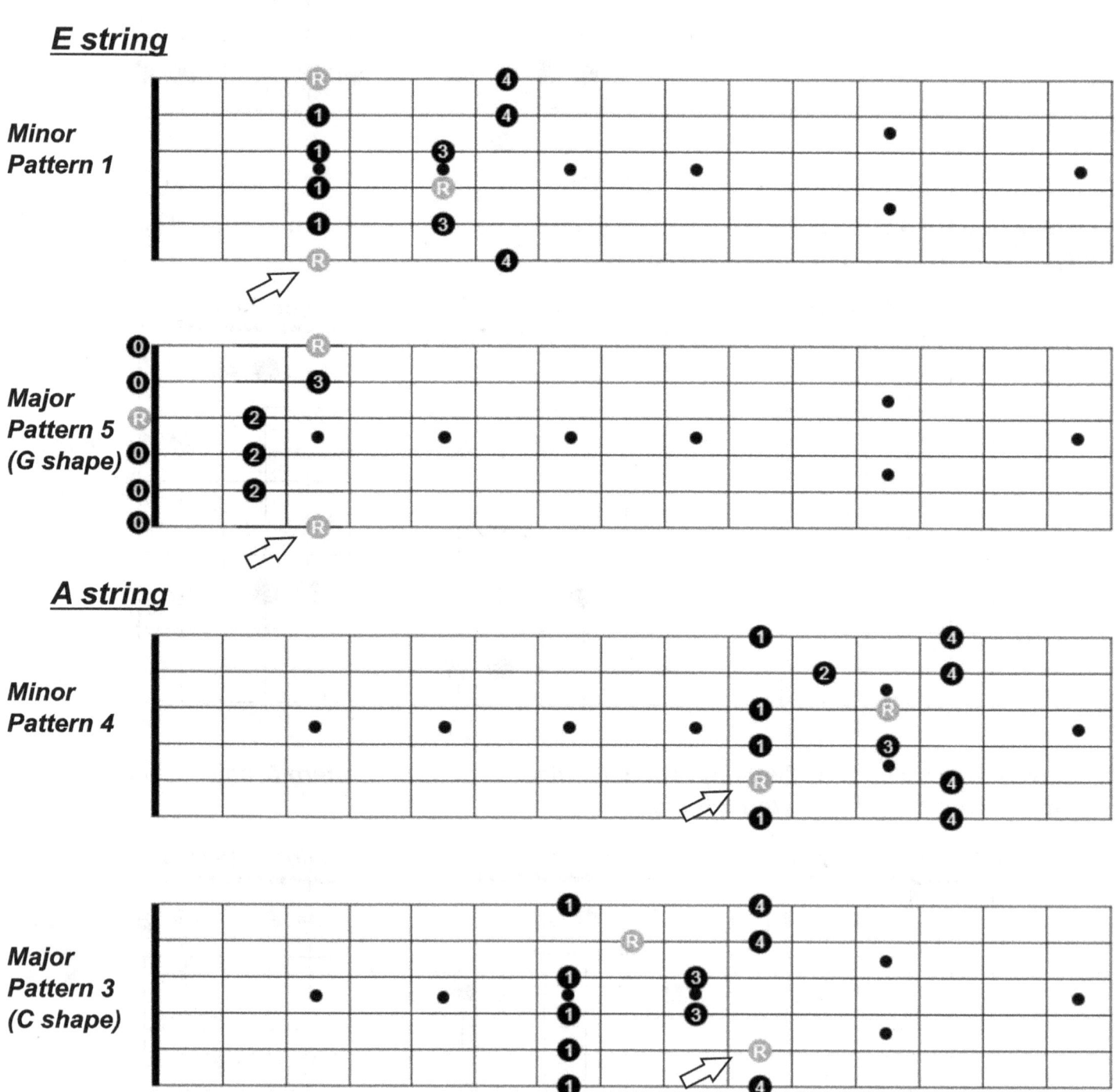

D string

Minor Pattern 2

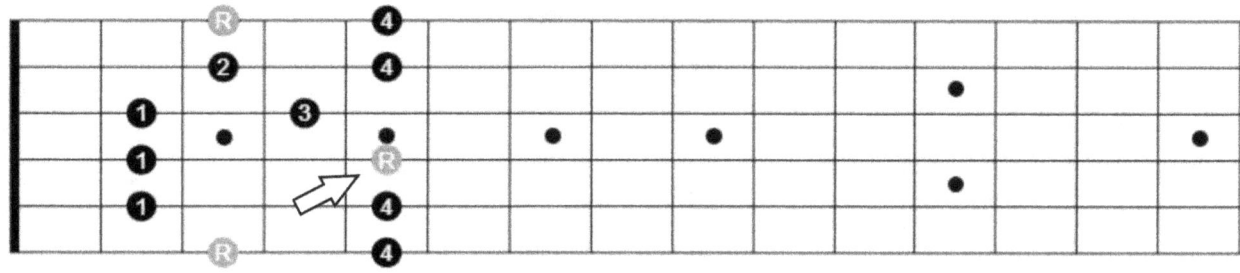

Major Pattern 1 (E shape)

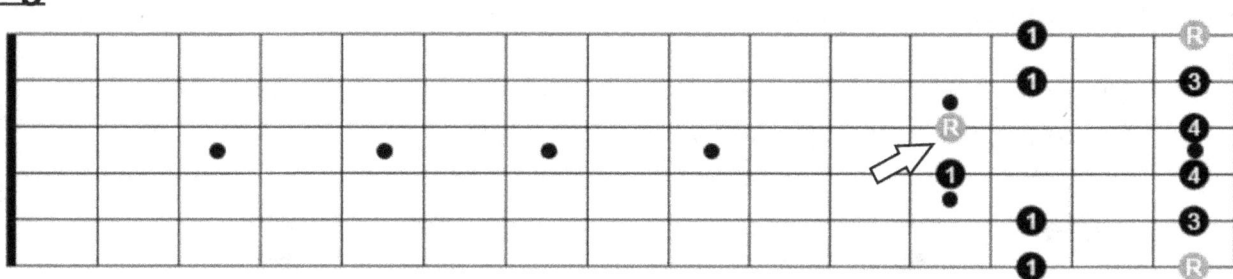

G string

Minor Pattern 5

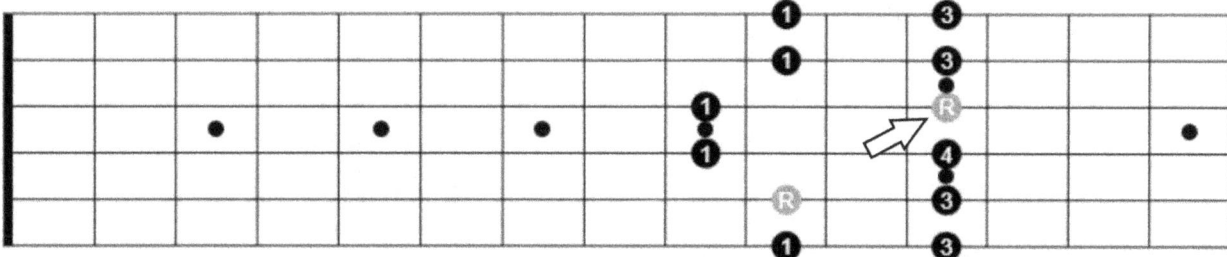

Major Pattern 4 (A shape)

B string

Minor Pattern 3

Major Pattern 2 (D shape)

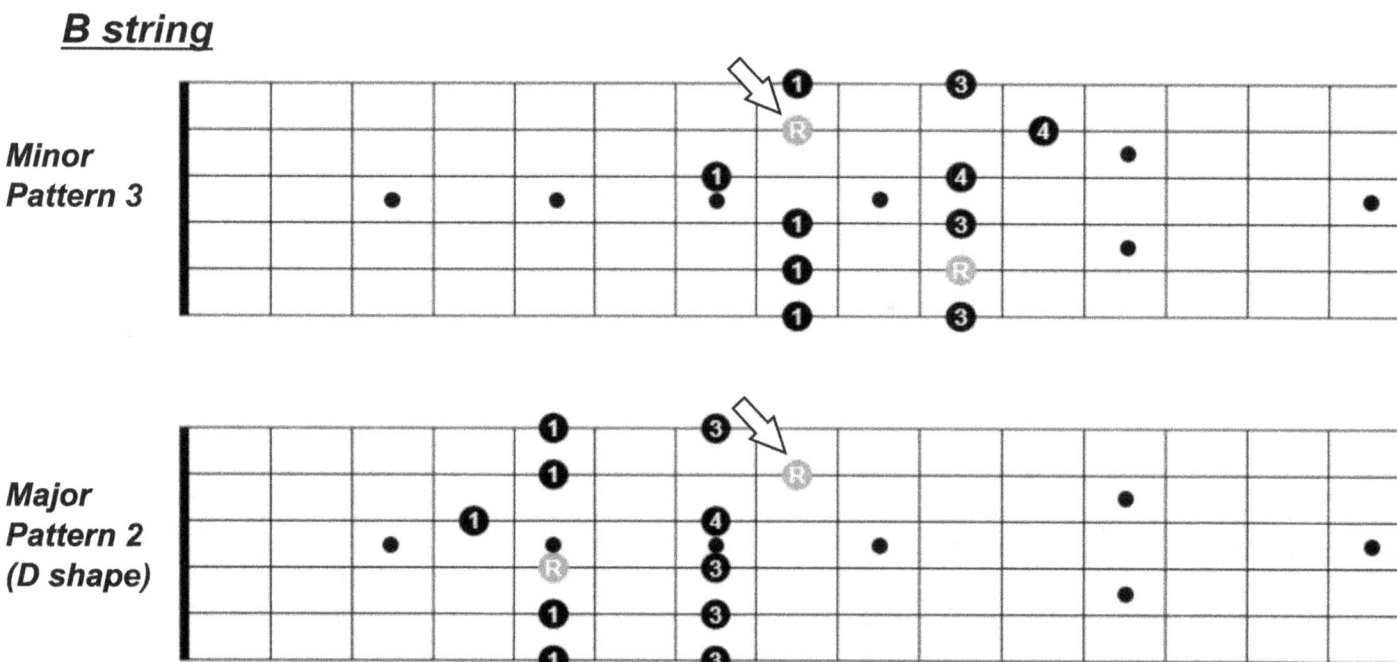

Next, we'll group the **minor and major pentatonic patterns** together so you can see how the **pattern numbers** relate to the **root** and **octave** locations. In these next exercises, you'll play both a **minor** and **major** pentatonic scale from the same root, but use different patterns for each.

Start from the ⓡ with the ⇨, ascend to the highest note in the pattern, descend to the lowest note in the pattern, and then return to your starting root.

E string   Minor Pattern 1   Major Pattern 1

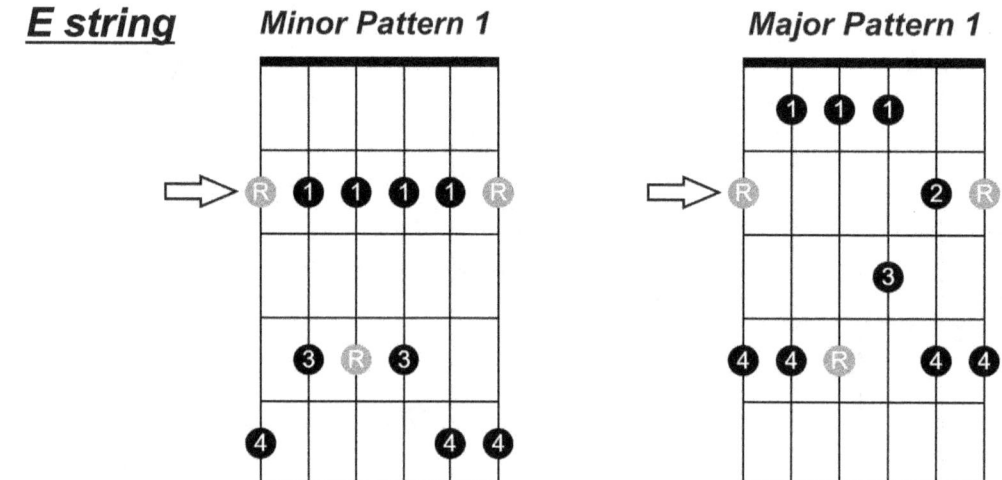

120

A string Minor Pattern 4 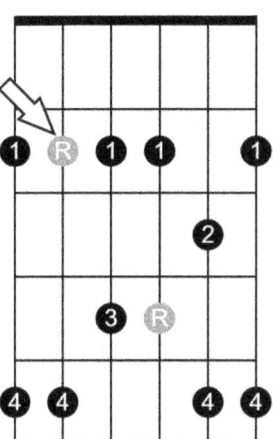 Major Pattern 4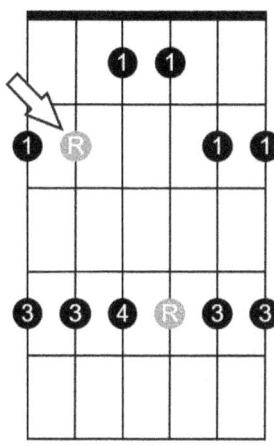

D string Minor Pattern 2 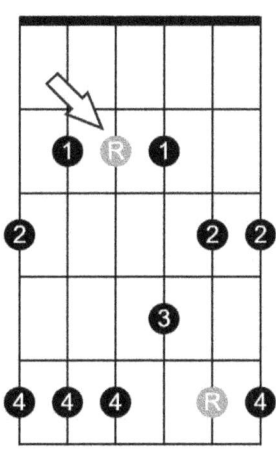 Major Pattern 2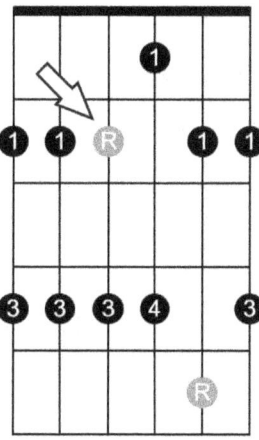

G string Minor Pattern 5 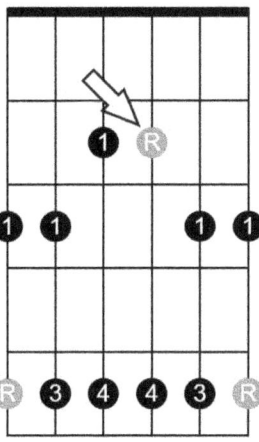 Major Pattern 5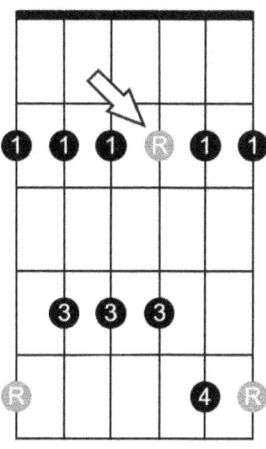

B string

Minor Pattern 3   *Major Pattern 3*

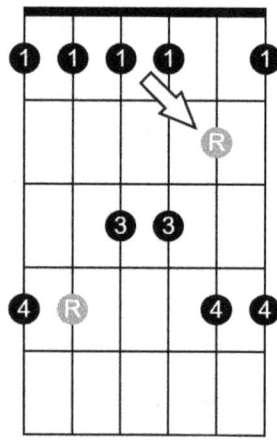

MINOR CAGED

The **minor CAGED system** is a powerful way to map out minor chords, arpeggios, and scales across the guitar fretboard. It helps you visualize the connections between chords and scales, making it easier to move fluidly up and down the neck.

For the minor CAGED shapes, think of them as **minor versions of the major CAGED shapes** you already know. The shapes you'll use most often are **Am** and **Em**, which should already be familiar. However, it's important to also get comfortable with the other shapes for the next section.

Note: It's not physically possible to play the **Cm** or **Gm** shapes as full chords in the standard positions shown below. The fingerings listed for those two shapes are my recommended versions if you're **arpeggiating** them—playing each note individually from low to high—instead of strumming them as full chords.

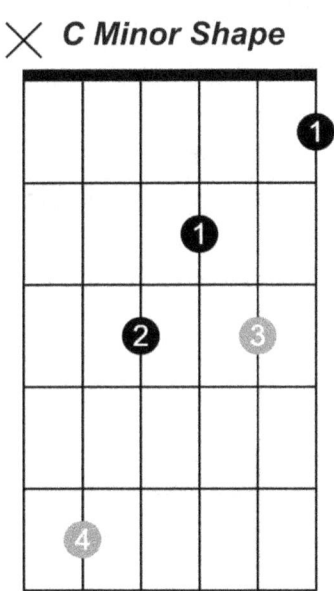
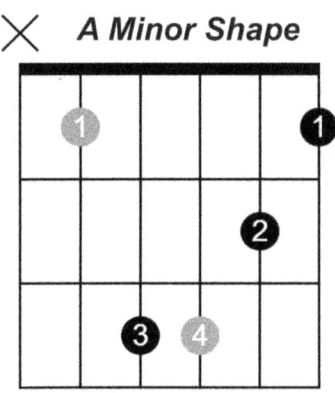
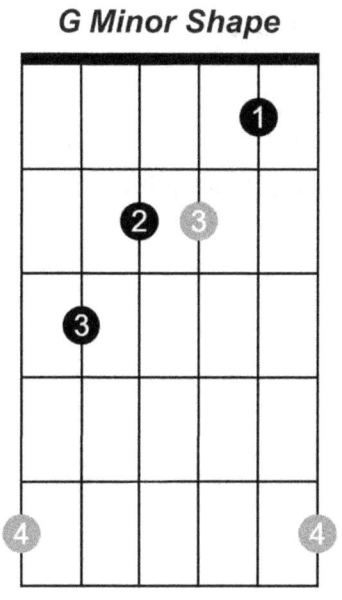
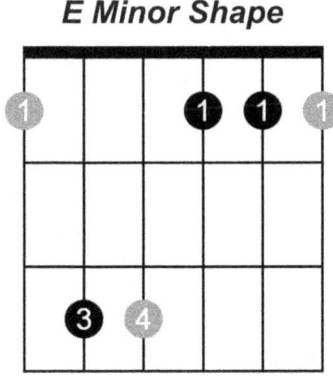
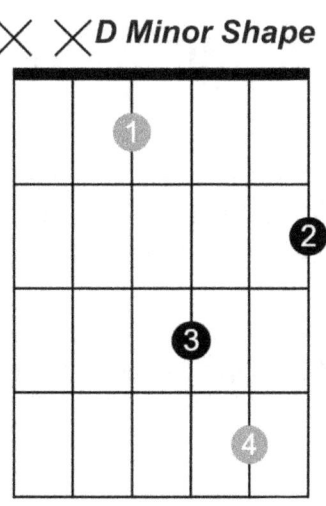

123

INVERSIONS

An *inversion* is when the notes of a chord (specifically a triad) are rearranged so that a note other than the root becomes the lowest note in pitch. A basic major or minor chord consists of three notes: the 1st, 3rd, and 5th scale degrees—also known as the root, 3rd, and 5th.

Let's use a C major chord as an example. In root position, the root note (C) is the lowest note, regardless of the order of the other two. So whether the notes are arranged as C–E–G or C–G–E (or even C–E–G–C–E, as in an open position C chord on guitar), it's still in root position because C is the lowest pitch.

1st Inversion
A *1st inversion* occurs when the **3rd** of the chord (E in a C major chord) is the **lowest note**. Example voicings include E–G–C or E–C–G. The key detail is that E is now the lowest note. This is written as ***C/E***.

2nd Inversion
A *2nd inversion* happens when the **5th** (G in a C major chord) becomes the **lowest note**. Example voicings include G–C–E or G–E–C. In this case, G is the lowest note. This is written as ***C/G***.

In summary

Root position: [1]- 3 - 5 *or* [1]- 5 - 3

1st inversion: [3]- 1 - 5 *or* [3]- 5 - 1

2nd inversion: [5]- 1 - 3 *or* [5]- 3 - 1

Another name for inversions is slash chords. You've maybe seen one of these common chords: C/G or D/F#. These are called slash chords, which just get their name from the "/" symbol.

C/G = C chord with the lowest note being G, which makes it a 2nd inversion
D/F# = D chord with the lowest note being F#, which makes it a 1st inversion

ACE-ING YOUR INVERSIONS

This method will help you play *inversions* all over the neck by using pieces of the closed *A, C, and E shapes* from the CAGED system. By focusing on these three chord shapes, you'll be able to play inversions on both *strings 1–2–3* and *strings 2–3–4*.

When playing these as inversions, you'll *visualize the entire chord shape* on the neck, but only play the *three triad notes* (shown in gray). This keeps the shapes compact, clear, and easy to move around the fretboard.

Let's start with the *major inversions* on *strings 2, 3, and 4*:

E Shape → **E Shape** — Root position — Fingering: 3, 2, 1

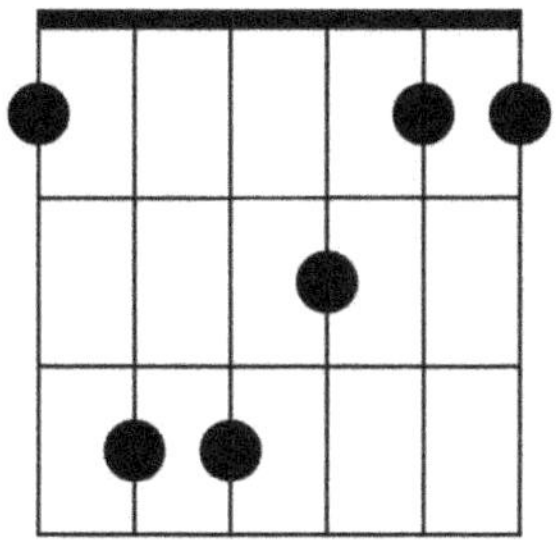

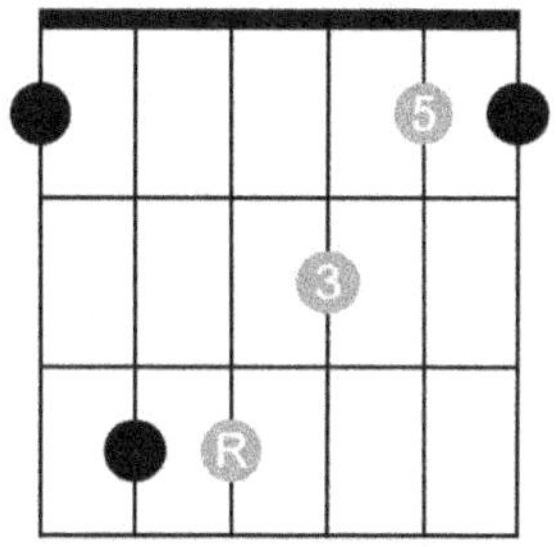

C Shape → **C Shape** — 1st inversion — Fingering: 3, 1, 2

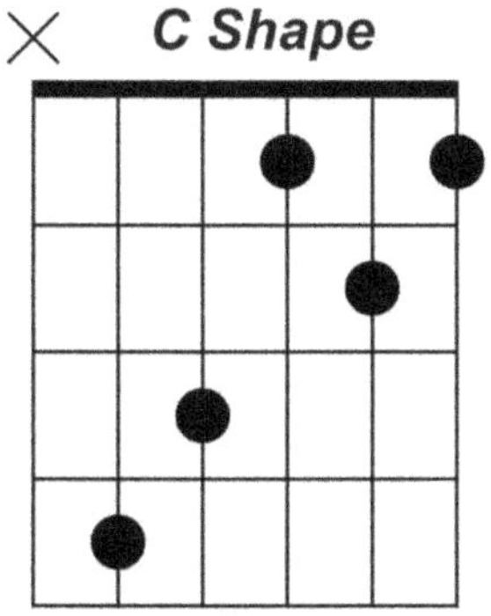

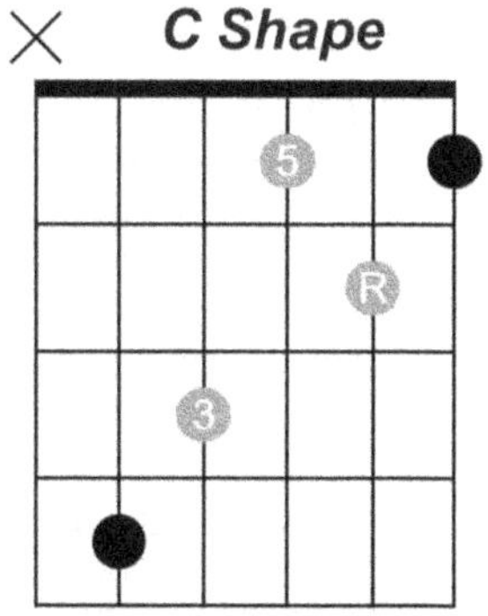

A Shape → **A Shape** — 2nd inversion — Fingering: 3, 3, 3 or 1, 1, 1

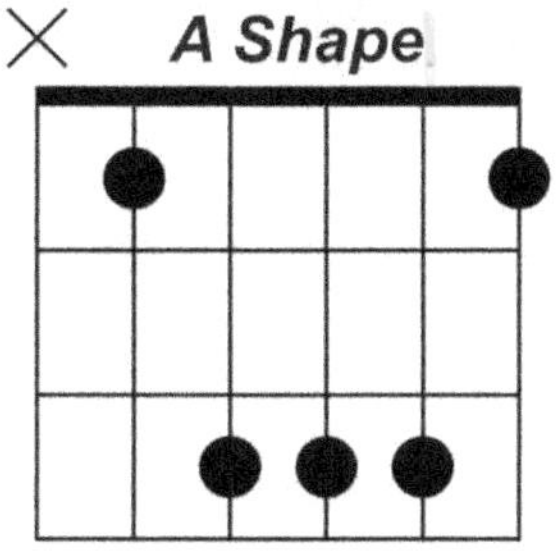

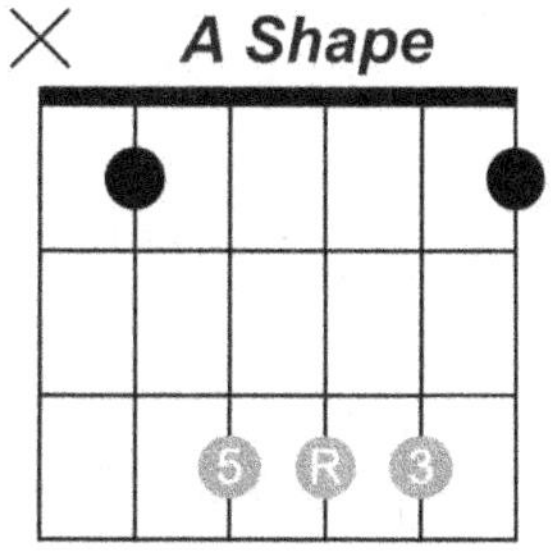

125

To play these inversions quickly and confidently, focus on the *lowest root note of the full chord shape*. This simplifies your thinking by narrowing the root location to just *two strings*:

• *E string root* for the *E shape*

• *A string root* for the *A and C shapes*

Below are all three inversion shapes for an *F chord*, shown with their corresponding root note positions.

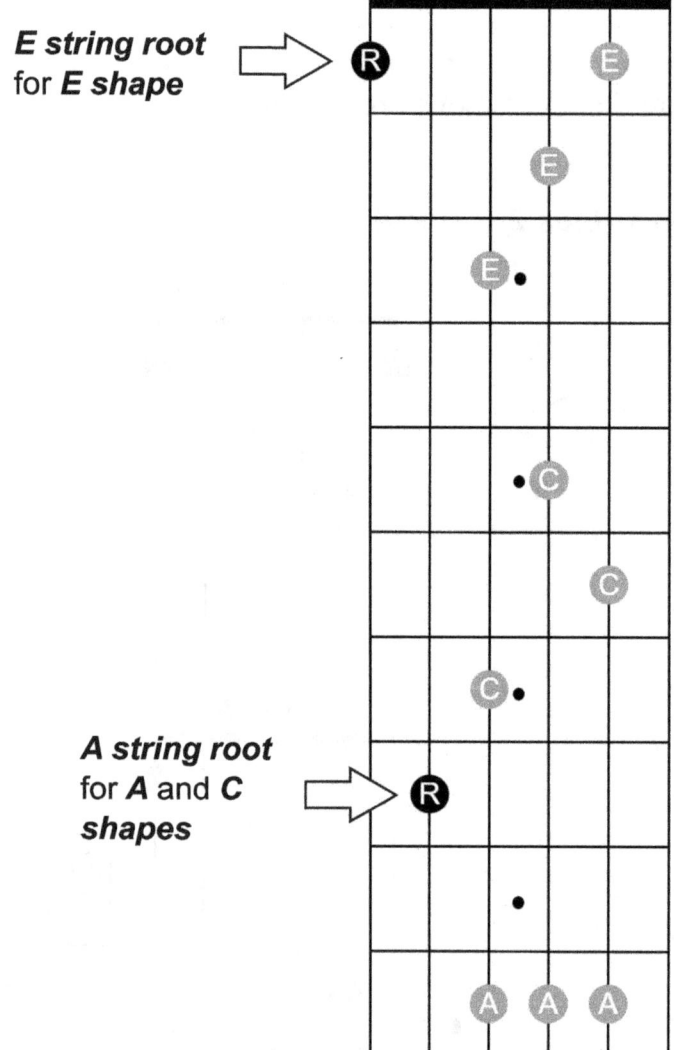

Exercise

A great way to practice these inversions is to *pick a chord and cycle through all three shapes*. Let's use a *D chord* as an example.

1. On the A string: Find a *D* at the 5th fret. From this root, play the *C shape* and the *A shape* inversions.

2. On the E string: Find a *D* at the 10th fret. From this root, play the *E shape* inversion.

Repeat this process with different chords to build fluency across the fretboard.

Next, we'll use these *same inversion shapes*, but convert them into *minor shapes*.

Remember: the only difference between a *major* and *minor* chord is the *third*.
Since the original shape is major, simply *lower the third by one fret* in each inversion to make it minor.

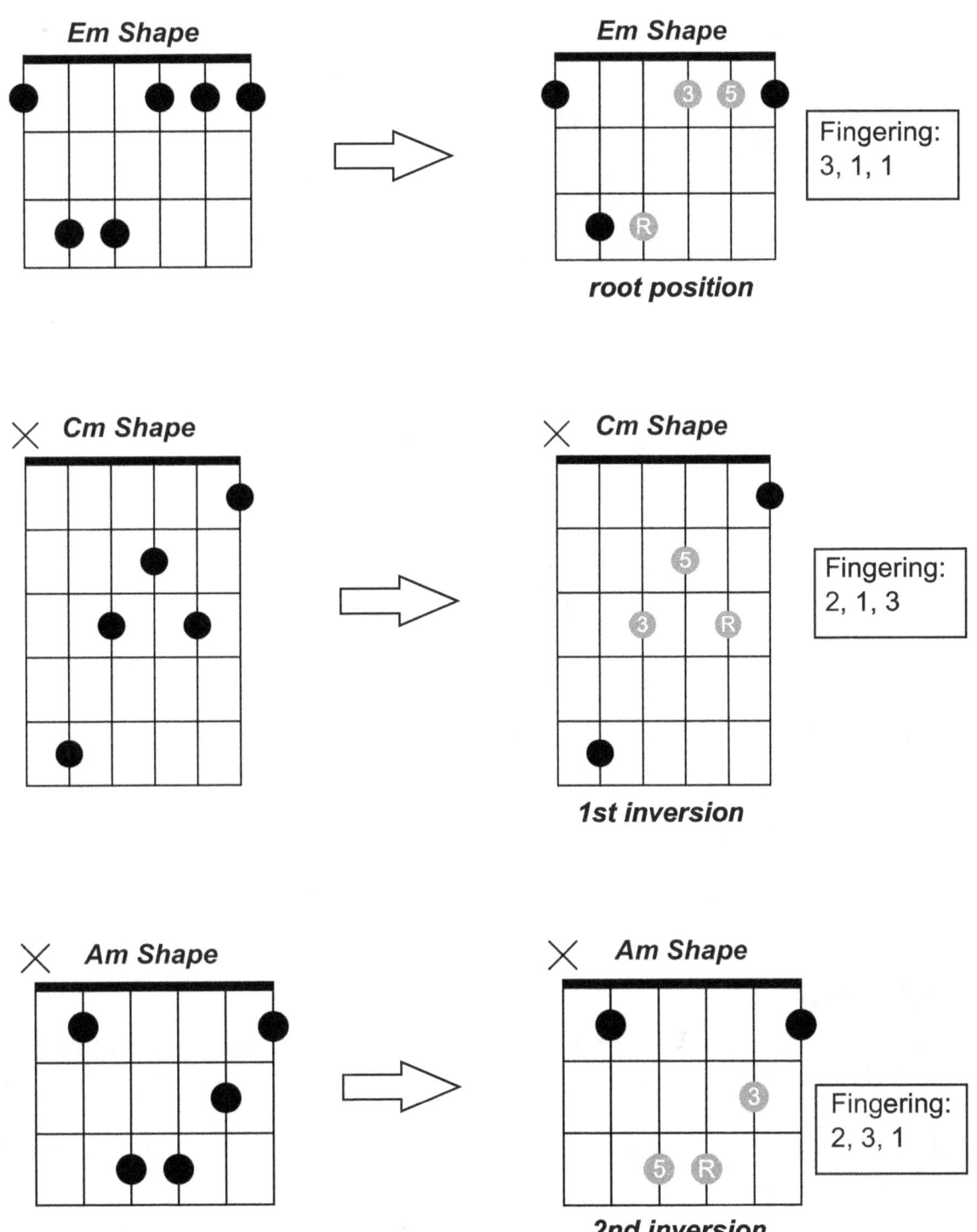

Again, to execute these quickly, *focus on the lowest root of the full shape*.

This narrows your root note down to just *two strings*:

• *E string root* for the *Em shape*

• *A string root* for the *Am* and *Cm shapes*

Below are all three inversion shapes for an *F minor chord*.

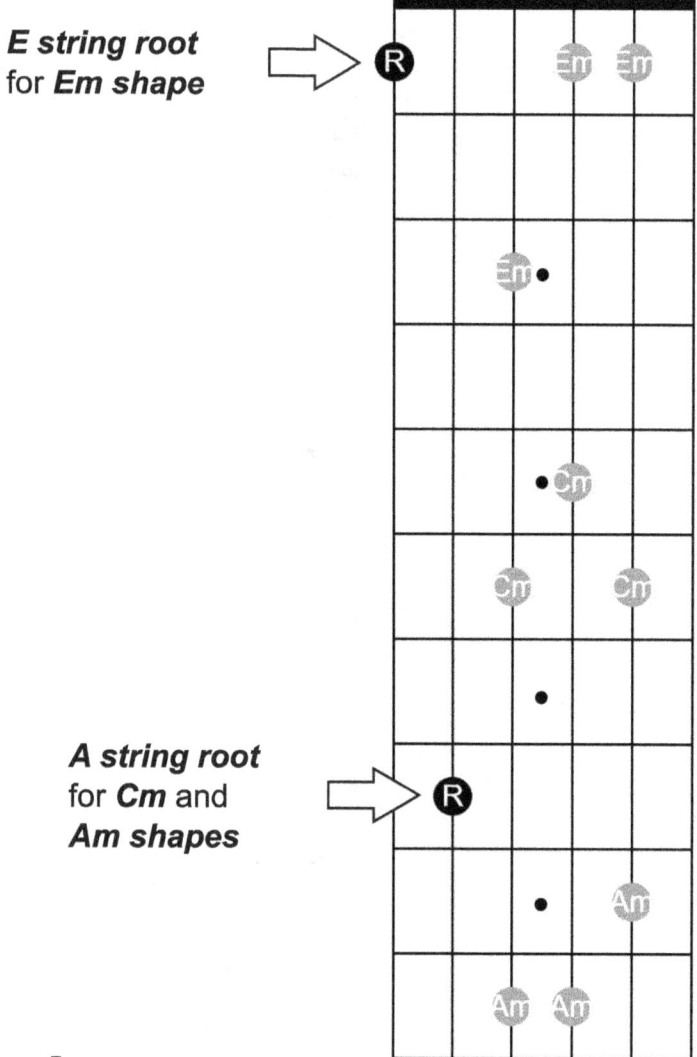

Exercise

A great way to practice these inversions is to *pick a chord and cycle through all three shapes*. Let's use a *D minor chord* as an example.

1. On the A string: Find a *D* at the 5th fret. From this root, play the *C minor shape* and the *A minor shape* inversions.

2. On the E string: Find a *D* at the 10th fret. From this root, play the *E minor shape* inversion.

Repeat this process with different chords to build fluency across the fretboard.

Next, we'll look at *major inversions on strings 1, 2, and 3*.

As you play these, keep *visualizing the full A, C, and E shapes*—even though you'll only be playing the 3 triad notes.

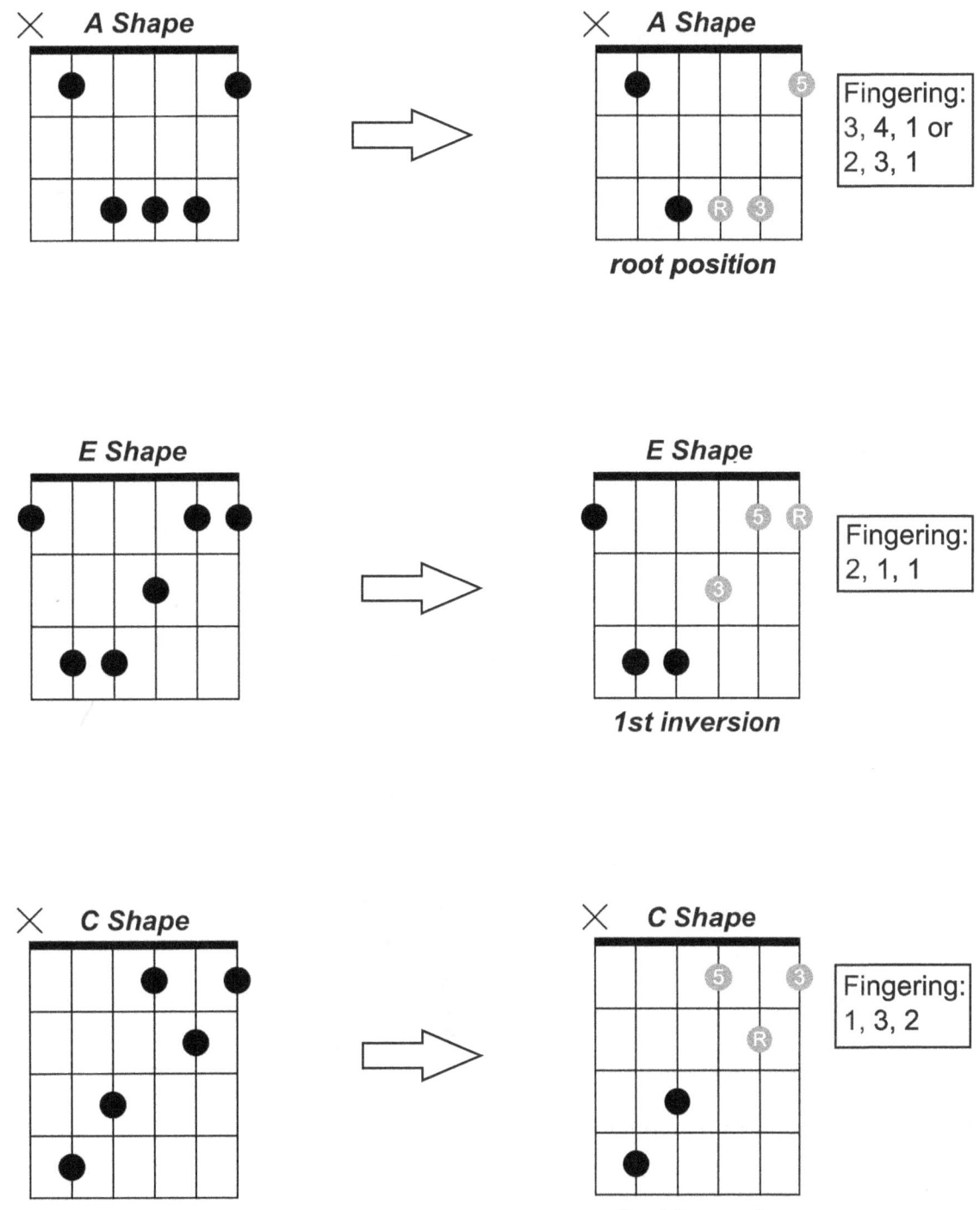

To play these quickly, focus on the **lowest root of the full chord shape**, just as before.

This narrows your search to two strings:

• **E string root** for the **E shape**

• **A string root** for the **A** and **C shapes**

Below are all three inversion shapes for an **F chord**.

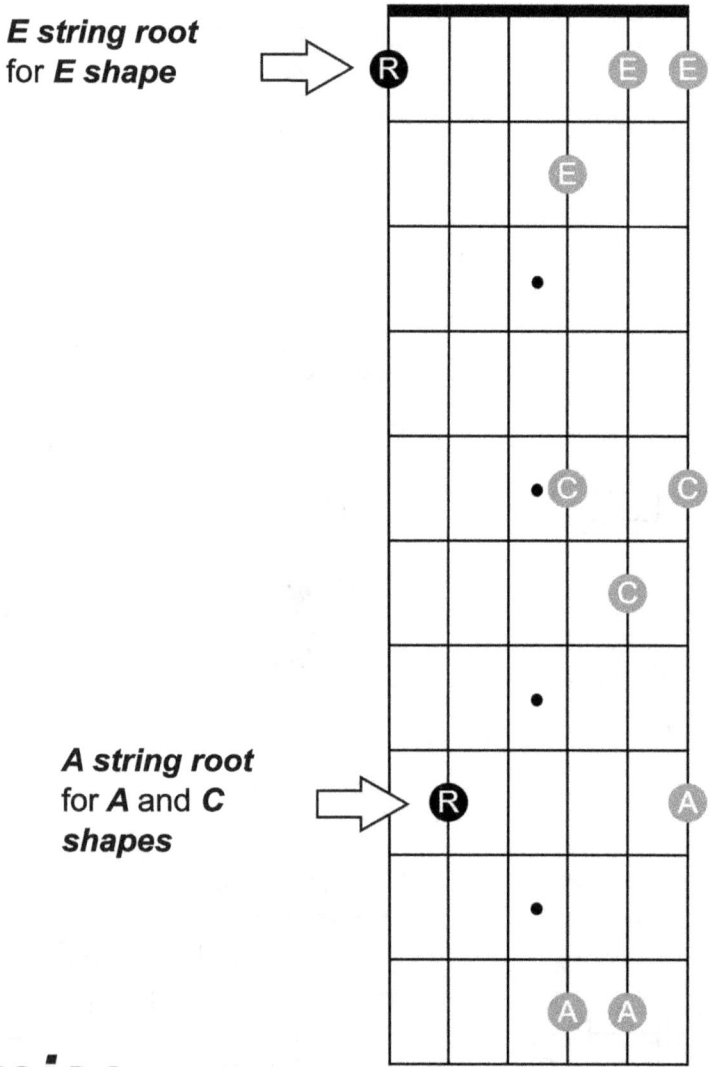

Exercise

A great way to practice these inversions is to **pick a chord and cycle through all three shapes**. Let's use a **G chord** as an example.

1. On the A string: Find a **G** at the 10th fret. From this root, play the **C shape** and the **A shape** inversions.

2. On the E string: Find a **G** at the 3rd fret. From this root, play the **E shape** inversion.

Repeat this process with different chords to build fluency across the fretboard.

Next, we'll explore *minor inversions* on *strings 1, 2, and 3*.

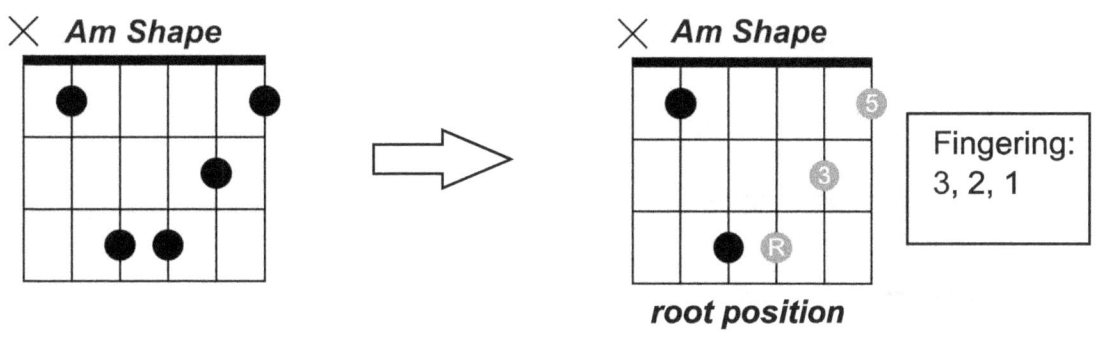

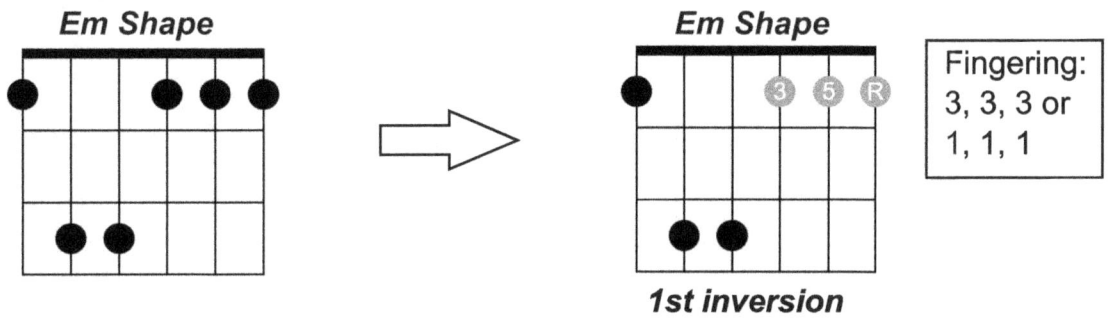

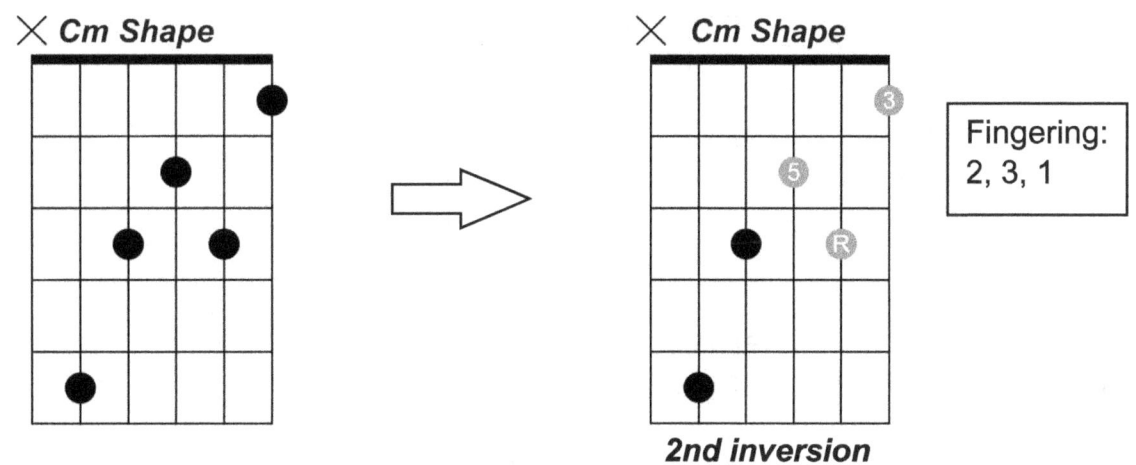

To play these quickly, focus on the **lowest root of the full chord shape**, just as before.

This narrows your search to two strings:

• **E string root** for the **E shape**

• **A string root** for the **A** and **C shapes**

Below are all three inversion shapes for an **F minor chord**.

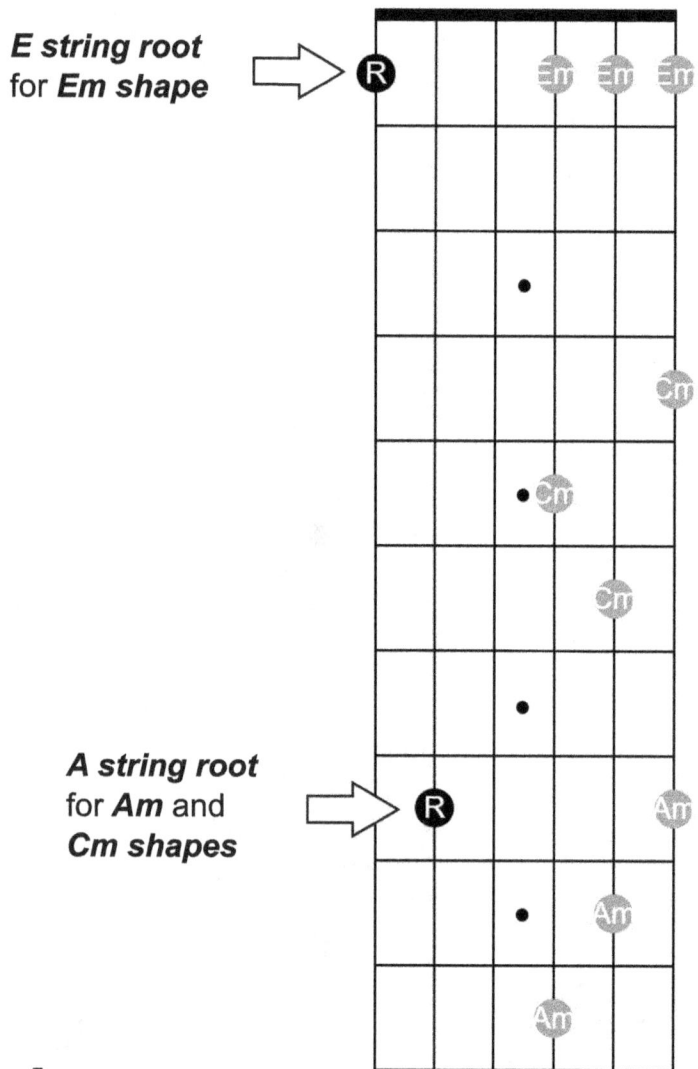

Exercise

A great way to practice these inversions is to **pick a chord and cycle through all three shapes**. Let's use a **G minor chord** as an example.

1. On the A string: Find a **G** at the 10th fret. From this root, play the **C minor shape** and the **A minor shape** inversions.

2. On the E string: Find a **G** at the 3rd fret. From this root, play the **E minor shape** inversion.

Repeat this process with different chords to build fluency across the fretboard.

EXERCISES USING INVERSIONS

A great exercise is playing a *1-4-5 progression using inversions*.

For this, stick to the same string groupings. We'll start in the key of *C* and focus on *inversions on strings 2–3–4*.

The chords you'll play are *C, F, and G*. The goal is to use *all three inversion shapes*—one for each chord—while *moving your hand as little as possible*.

First, we'll start off in *root position* to play the *1 (C) chord*:

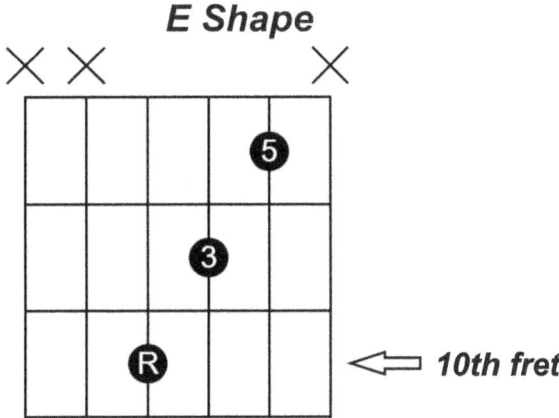

Next, we'll go to the *4 (F) chord*, so you'll use the *A shape (2nd inversion)*. You don't have to move your hand at all, just use your 3rd finger to play this chord:

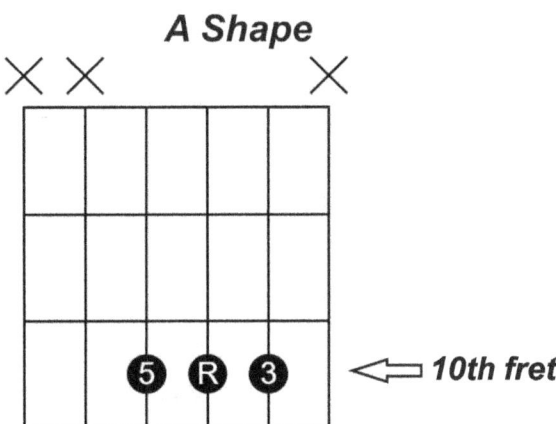

133

Since you've used the E and A shapes, you'll have to use the **C shape (1st inversion)** next for the **5 (G) chord**:

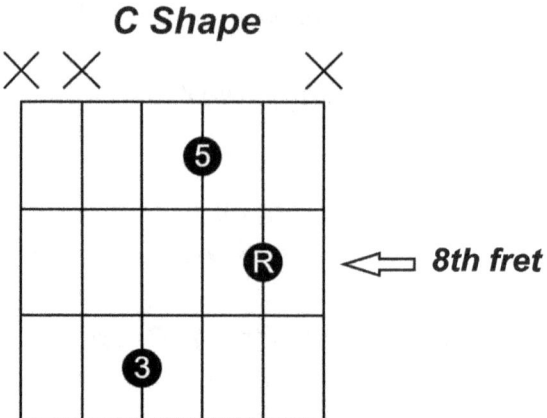

Notice that you only had to slide your hand back 1 fret. So we just played a 1-4-5 by moving the hand only 1 fret.

Next we'll use the **C shape (2nd inversion)** for the **1 (C) chord**:

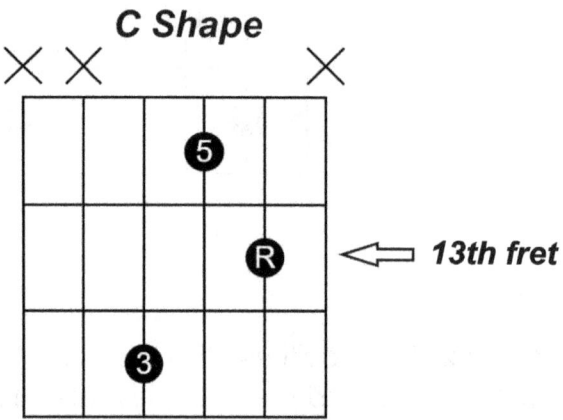

Now you just need to move the hand 1 fret higher and use your **E shape (root position)** to play the **4 (F) chord**:

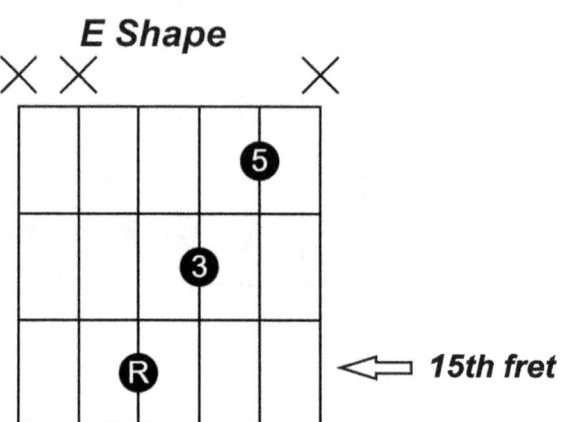

Now, to play the **5 (G) chord**, you'll move your hand back 1 fret and use your index finger to play the **A shape (2nd inversion)**:

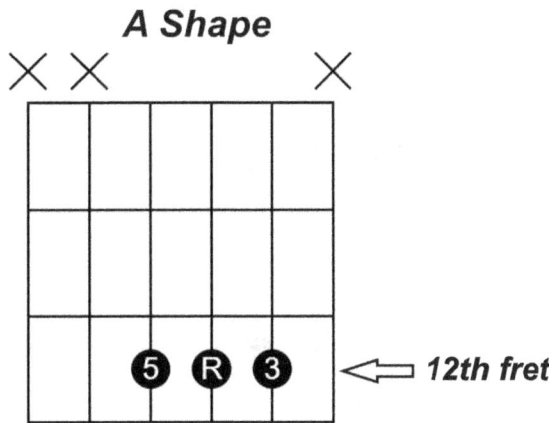

Again, we did a 1-4-5 progression and all 3 shapes were within 1 fret of each other.

Lastly, you'll play the **1 (C) chord** using the **A shape (2nd inversion)**, using your index finger for this shape:

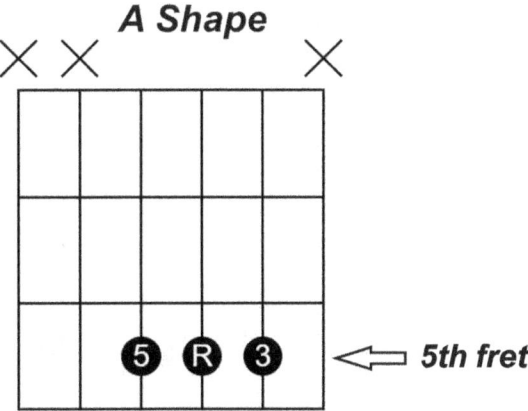

For the **4 (F) chord**, you won't have to move your hand at all, just place the **C shape (1st inversion)** from where your index finger is:

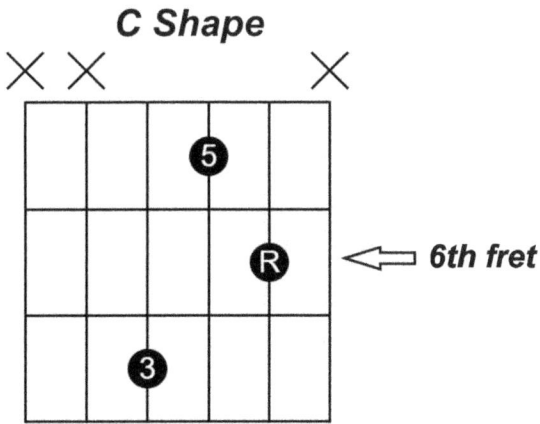

The **5 (G) chord** will be 2 frets lower, using the **E shape (root position)**:

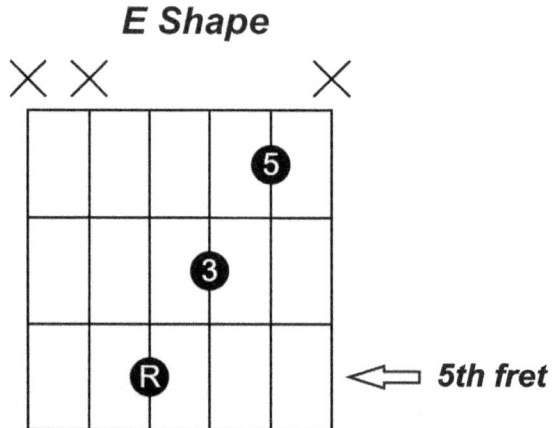

After completing the exercise, you can now see how close all of these chords are using these shapes. It would be a good idea to try this exercise in other keys, and using the minor shapes.

Next, we'll take a look at this same exercise using **strings 1-2-3**. We'll keep it in the **key of C** and start with the **E shape (1st inversion)** for the **1 (C) chord**:

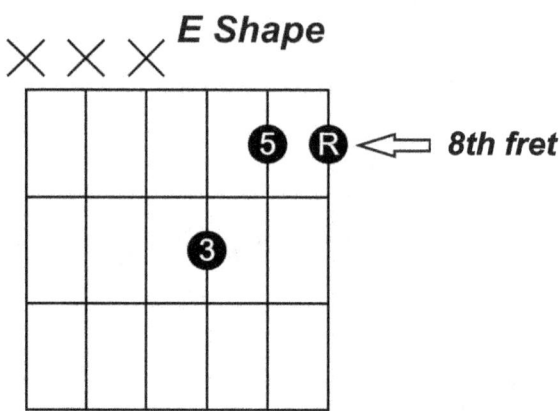

Now we'll use the **A shape (root position)** for the **4 (F) chord**; you won't have to move your index finger:

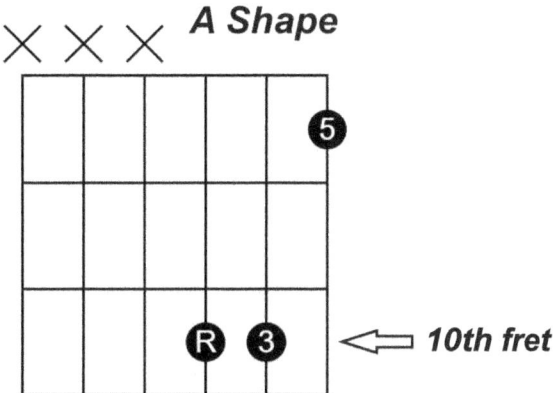

Lastly we'll use the **C shape (2nd inversion)** for the **5 (G) chord**; you'll need to move back 2 frets:

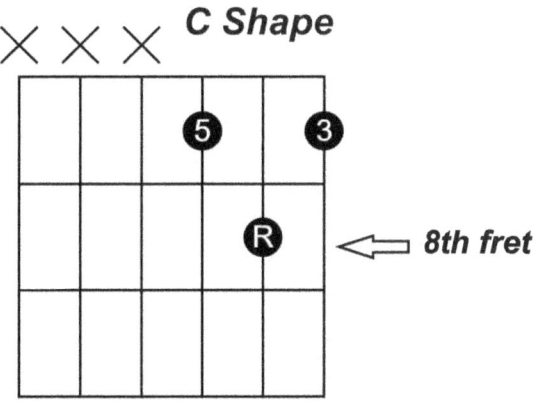

Next we'll use the **C shape (2nd inversion)** for the **1 (C) chord**:

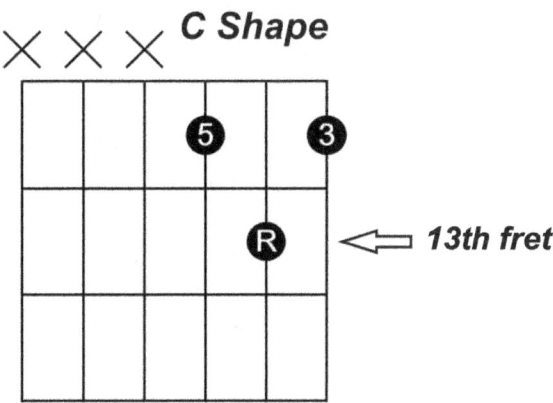

Now we'll use the **E shape (1st inversion)** for the **4 (F) chord**; you'll move your hand up 1 fret:

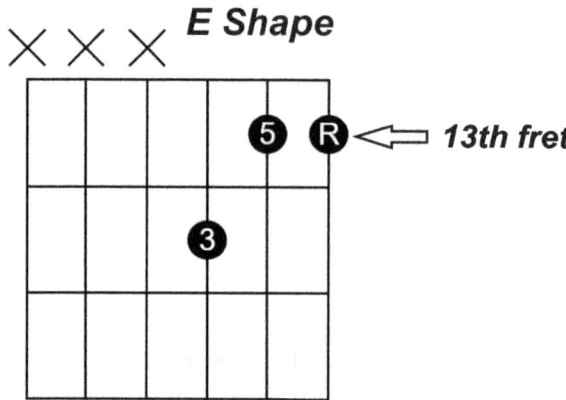

To play the **5 (G) chord**, you'll move 1 fret lower and play the **A shape (root position)**:

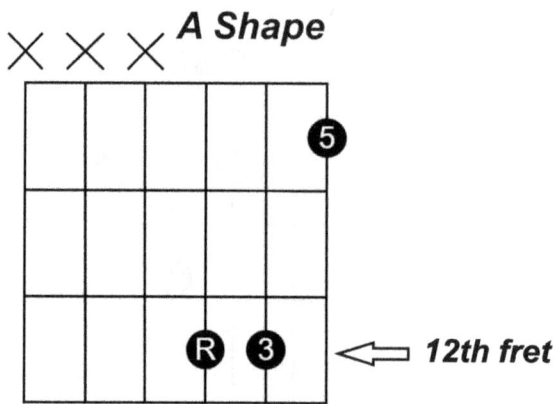

Lastly, you'll do this exercise starting with the **A shape (root position)** for the **1 (C) chord**:

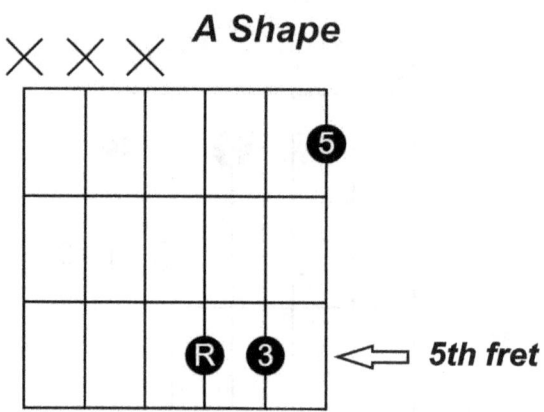

Slide your hand 1 fret higher and use the *C shape (2nd inversion)* to play the *4 (F) chord*:

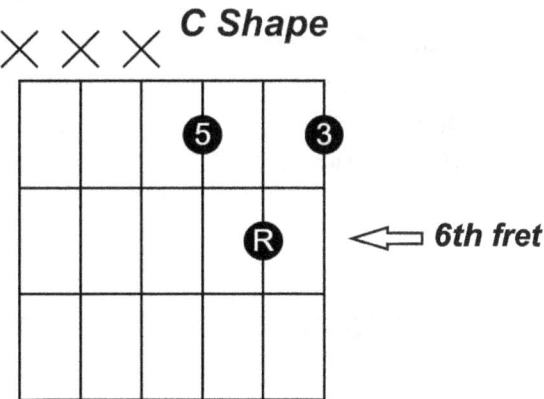

Slide your hand 3 frets lower and use the *E shape (1st inversion)* for the *5 (G) chord*:

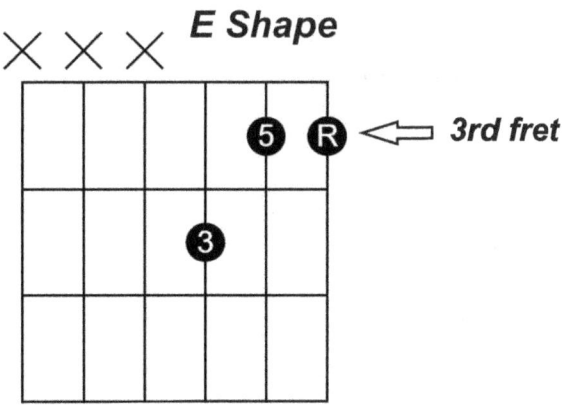

A FEW MORE NOTES ON INVERSIONS...

"Can't I just hold down the full chord shape and strum only the strings in the inversion?"
Technically, yes—for the **A** and **E shapes**, that can work. But for the **Cm shape** and **Gm shape**, it's not quite that simple. Plus, relying on this approach will eventually limit your playing. It's much better to **visualize the fretboard** and understand how these inversions fit within the full chord shape.

"What about inversions on strings 4–5–6?"
Those do exist, but inversions on **strings 1–4** are far more common and practical.

"How are these inversions typically used?"
Often, they serve as a **secondary guitar part**. When one guitarist plays open chords down low, using inversions up higher adds **variety and texture** with higher voicings.

"What songs use these inversion parts?"
Here are a few examples that feature prominent inversion parts:

In A Little While — U2

Another Brick in the Wall — Pink Floyd

Don't Speak — No Doubt

Tighten Up — The Black Keys

Brown Eyed Girl — Van Morrison

GENERAL MUSIC THEORY

Everything you've learned so far is incredibly useful—but to unlock its full potential, you need to apply it more broadly.

Learning **music theory** is the key to truly understanding the guitar neck and the patterns you've studied.

In the next section, we'll cover the **basic rules of music theory** to help deepen your grasp and take your playing to the next level.

KEY SIGNATURES

A *key signature* tells you which notes are sharp or flat in a given key. A *key* itself is a collection of notes built using a specific pattern of whole and half steps.

Most people learn major scales using the pattern:
Whole, Whole, Half, Whole, Whole, Whole, Half

While this method works, I've found that a better approach is to first **memorize the order of sharps.**

ORDER OF SHARPS

The order of sharps (#) will *always* go in this order:

F C G D A E B

You can use the saying **F**at **C**ats **G**o **D**own **A**lleys **E**ating **B**irds.

Helpful tips:

- If a key has *1 sharp*, it will always be *F#*.

- If it has *2 sharps*, they will be *F#* and *C#*.

- If it has *3 sharps*, they will be *F#*, *C#*, and *G#*, and so on.

- You always add sharps starting from the **beginning of the list and moving to the right**.

- For example, a key will **never have just C#** without also having F#—if there's a C#, there's always an F#.

RULE FOR SHARPS

Finding the Key Signature When You Know the Key:

• **Step 1:** Go down a half step (1 fret) from the key. This note is the *last sharp* in the key signature.

• **Step 2:** List the sharps in order from the beginning of the sharp list up to that last sharp.

Example:
If the key is **A**, go down a half step from A, which is **G#**—this is the last sharp. Then list the sharps from the start: **F#, C#, G#**.

Finding the Key When You Know the Key Signature:

• **Step 1:** Look at the last sharp in the key signature.

• **Step 2:** Go up a half step (1 fret) from that sharp. That note is the key.

Examples:

• If there is *1 sharp (F#)*, go up a half step to **G**—the key is G major.

• If there are *2 sharps (F#, C#)*, go up a half step from C# to **D**—the key is D major.

Exercise

Sharps	Key
1. F#	G
2. F# C#	D
3. F# C# G#	___
4. F# C# G# D#	___
5. F# C# G# D# A#	___
6. F# C# G# D# A# E#	___
7. F# C# G# D# A# E# B#	___

"What's the deal with E# and B#?" is a very common question. Yes, they are notes. You will almost always refer to an E# as an F and a B# as a C, unless you are in the key of F# or C#.

Answers:
3. A 4. E 5. B 6. F# 7. C#

ORDER OF FLATS

The order of flats (♭) will **always** go in this order:

B E A D G C F

You can use the sayings:

BEAD, **G**o **C**all **F**red

or

Battle **E**nds **A**nd **D**own **G**oes **C**harles' **F**ather

The order of flats is also the order of sharps reversed.

Helpful tips:

• If a key has *1 flat*, it will always be *B♭*.

• If it has *2 flats*, they will be *B♭* and *E♭*.

• If it has *3 flats*, they will be *B♭*, *E♭*, and *A♭*, and so on.

• You always add flats starting from the ***beginning of the list and moving to the right***.

• For example, a key will ***never have just E♭*** without also having B♭—if there's a E♭, there's always a B♭.

RULE FOR FLATS

Finding the Key with Flats

Rule: The *second-to-last flat* in the key signature tells you the key.

• Example: 2 flats (B♭, E♭) → second-to-last is **B♭** → key of **B♭**.

• Example: 3 flats (B♭, E♭, A♭) → second-to-last is **E♭** → key of **E♭**.

This works best when reading a piece of sheet music with the key signature shown.

Finding the Flats in a Known Key

• Start with the key name.

• List the flats in order *(B♭, E♭, A♭, D♭, G♭, C♭, F♭) until you go one flat past the key*.

• Example: Key of **A♭** → flats are **B♭, E♭, A♭, D♭**.

Exceptions to the Rules
Two keys don't follow the sharp or flat rules:

• **C major** – no sharps or flats

• **F major** – one flat (**B♭**)

Exercise

Using the key listed below, use the order of flats and go one flat past the key to get the key signature.

Key	Flats
1. F	B♭
2. B♭	B♭ E♭
3. E♭	___
4. A♭	___
5. D♭	___
6. G♭	___
7. C♭	___

Answers:
3. B♭ E♭ A♭
4. B♭ E♭ A♭ D♭
5. B♭ E♭ A♭ D♭ G♭
6. B♭ E♭ A♭ D♭ G♭ C♭
7. B♭ E♭ A♭ D♭ G♭ C♭ F♭

Now you know what is sharped or flatted in a key. But, also remember that *every note of the musical alphabet*—A, B, C, D, E, F, and G—*must be represented* in a key.

So, if we take the notes in a *G major scale*, we first start by thinking about what is sharped (*F#*). Then we use all of the notes in the musical alphabet, sharping the F, and we get: *G A B C D E F#*. These are the notes in a G major scale.

Let's do the same for a *D major scale* using all of the steps.
• First, go down a half step from a D; this brings you to a C#. This is your last sharp.
• Now name the sharps from the beginning of the list until you reach the C#: F# and C#.
• Next use all of the notes in the musical alphabet and be sure to sharp the F and C:
D E F# G A B C#. These are the notes in a D major scale.

This same method works for flats as well. Let's do the same for an *E♭ major scale* using all of the steps:
• First, list the flats in order until you go one past your key: B♭ E♭ A♭
• Next use all of the notes in the musical alphabet and be sure to flat the B, E, and A:
E♭ F G A♭ B♭ C D. These are the notes in an E♭ major scale.

> *Additional rule:* You can *never* have sharps and flats in a key. It must be one or the other.

All of the keys you have learned so far are *major keys*. It is implied that it is a major key even if you don't say "major" before it.

 "What's the deal with F♭ and C♭?" is a very common question. Yes, they are notes. You will almost always refer to an F♭ as an E and a C♭ as a B, unless you are in the key of F♭ or C♭.

145

CIRCLE OF 5THS AND 4THS

The **Circle of 5ths** is a visual tool that organizes key signatures and helps you see the relationship between keys.

Steps to Build the Circle of 5ths:

1. *Start at "Noon" with C major* – C has no sharps or flats.

2. *Move clockwise in perfect 5ths:*

• From C, go up a perfect 5th to **G** – place G to the right of C.

• From G, go up a perfect 5th to **D** – place D to the right of G.

• From D, go up a perfect 5th to **A**, and so on.

3. Continue going up in perfect 5ths until you loop all the way back to C.

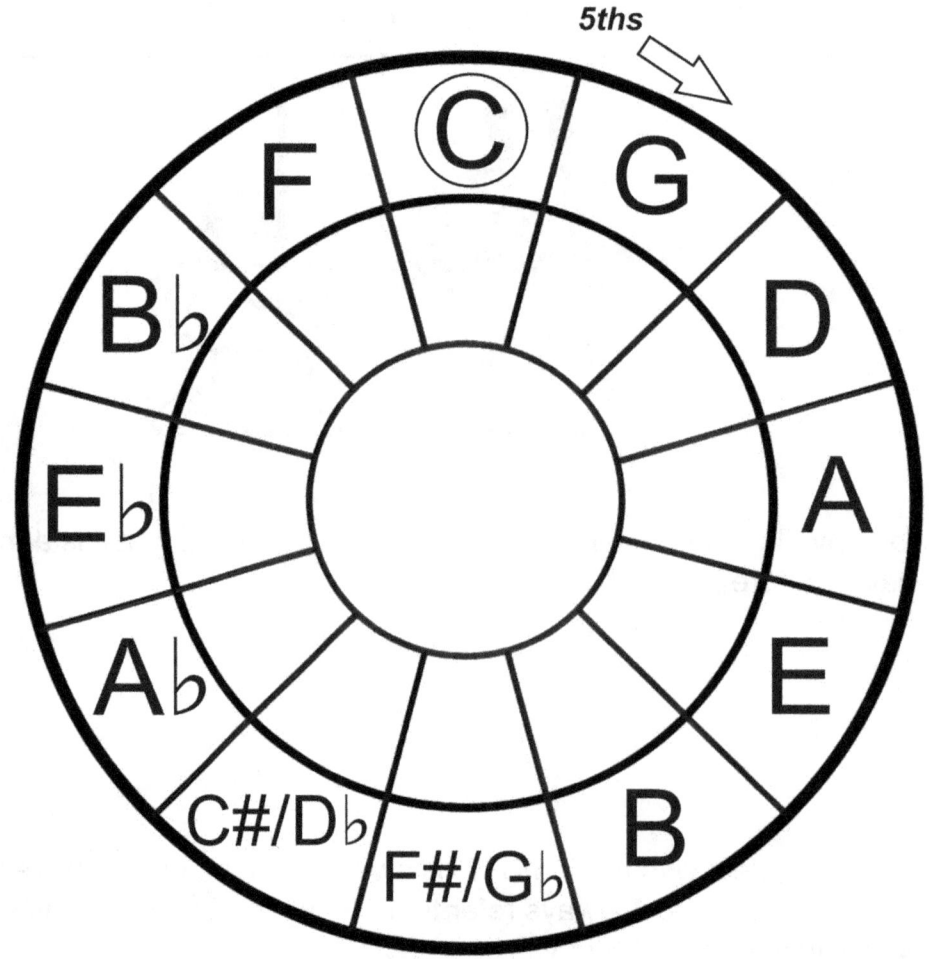

Why Use the Circle of 5ths and 4ths?
The Circle of 5ths not only helps you see how keys are related, but it also shows how you will eventually loop back to C.

Recommendation:

- Use the *Circle of 5ths* for keys with *sharps*.

- Use the *Circle of 4ths* for keys with *flats*.

There is some overlap—certain keys can be written with either sharps or flats.

Next Steps:

- First, we'll fill in the circle with the sharp keys using the Circle of 5ths.

- Later, we'll explore the Circle of 4ths for the flat keys.

Filling in the Circle with Sharp Keys
To fill in the Circle of 5ths, use the *order of sharps*: **F C G D A E B**

The number of sharps in each key increases as you move clockwise:

- *G* → 1 sharp (F#)

- *D* → 2 sharps (F#, C#)

- *A* → 3 sharps (F#, C#, G#)

- *E* → 4 sharps (F#, C#, G#, D#)

- *B* → 5 sharps (F#, C#, G#, D#, A#)

- *F#* → 6 sharps (F#, C#, G#, D#, A#, E#)

- *C#* → 7 sharps (F#, C#, G#, D#, A#, E#, B#)

CIRCLE OF 5THS

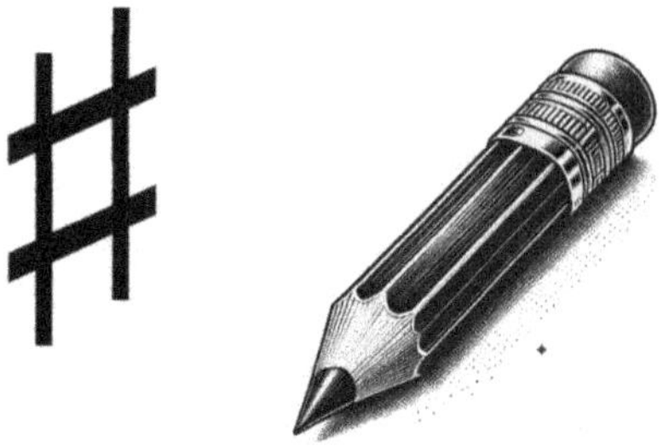

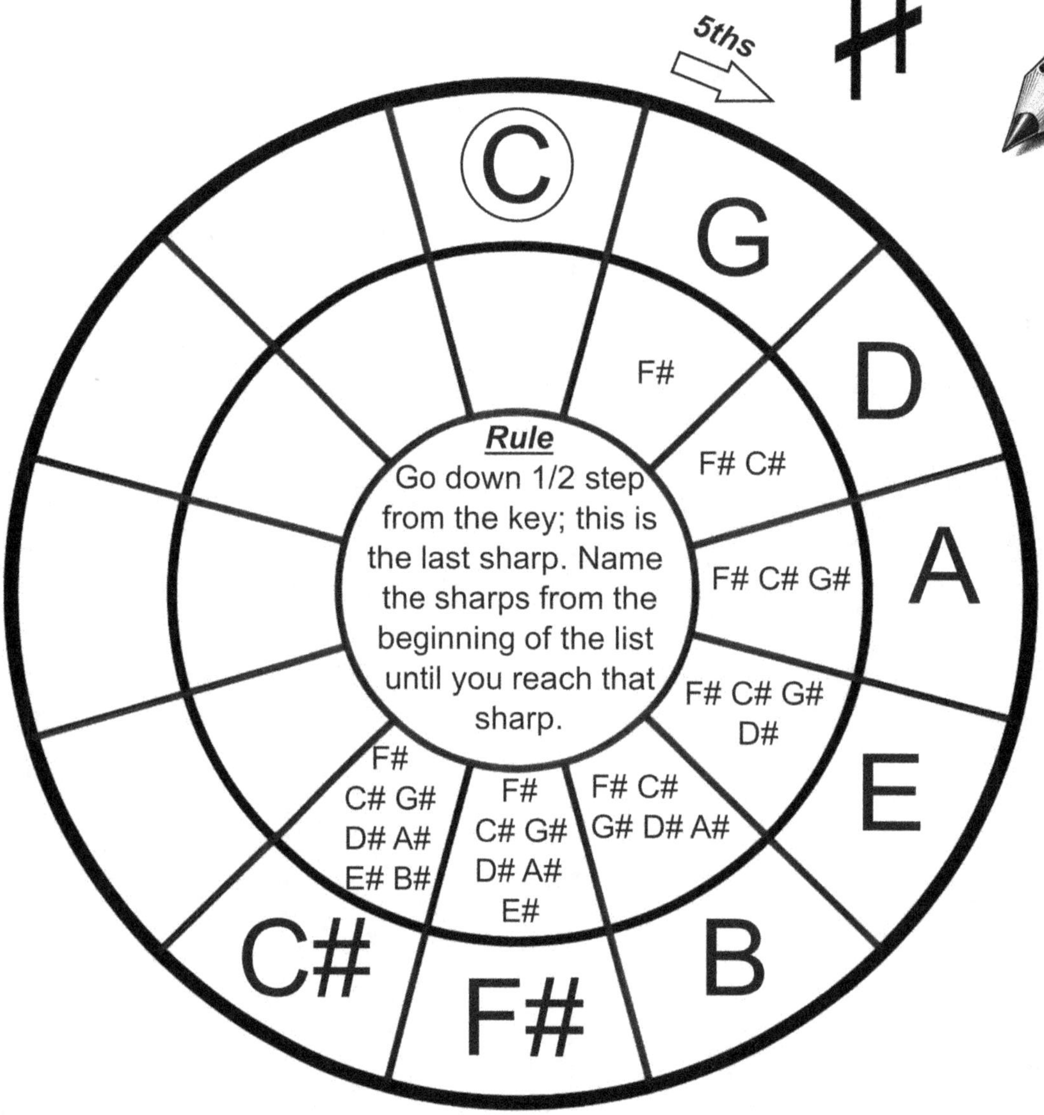

5ths →

Circle diagram:

Outer ring (clockwise from top): C, G, D, A, E, B, F#, C#

Middle/inner rings (sharps for each key):
- C: (none)
- G: F#
- D: F# C#
- A: F# C# G#
- E: F# C# G# D#
- B: F# C# G# D# A#
- F#: F# C# G# D# A# E#
- C#: F# C# G# D# A# E# B#

Rule
Go down 1/2 step from the key; this is the last sharp. Name the sharps from the beginning of the list until you reach that sharp.

Helpful tip:
If you imagine the Circle of 5ths as a clock:

- **1 o'clock** = G (**1 sharp**)

- **2 o'clock** = D (**2 sharps**)

- **3 o'clock** = A (**3 sharps**)
...and so on.

The "hour" tells you how many sharps are in the key.

Here's a step-by-step version for the *circle of 4ths*:

1. *Start at C*—Place the key of C in the top ("noon") position since it has no sharps or flats.

2. *Move up a perfect 4th*—From C, go up a 4th to *F* and place it one position to the left of C.

3. *Repeat the process*—From F, go up a 4th to *B♭*. From B♭, go up a 4th to *E♭*, and so on.

4. Complete the circle—Continue moving in 4ths until you eventually return to C.

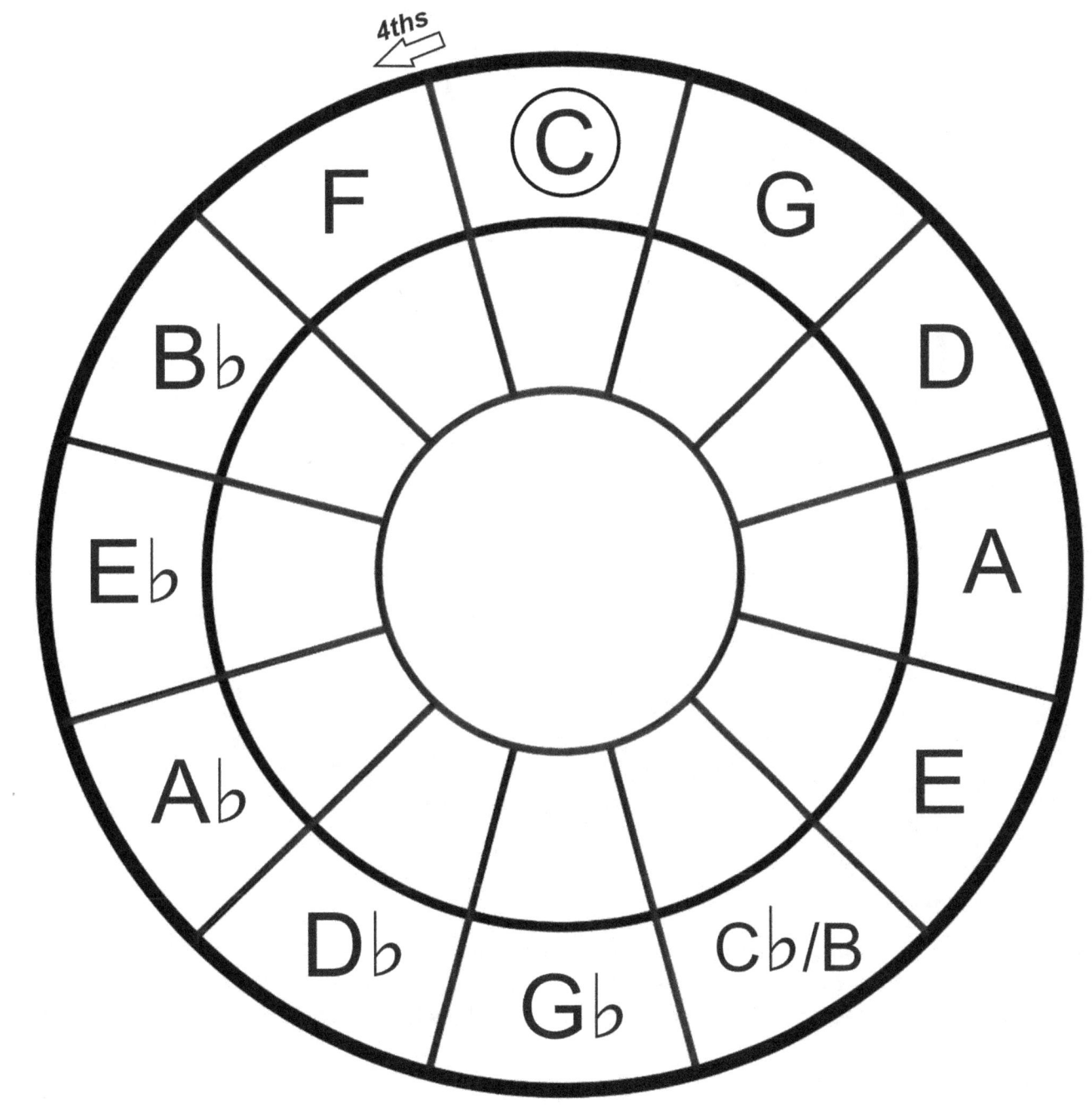

CIRCLE OF 4THS

- Start with **C** at the top (0 flats).

- Move left in 4ths and assign flats according to the order of flats: **B♭, E♭, A♭, D♭, G♭, C♭, F♭** (though F♭ is rare).

- Each step left adds one flat.

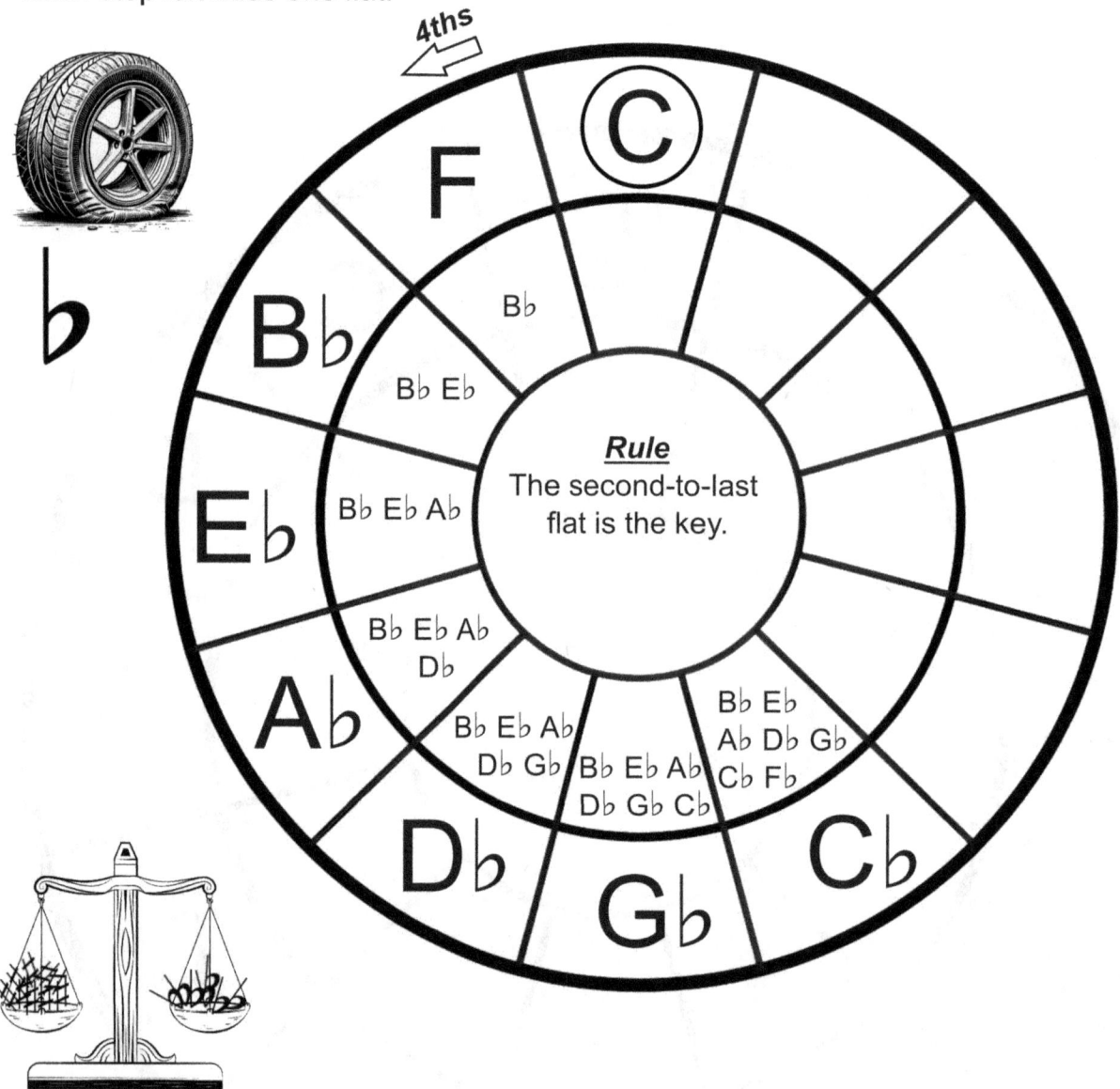

Rule
The second-to-last flat is the key.

Helpful Tip – Choosing Between Enharmonic Keys
When you're unsure which version of a key to use—such as D♭ vs. C#, G♭ vs. F#, or C♭ vs. B—pick the key with fewer accidentals (sharps or flats). This keeps notation cleaner and easier to read.

- **C♭ vs. B**: Choose **B** (5 sharps) instead of **C♭** (7 flats).

- **D♭ vs. C#**: Choose **D♭** (5 flats) instead of **C#** (7 sharps).

- **G♭ vs. F#**: Either can work—they both have 6 accidentals (G♭ has 6 flats, F# has 6 sharps).

This is the full circle with both sharps and flats:

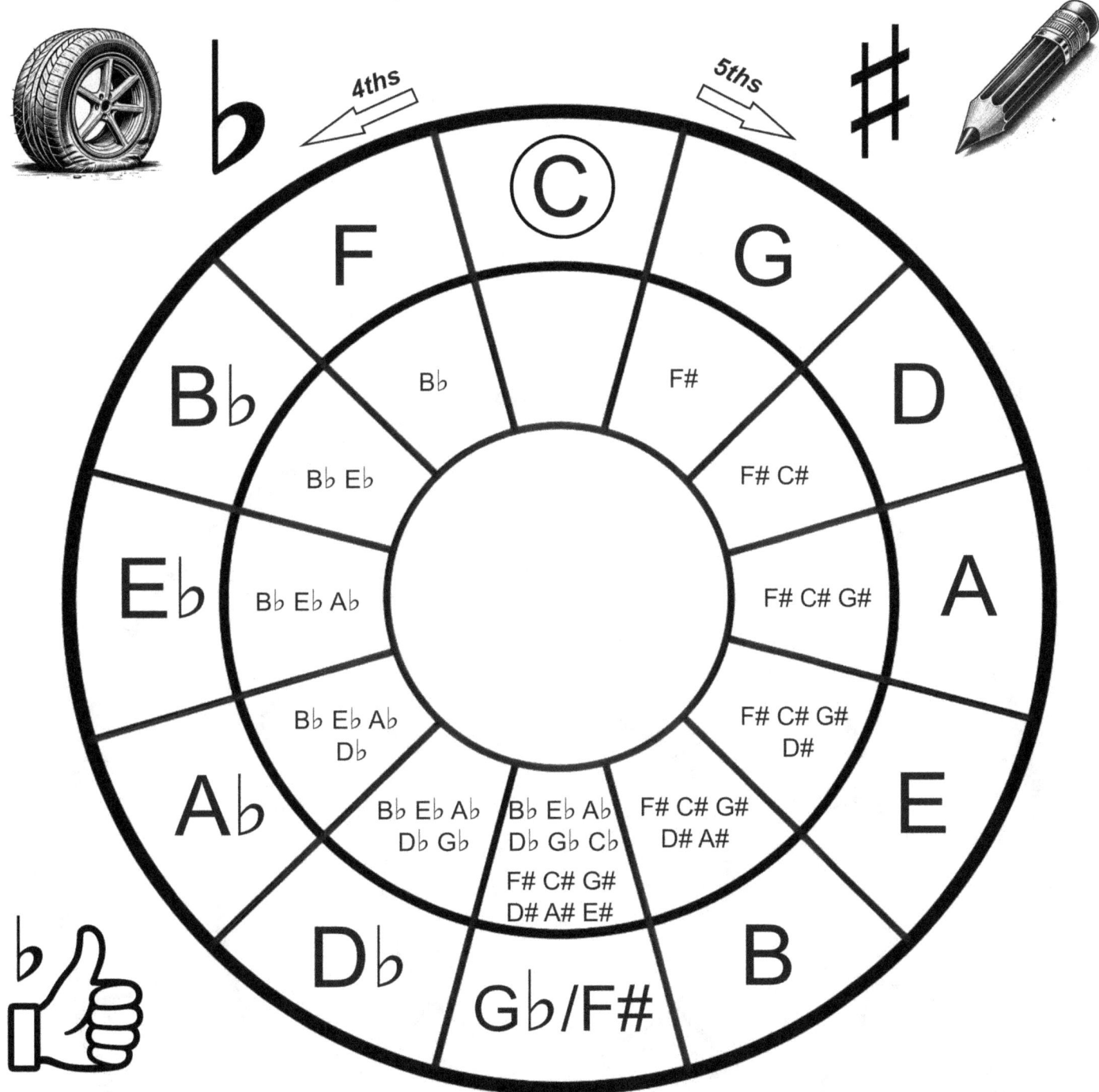

General Rule – Choosing Sharp or Flat Key Names
If you're unsure whether to name a key by its sharp or flat version, *default to the flat name*.

For example:

• Instead of **G#**, use **A♭**.

• Keys like G# technically exist, but they require the use of *double sharps*—notes that are raised by a whole step instead of a half step. This makes reading and writing music more complex, so the flat equivalent is preferred whenever possible.

Exercise

List the order of sharps: __ __ __ __ __ __ __

Rule for finding key with sharps: _____

List the order of flats: __ __ __ __ __ __ __

Rule for finding key with flats: _____

Fill in the circle below with both sharped and flatted keys:

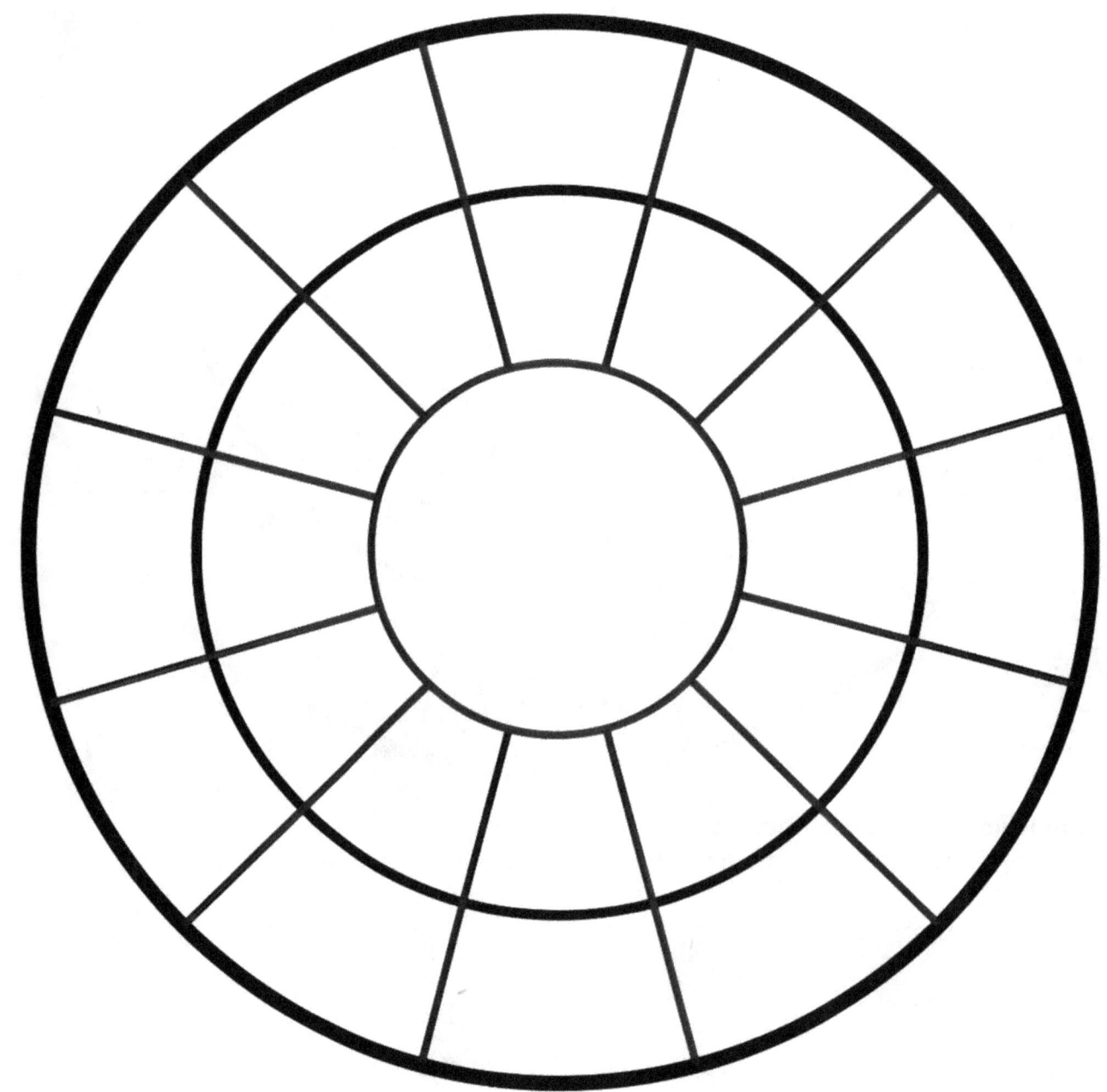

CHORDS IN A KEY

In every key, the chord qualities (major, minor, diminished) are the same and go in the same order. This is because when the chords are built, they are built using the notes in a major scale. Numbers are given to the chords based on their scale degree. So if we're in the key of C, the C will be the 1, Dm will be the 2, Em the 3, etc. This is known as the Nashville Number System, which is detailed in the next chapter.

<u>***In every key, the chords follow this rule***</u>:

• *1 = Major (I)*

• *2 = minor (ii)*

• *3 = minor (iii)*

• *4 = Major (IV)*

• *5 = Major (V)*

• *6 = minor (vi)*

• *7 = diminished (vii)*

The chords in the key of C will be as follows: I   ii   iii   IV V vi   vii
                                                                C Dm Em F   G Am Bdim

• *I, IV, and V* are the **major chords** in *every key*

• *ii, iii, and vi* are the **minor chords** in *every key*

• *vii* is a **diminished chord** in *every key*

Why the Pattern Never Changes
Because every major scale uses the same step pattern, the way chords are built stays consistent across keys. Chord quality depends on the spacing between the notes:

• **Major Chord** = Root → *2 whole steps* → + *1½ steps*

  • Example: C → E → G

• **Minor Chord** = Root → *1½ steps* → + *2 whole steps*

  • Example: D → F → A

• **Diminished Chord** = Root → *1½ steps* → + *1½ steps*

  • Example: B → D → F

It's helpful to know the rules for building major, minor, and diminished chords, but most of the time you can figure them out faster by simply using the **notes in the scale of the key you're in**.

The shortcut: **Always skip a note in the scale** to get to the next note in the chord.

Example – Key of C Major (C D E F G A B):

- *I (C major)* = C → E → G   Ⓒ D Ⓔ F Ⓖ A B
- *ii (D minor)* = D → F → A   C Ⓓ E Ⓕ G Ⓐ B
- *iii (E minor)* = E → G → B   C D Ⓔ F Ⓖ A Ⓑ
- *IV (F major)* = F → A → C   Ⓒ D E Ⓕ G Ⓐ B
- *V (G major)* = G → B → D   C Ⓓ E F Ⓖ A Ⓑ
- *vi (A minor)* = A → C → E   Ⓒ D Ⓔ F G Ⓐ B
- *vii° (B diminished)* = B → D → F   C Ⓓ E Ⓕ G A Ⓑ

By "skipping" a note each time, you're stacking every other note in the scale, which is the quickest way to build chords in any key.

The great part about using this method is you can easily **add the 7s** of the chords by just **skipping one more letter**.

- *I (C major 7)* = C → E → G → B   Ⓒ D Ⓔ F Ⓖ A Ⓑ
- *ii (D minor 7)* = D → F → A → C   Ⓒ Ⓓ E Ⓕ G Ⓐ B
- *iii (E minor 7)* = E → G → B → D   C Ⓓ Ⓔ F Ⓖ A Ⓑ
- *IV (F major 7)* = F → A → C → E   Ⓒ D Ⓔ Ⓕ G Ⓐ B
- *V (G dominant 7)* = G → B → D → F   C Ⓓ E Ⓕ Ⓖ A Ⓑ
- *vi (A minor 7)* = A → C → E → G   Ⓒ D Ⓔ F Ⓖ Ⓐ B
- *vii° (B half diminished 7)* = B → D → F → A   C Ⓓ E Ⓕ G Ⓐ Ⓑ

Alternate way of Finding the 7th of a Chord
• **Method**: Count backward from the root note—go down one letter name in the musical alphabet making sure to use the key signature.
• **Example**: The 7th of **C** is **B**.

Two Types of 7ths
1. Major 7th (maj7)

• Only found in **major chords** built on the **1st** and **4th** degrees of the scale.
• **How to find:** Go down **½ step** (1 fret) from the root.

2. Minor 7th (m7)

• Used for **all other diatonic chords**, including:

  • **V chord** → Dominant 7 (e.g., G7 in C major)
  • **ii, iii, vi chords** → Minor 7
  • **vii chord** → Half-diminished (m7♭5 or ø7)

• **How to find:** Go down **1 whole step** (2 frets) from the root.

The chords in *any* key with 7s will be as follows:

I	ii	iii	IV	V	vi	vii
maj7	m7	m7	maj7	7	m7	m7♭5 or ø7
(major 7)	(minor 7)	(minor 7)	(major 7)	(dominant 7)	(minor 7)	(minor 7 flat 5, or half diminished)

The chords in the **key of C** with 7s will be as follows:

I	ii	iii	IV	V	vi	vii
Cmaj7	Dm7	Em7	Fmaj7	G7	Am7	Bm7♭5

In any major key there are 4 different types of seventh chords:

Major 7: I, IV (major chord with a major 7th)

Dominant 7: V (major chord with a minor 7th)

Minor 7: ii, iii, vi (minor chord with a minor 7th)

Half-diminished (m7♭5): vii (diminished triad plus a minor 7th)

Once you are comfortable using this method in the key of C, try it in other keys. The only thing you'll need to remember is the **key signature** (i.e., what is **sharped** or **flatted**).

CHORD SYMBOL SHORTCUTS

Major
C CM C$^\Delta$

Major 7
C^{maj7} C^{ma7} C$^{\Delta7}$ CM^7

Minor
C- Cm Cmi

Minor 7
C-^{7} Cm^7 Cmi^7

Dominant 7
C^7

Diminished
C$^\circ$ Cdim Cm$^{(\flat5)}$ Cm$^{(-5)}$

Half Diminished, Minor 7 Flat 5
C$^{\varnothing7}$ Cm$^{7\flat5}$ C-$^{7\flat5}$

Helpful tip:

• A **diminished triad** (root, minor 3rd, diminished 5th) becomes **half-diminished** when you add a **minor 7** (also called **m7♭5** or **ø7**).

• If you take that minor 7 and **lower it by a half step**, the chord becomes **fully diminished** (also called a **diminished 7** or **o7**).

CHORDS IN ALL COMMON MAJOR KEYS WITH 7S

C : C^{maj7} Dm^7 Em^7 F^{maj7} G^7 Am^7 B^{ø7}

G : G^{maj7} Am^7 Bm^7 C^{maj7} D^7 Em^7 F#^{ø7}

D : D^{maj7} Em^7 F#m^7 G^{maj7} A^7 Bm^7 C#^{ø7}

A : A^{maj7} Bm^7 C#m^7 D^{maj7} E^7 F#m^7 G#^{ø7}

E : E^{maj7} F#m^7 G#m^7 A^{maj7} B^7 C#m^7 D#^{ø7}

B : B^{maj7} C#m^7 D#m^7 E^{maj7} F#^{7} G#m^7 A#^{ø7}

F : F^{maj7} Gm^7 Am^7 B♭^{maj7} C^7 Dm^7 E^{ø7}

B♭ : B♭^{maj7} Cm^7 Dm^7 E♭^{maj7} F^7 Gm^7 A^{ø7}

E♭ : E♭^{maj7} Fm^7 Gm^7 A♭^{maj7} B♭^{7} Cm^7 D^{ø7}

A♭ : A♭^{maj7} B♭m^7 Cm^7 D♭^{maj7} E♭^{7} Fm^7 G^{ø7}

D♭ : D♭^{maj7} E♭m^7 Fm^7 G♭^{maj7} A♭^{7} B♭m^7 C^{ø7}

G♭ : G♭^{maj7} A♭m^7 B♭m^7 C♭^{maj7} D♭^{7} E♭m^7 F^{ø7}

Helpful tips:

- **Flat keys:** With the exception of **F**, all flat keys start with a **flatted note** (e.g., B♭, E♭, A♭…).

- **Sharp keys:** With the exception of **F#** and **C#**, all sharp keys start with a **natural note** (e.g., G, D, A…).

NASHVILLE NUMBER SYSTEM

The **Nashville Number System** is an informal way to communicate chord progressions using numbers instead of chord names. Developed in the late 1950s by Neal Matthews Jr., it became popular in studio settings as a quick, flexible way to chart songs and transpose (change the key) easily.

To use this system effectively, you'll need to:

• Know your key signatures

• Understand the order of major and minor chords in a key

Once you have that down, the system becomes straightforward.

Example: I – vi – ii – V in the Key of C

• First, recall the key signature for C major—**no sharps or flats**.

• Then, think of the diatonic chords in the key of C:

```
I   ii   iii   IV   V   vi   vii
C   Dm   Em    F    G   Am   Bdim
```

So the progression *I – vi – ii – V* is:

C – Am – Dm – G

Now Transpose to the Key of G:

• The key of G major has one sharp: F#

• The diatonic chords in G are:

```
I   ii   iii   IV   V   vi   vii
G   Am   Bm    C    D   Em   F#dim
```

Now the same progression *I – vi – ii – V* becomes:

G – Em – Am – D

What About Chords That Don't Fit the Key?

The Nashville system works best with **diatonic chords**—chords that naturally occur in the key. But if a chord appears **outside the key** (a **non-diatonic** chord), you'll need to be more specific.

For example, in the key of G, an **E major chord** doesn't fit the key signature—E minor would be the vi chord. So if **E major** appears in your progression, you would write it as **VI** (uppercase for major) and possibly add a note to indicate it's non-diatonic.

Tips for Learning

At first, the system might feel overwhelming. Start simple:

• Begin with songs in C or G using open chords.

• Choose easy songs with repetitive progressions.

• Say the numbers out loud as you play.

• Gradually work up to songs with barre chords and more complex progressions.

FINDING THE KEY OF A SONG USING CHORDS

It's always helpful to know the key you're playing in. Knowing the key tells you:

• Which chords are most likely to appear in the song.

• What notes will fit if you want to improvise.

Step 1: Look for the three major chords.
If you have sheet music with a key signature, you can identify the key quickly by counting sharps or flats. But if you're looking at a *lyric sheet with chord symbols only*, that method won't work for two reasons:

1. Some chords in the key might not appear in the song at all.

2. Sharps or flats can be "hidden" inside a chord. (Example: a D major chord contains F♯.)

Instead, find the *three major chords in the song*—these will almost always be the I, IV, and V chords. Next, put the *two major chords that are next to each other* in the musical alphabet in spots *IV and V*, leaving the *remaining major chord* as the *I chord*.

Example:
Song: *Let It Be* by The Beatles (verse progression)

C G | Am F | C G | F C

Major chords: C, G, F

• F and G are next to each other in the musical alphabet → these are the IV and V chords.

• The remaining major chord, C, must be the I chord.

Result: Key = *C major*

Remember: In every major key, the I, IV, and V chords are *major*.

Exercise
Let's take a few other progressions and see if you can name the key:

1. G | Em | D | C ____
2. D | A | D | G ____
3. B | A | E | F#m ____
4. B♭ | F | C | Dm ____
5. E | B | G#m | F# ____
6. E | C#m | D | A ____

Answers:
1. G 2. D 3. E 4. F 5. B 6. A

You won't always find three major chords in a song.
When that happens, use both the *major and minor chords to figure out the key*.

Example:
Progression: G | C | Dm | Am

The two major chords are **G** and **C**.

Since they are *not* next to each other in the musical alphabet, they can't be the IV and V chords. That means the song must be in either G or C.

In the key of G, the V chord would be **D major**—but here we have Dm, so it can't be G major.

That leaves **C major** as the key.

In C major, this progression is:
V – I – ii – vi

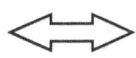

Helpful tip: If a song starts and ends on the same chord, that is most likely the key of the song.

Exercise

Name the key of these progressions:

1. D | C | Am | Bm ___

2. F#m | E | A | Bm ___

3. C | F | Am | Gm ___

4. Eb | Cm | F | Gm ___

5. D | C#m | Bm | A ___

6. G | F | Am | Dm ___

Answers:
1. G 2. A 3. F 4. Bb 5. A 6. C

Sometimes, songs have *more than three major chords*. When this happens, focus on the **three major chords that occur most often** and use those to determine the I–IV–V.

Keep in mind:

• Not every song stays in a single key.

• Some songs have **key changes**.

You'll learn more about this in the section on **diatonic vs. non-diatonic chords**.

161

RELATIVE MINORS

Every *major key* has a *relative minor key*. The term *relative* means that the two keys are related—they share the *same notes*, including any sharps or flats. The relative minor scale is also called the *natural minor scale*, and it uses the same set of notes (and usually the same chords) as its major counterpart, with just a few exceptions.

How to Find the Relative Minor
The easiest way to find the relative minor of any major key is to go to the *6th note* of the major scale.

Example:
The notes in the *C major scale* are:
C – D – E – F – G – A – B

The 6th note is *A*, so *A minor* is the relative minor of *C major*.

If you play the *A natural minor scale*, you'll get:
A – B – C – D – E – F – G

These are the *same notes* as C major, just starting and ending on *A* instead of *C*.

Here is one way to play a one octave major scale:

The numbers represent the intervals in the *major scale*:

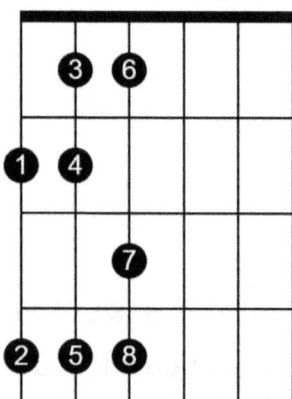

This is how you play a *major 6th*, which will tell you the *relative minor*.

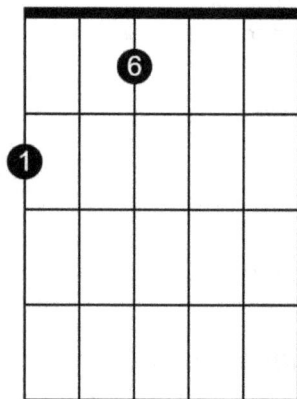

One reason guitarists like to know the *relative minor* is so they can choose where to play a solo. If you know your *major key*, you have two soloing options:

• Play a *major pentatonic* in that key.

• Play a *minor pentatonic* in the *relative minor key*.

Both scales use *exactly the same notes in the same order*—only the tonal center changes.

162

As we learned previously, the chords in the key of **C major** are:

I	ii	iii	IV	V	vi	vii
C	Dm	Em	F	G	Am	Bdim

The **relative minor** of C major is **A minor**, which uses the same notes but starts on **A**. So, the chords in the key of **A minor** (natural minor) are:

i	ii	III	iv	v	VI	VII
Am	Bdim	C	Dm	Em	F	G

Adding the Dominant V Chord
A common variation in minor key progressions is replacing the **v chord (minor)** with a **V chord (major)**. This creates a stronger pull back to the tonic chord (i). This change comes from the **harmonic minor scale**, which is the **natural minor scale with a raised 7th**.

Example:

The **A natural minor scale** is:
A – B – C – D – E – F – G

The **A harmonic minor scale** raises the 7th note (G → G♯):
A – B – C – D – E – F – G♯

This raised 7th changes the **E minor chord (v)** to **E major (V)**, creating stronger resolution to Am. Add a minor 7th (D) to E major, and it becomes **E7**, a **dominant 7th chord**. When a song begins on the relative minor chord, it's usually considered to be in the relative minor key.

Determining the Key: Major or Minor?
If a song **starts on the relative minor chord**, it's often in the **minor key**, even if the chords also belong to the major key.

To figure out whether a progression is in a **major** or **minor** key, listen for the **home chord**—the one the progression wants to return to.

Example progression:
Am | F | C | G

Even though all of these chords exist in both **C major** and **A minor**, your ear naturally hears **Am** as the resolution point. This suggests the progression is in **A minor**.

Exercise

Find the relative minor of these major keys:

1. A ___
2. C ___
3. G ___
4. E ___
5. D ___
6. B♭ ___
7. F ___
8. E♭ ___

Quick guitar trick:
To find the relative minor of a major key on the low E string, place your **pinky** on the **major key root note**. Treat that note as the **second note of minor pentatonic Pattern 1**. Your **first finger** will now be on the **relative minor root**.

Pattern 1

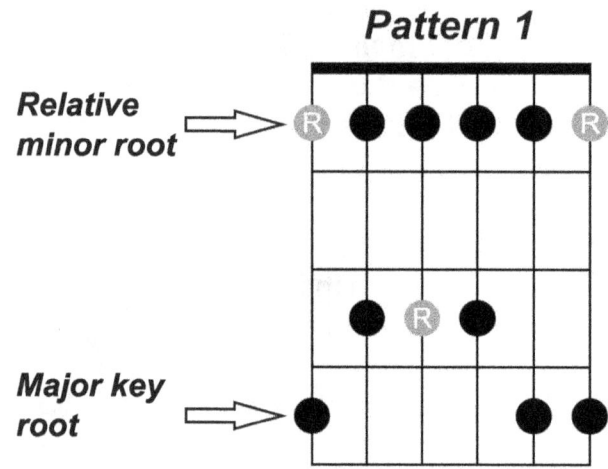

Answers:
1. F#m 2. Am 3. Em 4. C#m 5. Bm 6. Gm 7. Dm 8. Cm

DIATONIC CHORDS VS. NON-DIATONIC CHORDS

A *diatonic chord* is one that **fits within a key**. A *non-diatonic chord* is one that **does not fit within a key**.

A non-diatonic chord could be a major chord in place of a minor, a minor in place of a major, or a sharped or flatted chord that doesn't fit with the key signature. For an example, we'll first start with the chords in the key of C:

C Dm Em F G Am Bdim

Any chord outside of these 7 chords is considered a <u>non-diatonic</u> chord. Some examples are: Cm, D, E, F#m, Gm, etc.

Recognizing popular non-diatonic chords will help you determine the key. Non-diatonic chords might get used to add interest to a song, alter a melody, or because a songwriter isn't familiar with how key signatures work and they just use what sounds good to their ear! Regardless of the reason, there are a few rules that are commonly followed.

1. Secondary Dominants

A *V chord* (5 chord) naturally wants to resolve to a *I chord* (1 chord). This is one of the strongest movements in music.

But here's where the number system can get a little confusing:
In this case, the "1" doesn't always mean the tonic (home chord) of the current key—it can mean the target chord you're moving toward.

When you temporarily use a V chord that belongs to a *different key*—not the key you're currently in—it's called a *secondary dominant*.

Examples:

• To move to *A major*, play *E7* before it. Why? Because *E is the 5 of A*.

• To move to *E* major, play *B7* beforehand. *B is the 5 of E*.

These V chords "borrow" their role from the new key, even if you're not fully modulating.

You don't always have to use a dominant 7th chord—a major chord can also create this effect. However, dominant 7th chords (like E7, B7, etc.) create a stronger pull toward the chord they resolve to.

Why Use Secondary Dominants?
This technique is especially useful when:

- You want to move to a chord outside the current key

- You're changing keys within a song (modulation)

- You want to add tension or surprise to a chord progression

2. The Minor iv Chord (iv → I Resolution)

A *minor iv chord* often creates a strong, emotional pull back to the *I chord*. One common and expressive way to use it is in the progression: *IV → iv → I*

Even though the iv chord is *non-diatonic* in a major key (it contains a note outside the key), it works due to the **chromatic voice leading** between chords.

Example in C Major:

F (IV) = F A̲ C

Fm (iv) = F A̲♭ C

C (I) = C E G̲

Notice the chromatic motion in the middle voice:

- *A (from F major)* moves down a half step to *A♭ (in F minor)*

- *A♭ (in F minor)* then moves down another half step to *G (in C major)*

This smooth, descending chromatic line (A → A♭ → G) gives the progression a rich, expressive sound that feels both emotional and resolved.

3. Chromatic Voice Leading

Chromatic voice leading involves using chord tones to create smooth, step-by-step chromatic movement—either ascending or descending. Chromatic simply means moving by a half step (one fret up or down on the guitar).

Here's an example of descending chromatic voice leading, where we follow a single note as it moves down one half step at a time through a progression.

- We start with a **D major** chord, where the lowest note played is D.

- The note a half step below D is C#. Instead of moving to a C# chord, we look for a chord that contains C#—in this case, **A major**, where C# is the 3rd.

- A half step below C# is C, so we move to **C major**, which includes that note.

- A half step below C is B. **G major** works well here, since B is its 3rd.

- The next half step down is B♭, so we use **B♭ minor** to keep the chromatic motion going.

- Below B♭ is A, which is the 3rd of an **F major** chord.

- The next note below an A is an A♭, and we'll use a **A♭ major** chord.

- Finally, A♭ moves down to G, and we resolve on **G major**.

Full progression:

D | A | C | G | B♭m | F | A♭ | G

Chromatic movement:

D → C# → C → B → B♭ → A → A♭ → G

This progression doesn't stay within a single key, but that's the point—chromatic voice leading prioritizes smooth movement over key consistency. You can use this technique for a full progression or just a short section.

The same approach works in reverse for ascending chromatic voice leading: follow a single note upward by half steps, choosing chords that contain each note.

4. Mixing and Matching Chords from Related Keys

One way to add variety to your progressions is to **borrow chords from closely related keys**. A quick way to find these keys is to take the **IV and V chords** from your current key and treat them as the **I chord** of their own keys.

Example in C Major:

If you're in **C major**, the IV is **F** and the V is **G**.

This means you can borrow chords from **F major** and **G major**.

C: C - Dm - Em - F - G - Am - Bdim

F: F - Gm - Am - B♭ - C - Dm - Edim

G: G - Am - Bm - C - D - Em - F#dim

Borrowing in Action:

• From **F major**, you gain **Gm** and **B♭**

• From **G major**, you gain **Bm** and **D**

These extra chords fit smoothly because the keys are closely related, sharing many of the same notes.

In rock and pop, it's common to avoid diminished chords when borrowing. Focus on major and minor chords for a cleaner, more accessible sound.

On the following page is a listing of home keys with chords borrowed from related keys.

HOME KEYS WITH CHORDS FROM RELATED KEYS

Home Key	Chords from IV	Chords from V
C	Gm & B♭	Bm & D
G	Dm & F	F#m & A
D	Am & C	C#m & E
A	Em & G	G#m & B
E	Bm & D	D#m & F#
B	F#m & A	A#m & C#
F	Cm & E♭	Em & G
B♭	Fm & A♭	Am & C
E♭	B♭m & D♭	Dm & F
A♭	E♭m & G♭	Gm & B♭
D♭	A♭m & C♭	Cm & E♭
G♭	D♭m & F♭	Fm & A♭

PLAYING BARRE CHORDS IN A KEY

Eventually, you'll want to be comfortable playing **all of the chords in every key**. In this section, we'll focus on doing that using **barre chord patterns**.

Think of this as a **tool** to use alongside your knowledge of **key signatures** and the **notes in a key**.

You'll be working with the **E-shape** and **A-shape barre chords** we covered earlier in this book, along with the **minor 7♭5 chord** (also called a **half-diminished chord**).

E Major Shape

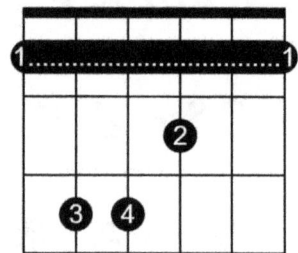

A Major Shape

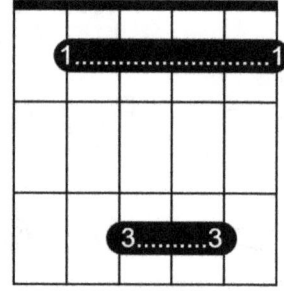

E Minor Shape

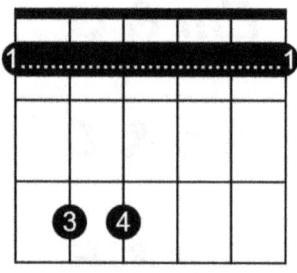

A Minor Shape

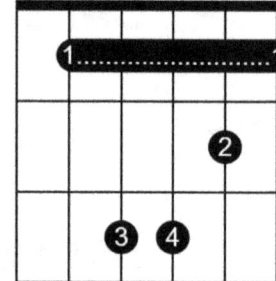

E Minor 7♭5 Shape

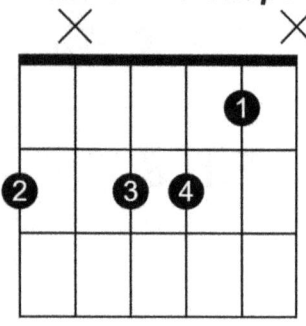

A Minor 7♭5 Shape

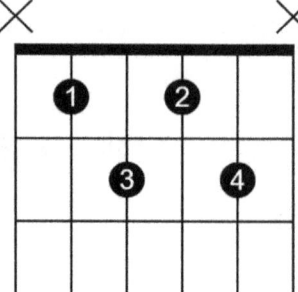

To lay out the *root notes for the chords* on the fretboard, we'll be using two *1-4-5 patterns*.

We will use these two patterns for the major chords in a key. You will only use one pattern at a time. If the *root is on the E string*, use **Pattern 1**. If the root is on the **A string**, use **Pattern 2**.

1-4-5 Pattern 1

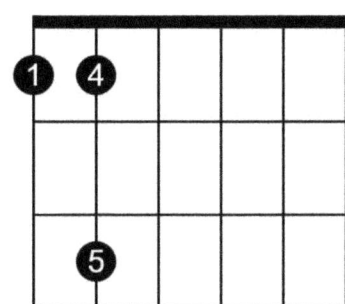

1-4-5 Pattern 2

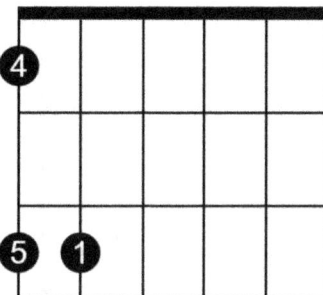

We use these same two patterns for the root notes for the minor chords in a key. The major pattern that you choose will tell you which minor pattern to use.

6-2-3 Pattern 1

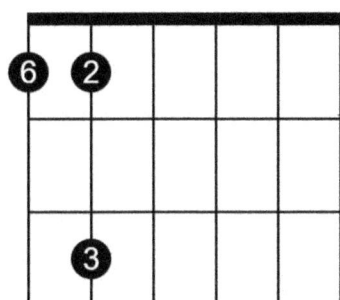

6-2-3 Pattern 2

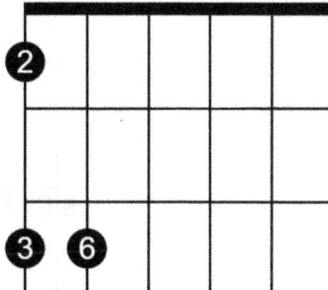

Notice that the 2 sets of shapes are the same; they just have different numbers assigned to the root notes.

Exercise

Outline the root notes for the chords in the key of A. Start with the 1-4-5 Pattern 1 to get the root notes for the major chords in the *key of A*, which means you start on the 5th fret of the E string.

1-4-5 in key of A

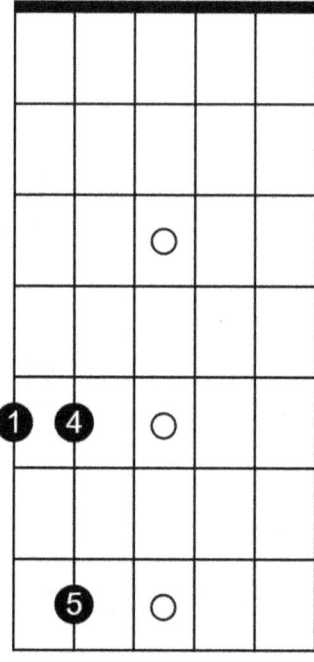

Next, to get the root notes for the minor chords in the key of A, move the 1 (A) down 3 frets (F#) and use the 6-2-3 Pattern 1.

6-2-3 in key of A

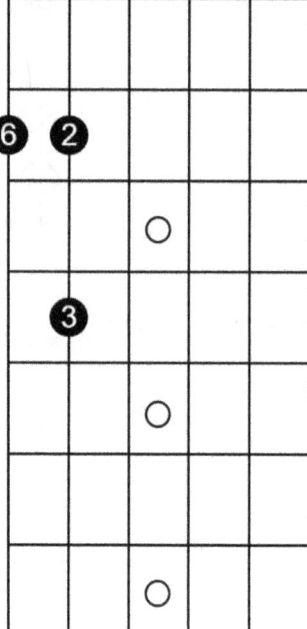

That covers everything except the 7 chord, which is always one fret lower than the 1 chord. Here are all of the root notes put together.

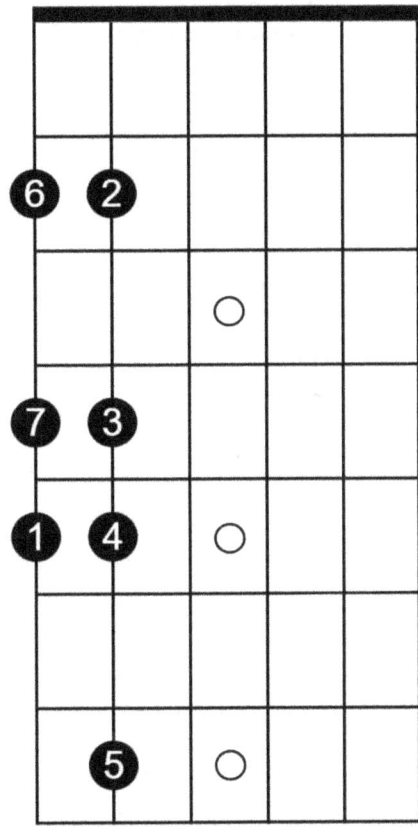

Root notes in the key of A

Now you just need to play the chord off of each numbered root note. If the number is on the E string, use an E shape. If the number is on the A string, use an A shape. The chords are:

I ii iii IV V vi vii
A Bm C#m D E F#m G#m$^{7\flat 5}$

Exercise

Next, use the second set of patterns to find the root notes for the chords in the **key of E**. Start on the 7th fret of the A string (E) to get the root notes for the major chords.

1-4-5 in key of E

To get the roots for the minor chords in the key of E, move your 1 down 3 frets (C#) and use the 6-2-3 pattern 2.

6-2-3 in key of E

All together, it looks like this. The same thing applies to the 7 chord as before; it will be 1 fret lower than the 1.

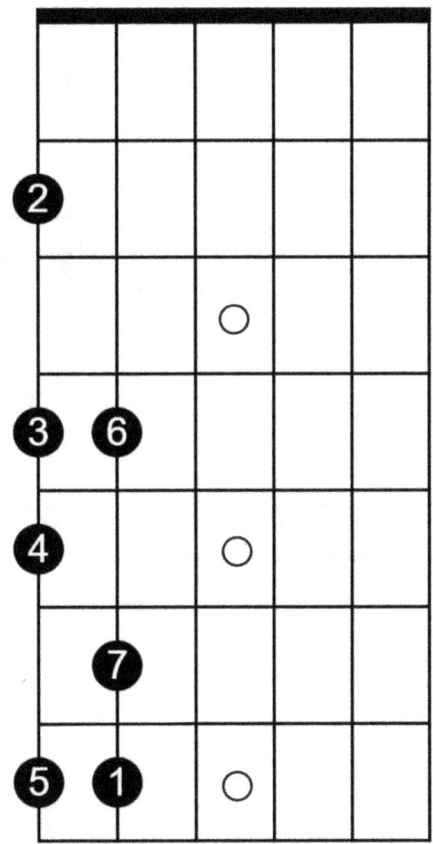

I ii   iii   IV V vi   vii
E F#m G#m   A B C#m D#m$^{7\flat5}$

Exercise

Another way to find the *root notes of a key* is using these *two patterns*:

1-4-5 Pattern 1
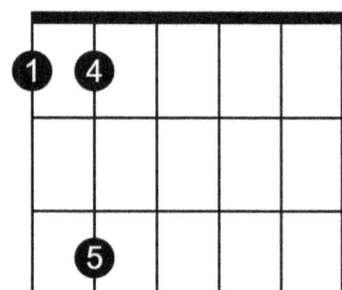

6-2-3 Pattern 2
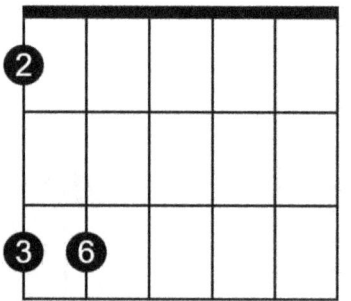

Root notes in the key of G
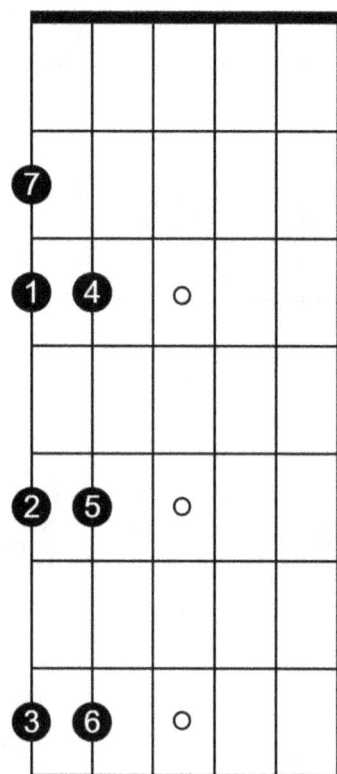

I ii iii IV V vi vii
G Am Bm C D Em F#m⁷♭⁵

Exercise

Lastly, another way to find the *root notes of a key* is using these *two patterns*:

1-4-5 Pattern 2

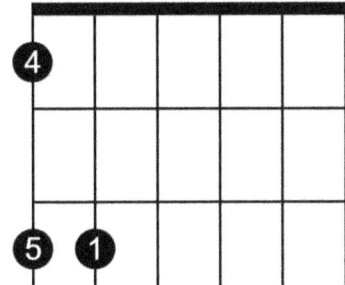

6-2-3 Pattern 1

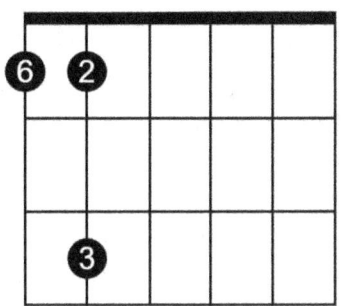

Root notes in the key of C

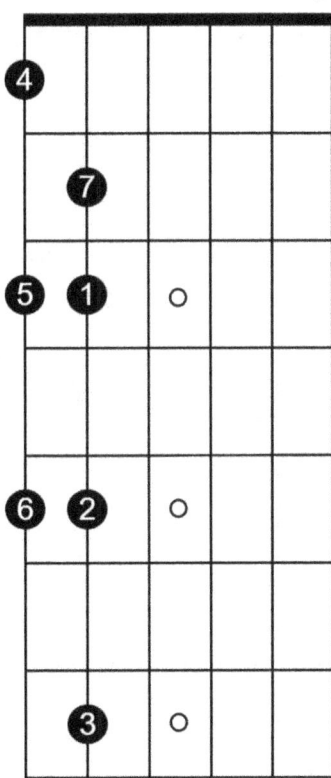

I	ii	iii	IV	V	vi	vii
C	Dm	Em	F	G	Am	Bm$^{7\flat 5}$

OPEN CHORD DICTIONARY

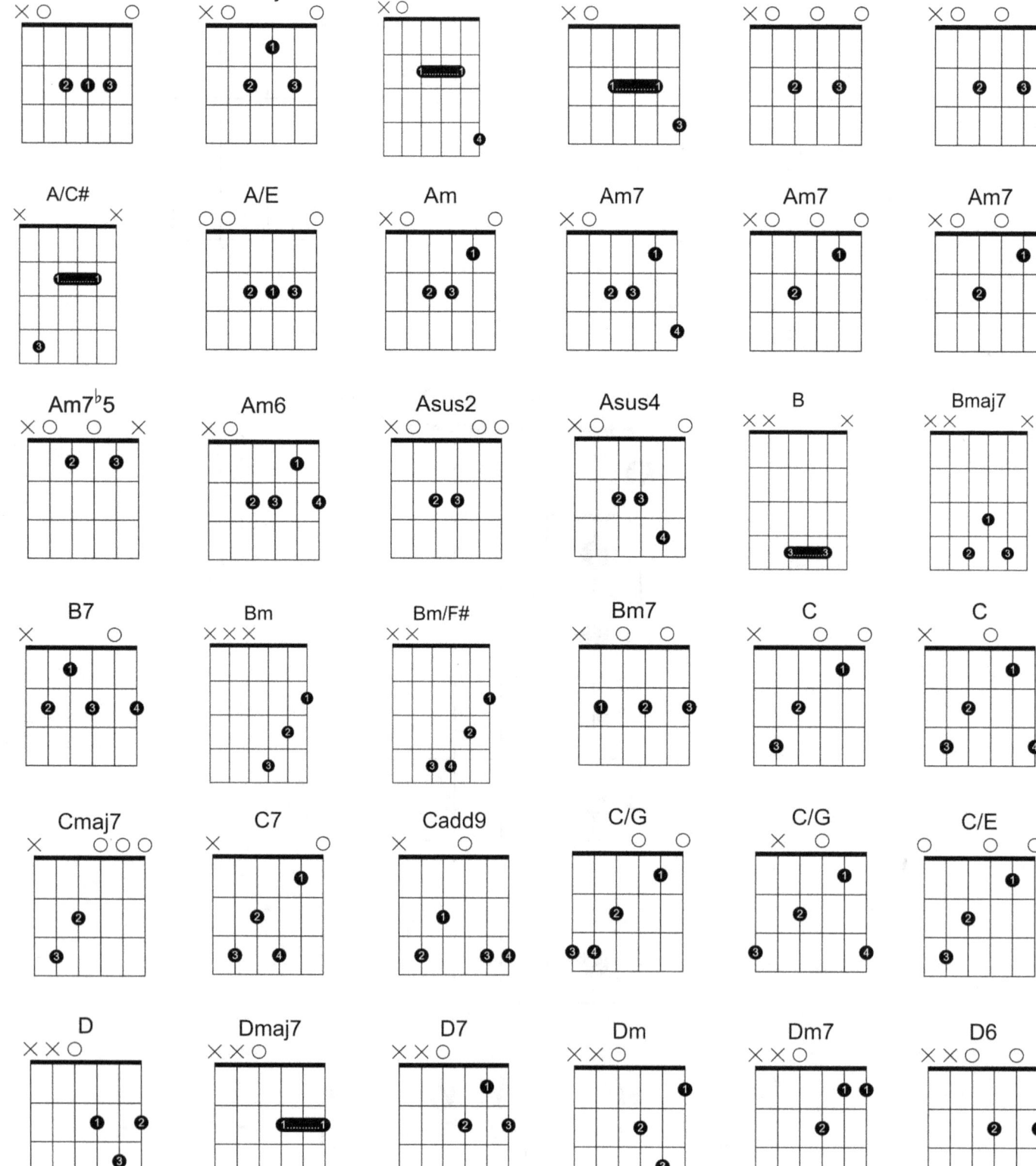

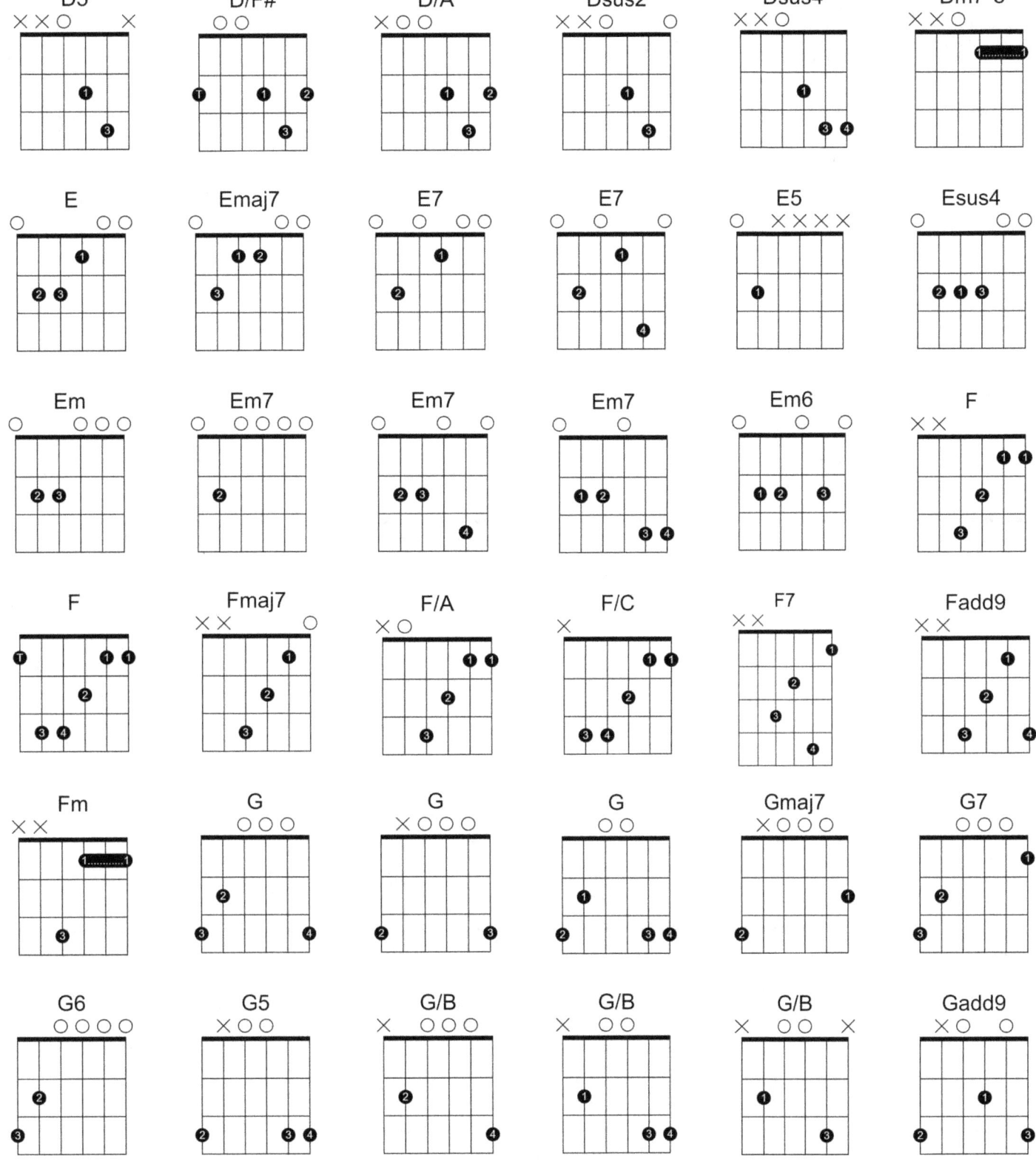

BLANK CHORDS

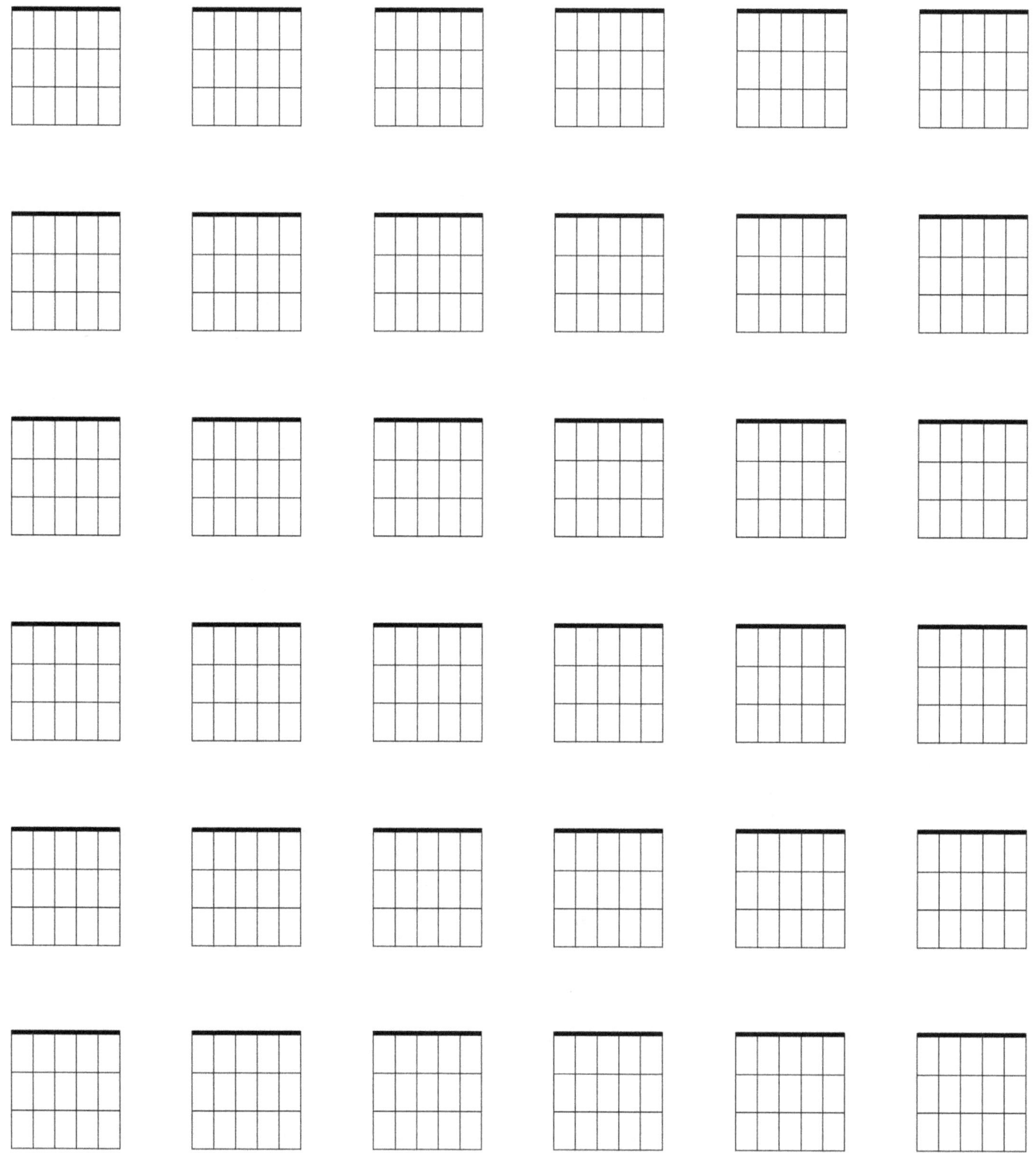

ACKNOWLEDGEMENTS

To my wife, Jenna Wade, whose love and patience made this project possible. Thank you for your endless encouragement, your careful editing, and for reminding me how much I still have to learn about grammar—and the proper use of a semicolon.

To my parents, John and Mona Wade, who against their better judgement let me follow my passion as a career.

To my good friend and partner in crime, Ryan Smith, for coffee chats, invaluable feedback, and for inspiring me.

To my cat Ollie, who reminded me that lap time was always more important than this book.

To all of my private students—especially Kate Hopper, Al Nairn, Jeff Olsen, Mary Strand, and David Wagner—thank you for sharing your wisdom, expertise, and feedback, for inspiring me daily, and for offering such encouragement and support for this project.

Enjoyed This Book?

If Guitar Theory Simplified helped you understand the fretboard more clearly, would you consider leaving a short, honest review on Amazon?

Reviews help other guitarists know whether this book is right for them — and they make a huge difference for independent authors like me.

Thank you for your support,
Mark Wade

www.ingramcontent.com/pod-product-compliance
Lightning Source LLC
Chambersburg PA
CBHW081131170426
43197CB00017B/2823